PRIMARY EDUCATION

PRIMARY EDUCATION

R.K. ROY

KALPAZ PUBLICATIONS
DELHI-110052

PRIMARY EDUCATION
(Education)

Published in 2007 in India by
Kalpaz Publications,
C-30, Satyawati Nagar, Delhi-110052
E-mail : Kalpaz@hotmail.com
Ph : 9212729499

Laser Typesetting: Grow Computers, Delhi
Printed at : Rajdhani Printers, Delhi

Contents

Preface

No education is possible without a set of values, and any education which purports to be value-free is likely to be based on hidden values of its own. Similarly, any approach to education which claims to be entirely derived from theories of development, or experience, or of curriculum is unlikely to be adequate. For either it is based on a fallacious argument, such as that because education is related to development, therefore education ought to depend on development: or it is based on an argument derived from other and still more basic premises.

All sound education should make pupils and students aware of the limitations of their knowledge and encourage a due sense of humility within the realms of learning—whether they are leaders of followers. School, parents and home should all united in an effort to enable the children to reach their fullest development a individuals, and also to become useful and upright citizens in their community.

There is a recognition of the child as a total being who has specific and differing needs within the realms of character and intellect, and additionally the need to be initiated into the world of work and life itself in such a way as to be able to cope practically as well as intellectually. The children are to be trained in habits of careful observation and clear reasoning so that they may gain same intelligent acquaintance with some of the facts and laws of nature and this is hardly followership. The school must further arouse in its pupils a lively interest in man's ideals, achievements, literature and history; it must give them 'some power over language as an instrument of thought and expression'—surely more keeping with education for leadership.

This volume on primary education analyses the bottlenecks in universalisation of primary education. It extensively reviews the studies in the area, analyses factors responsible for impeding progress of children's education and highlights existing policy options.

Editor

1
Early Childhood Education

School, parents and home should all unite in an effort to enable the children to reach their fullest development as individuals, and also to become useful and upright citizens in their community.

Developmental Theories in Early Education

Quite generally, theories of development and practice differ in their orientation to the developing individual. The orientation of practice is necessarily activist. It assumes that some aspects of behaviour or some types of knowledge are more or less desirable than others. One corollary is that these require certain environmental conditions which a skilled practitioner can bring about. Should children know how to fight, read, think, imagine, or love? If the answer is "yes", the task of a theory of practice is to describe what a practitioner must do to cultivate that know-how. By contrast, a theory of development is passivist in orientation. The core assumption is that behaviour changes as a function of encounters present in most environments. Suppose a behaviour ordinarily increases and then decreases during the early years. In explaining this pattern of change, the theory might state that the increase in crying is a by-product of the child's social awareness, a welcome mark of growing maturity. True, the intensity of distress may be related to the child's previous experiences or to the setting in which separation is occurring. A theory of development will offer general statements identifying experimental and setting factors and why they work the way they do. It will not offer principles for modifying or generating these factors. These theories differ in other ways as well. Theories of development are universalistic rather than particularistic, and, with respect to environmental forces, they are minimalist rather than maximalist. By the former, we mean that theories of development describe what is considered the "normal" course of growth and change. Even when developmental theories expand to consider individual differences, they deal with types of individuals and situations rather than with a particular individual at a particular moment in time. By the latter, we mean that developmental theories tend to view the environment as a set of minimal core features, the presence of which is necessary for development to occur.

In developmental theories, the environment enters into serious theoretical discussions when it fails to provide the minimum support needed for growth. Even in the study of individual differences, the goal of development theory is to specify the minimum band of environmental variation required to produce a given individual variation. By contrast, a theory of practice is concerned with the practitioner's perception of particular individuals.

More important in view of its activist orientation, a theory of practice is concerned with maximizing beneficial environmental variation. One goal of such a theory is to formulate strategies for constructing environments that ensure the greatest beneficial impact on the greatest number of individuals. Finally, a theory of development views the changing individuals as a product of the multiple practices of multiple practitioners. By contrast, a theory of practice adopts the perspective of one type of practitioner, and this perspective defines a theory of teaching, parenting, or policy making. The theory builds on what is known about the child, but it uses only that part which pertains to the environmental conditions controlled by the practitioner of interest in the theory. It is in this respect that a theory of practice may have its most significant impact on a theory of development.

A theory of practice must inevitably specify the realizable context in which development occurs. Although developmental theorists have recently called for an "ecology of child development", the emergence of useful ecological constructs may be dependent on the formulation of theories capable of providing rules for producing developmentally consequential contexts. The maximalist orientation of a theory of practice requires far more information about environmental arrangements than theories of development typically provide. If the task of a theory of practice is to construct rules for generating realizable arrangements outcomes, it may need to map the malleability of the environment in which children are reared. John Bowlby's attachment theory is a useful beginning point for a discussion of the interplay between theories of development and practice.

Attachment Theory

From ethology, Bowlby incorporated the view of attachment as an instinctual, species-characteristic behavioural system. According to this view, human infants are born with a predisposition to display various social behaviours such as smiling, sucking, clinging, following, and crying which act as signals bringing the infant into contact with the mother and eliciting nurturant behaviours from her. This evolution of this system of behaviours resulted from its contribution to the survival of the human infant during the long period of relative helplessness. Throughout the first few years of life, the behaviours which make up the attachment "system" undergo change and modification in response to the current situation, past experiences, and the development level of the child.

Control systems theory and the concept of "goal directed" behaviours were adopted by Bowlby to explain the process by which a child comes to employ a variety of strategies to maintain proximity to the mother. Development changes in the system are explained through Piaget's cognitive structural theory. The first stage refers to the period soon after birth when instinctual signals such as eye contact, rooting and sucking maintain maternal contact. During the second period, the infant learns to orient and signal to one or more discriminated figures. The third stage occurs along with person permanence when the infant becomes capable of internally representing the parent who is no longer in view. At this point, active behaviours on the part of the child to regain proximity and contact first occur. This stage lasts from around ten months to three or four years of age.

Development changes within this stage are marked by the child's gradually increasing ability to maintain elaborated internal representations of the parents during their absence, representations which serve to reduce concern over separation. Also, the child acquires continually more sophisticated signals to obtain the parent's attention. Bowlby characterizes the fourth and final stage as a "goal directed partnership." separations at this stage are less problematical as the child develops the ability to ascribe purpose to the parent's absence and eventual return. Most investigations of attachment have focused on the third phase when the presence of an attachment figure appears critical to the infant's sense of well-being. The child at this stage has been described as using this figure--whether mother, father, or regular caregiver–as a secure base from which to launch exploratory forays into the environment.

To picture the developmental process, one can imagine a circle around the child and mother. Under stress the circle becomes smaller and the child moves closer to the mother. Older children's circles become much larger as they use distal signals to "check in." Under stress the circle may contract but not as severely as before, as long as the child can explore the environment. Anderson described this behaviour in one- and two-year-olds at play in the park. Children would wander from the mother as they became absorbed with toys or other children. Once a certain distance was exceeded, however, the children re-established contact with the mother before returning to play.

Attachment research has identified ways in which children use discrete behaviours to signal their need for reassurance and proximity to adults. Sensitive adults observing these behaviours can use them as a guide to the feelings of the child. An understanding of these signals can help a caregiver respond in ways that assist the child in dealing with separations from home and parents. For example, attachment theory suggests that a young child who bursts into tears when the mother enters the center is signaling his need for comfort and contact with the mother, not displeasure or rejection of the classroom teacher.

Similarly, a child approaching the teacher to show a toy or standing silently by her side may be displaying variations of the "check in" behaviour described by Anderson. Rather than viewing these behaviours as expressions of excessive dependency, teachers might view them as the child's way of using the teacher as a secure base. The unique aspect of Bowlby's attachment paradigm is its explanatory focus on the development of social ties from the child's point of view. As a result of the intertwining of ethological and cognitive approaches, observed behaviours of the infant and child can be interpreted as indicators of the child's construction of a social reality. But individual children may differ considerably in the affective aspect of these constructions.

Bowlby's attachment theory has provided a fruitful framework for examining the growth of a child's social world. This work has proved useful not only in establishing expected age norms for particular behaviours but in determining patterns of individual differences as well. Perhaps the most productive work of this kind has been carried out by Mary Ainsworth and her colleagues. In a longitudinal study of mothers and infants, home observations were made at three-week intervals over the course of the first year. At one year, a laboratory session was designed to determine the infant's reaction to several short separations from the mother. Qualitative differences in the infant's responses were recorded. The largest group of infants responded to these separations much as attachment theory would predict. They actively engaged the mother on her return, signaling for pickup and comfort if upset, or using distal behaviours if the separation had been less stressful. The next two groups of infants were not as successful in using the mother for comfort and reassurance on her return and generally required a longer period to return to active play. One group of infants, referred to as "avoidantly attached," responded to reunion by withdrawing or by ignoring the mother. Another group, referred to as "ambivalently attached", responded to reunion with a mixture of both approach and resistant behaviours. Infants in this group displayed the greatest amount of distress over separation but were not comforted by maternal contact. Examination of home observation data indicated qualitative differences in the interactions of the mothers and infants in these groups. During the first year of life, the mothers of ambivalent and avoidant infants had responded less frequently or appropriately to bids for attention from their infants. These individual differences have been found among samples of infants ranging in age from twelve to twenty-four months of age. Moreover, these patterns have been found to be stable over time. But changes from secure to anxious attachment patterns do occur. Interestingly, these are related to stressful changes in the mother's and are likely to effect interactions with the child.

The study of individual differences in the organization of the attachment behaviour illustrates the contribution and limitations of developmental theories for a theory of practice in early education. Consider, for example, two complementary issues, the impact of short-term separation on the maintenance of a secure attachment bond to the mother, and the structure of a child-care experience that supports the child's sense of security. Bowlby's theory predicts that child care occurring before the fourth phase of attachment will involve a special emotional strain for the child. This strain will be greater when the child is younger and will reflect deficits in the child's rudimentary ability to represent the mother in her absence. A variety of factors, including familiarity with the caregiver and the surroundings, the presence of interesting toys, and duration of the separation, also determine the extent of the infant's distress. However, attempts to apply the theory to practical problems often ignore theoretically significant issues. Most attempts at examining the effects of separation due to child care have focused primarily on the fact of the child's enrollment, without attention to the multitude of other factors affecting the child's experience such as age of entrance, length of care, or nature of the care.

In one of the earlier studies Blehar reported that thirty-month-old-day-care children were more avoidant and forty-month-olds more resistant than their age-matched, home-reared controls. These results have not been replicated by other researches. The assessment situation used in these studies, however, was developed for use with twelve-to twenty-four-month-olds and so may be inappropriate for assessing attachment in older children. Since the strange situation procedure was inappropriate for the age group examined, these discrepant results are difficult to interpret.

Influence of Day Care: In view of Bowlby's analysis, an important issue concerns the influence of day care on the formation of the attachment relationship during the first year of life. Schwartz examined attachment in eighteen-month-old full-time, part-time, and non-day-care infants. The day-care children had been placed in day-care home before six months of age. When the three attendance groups were compared, only 9 per cent of the part-time children were classified as anxiously attached compared to 30 per cent of the non-day-care children and 40 per cent of the fulltime day-care children. Similar group differences were also noted when ratings of avoidant and resistant behaviours were examined. Full-time day-care infants displayed more avoidant behaviour than did their non-day-care or part-time peers. Further, there was a tendency for part-time children to display fewer resistant behaviours than non-day-care children. Thus, day-care attendance as such did not affect the likelihood that an infant would develop an anxious attachment relationship with the mother. Early enrollment on a full-time basis, however, did result in a greater frequency of behaviour which has been interpreted as signs of suppressed anger at the mother. By contrast, part-time care appears to support the child's bond to the mother. For middle and upper middle-class women like those in the present study part-time employment may serve to support their mothering role by offering periods of outside adult contact without the time constraints of full employment. These finding certainly have implications for mothers in-the age of children receiving care. The merits and social costs of full versus part-time employment and child care are issues that need further exploration.

On a basic level this might involve determining which forms of substitute care are appropriate to children in various age groups. A more subtle issue is whether certain ages, such as ten months of age when attachment behaviours initially appear or eighteen months when there is a sudden reappearance of intense separation protest, might represent crisis points when abrupt introduction to stage surrounding may be disruptive to the child's sense of security. Alternatively, these transitional periods may represent times when the child is ready to make developmental progress and the introduction to day care may facilitate the formation of secondary attachment.

Attachment theory also provides a powerful but as yet unrealized analytical tool for studying children's relationships with significant adults other than primary attachment figures. For example, the children in Schwartz's study attended day-care homes with a single alternate caregiver. Infants under one year of age placed with a single adult caregivers have been found to display less resistant behaviours towards the mother than infants cared for in group settings. Children at this age may not be able to use multiple and changing caregivers effectively as sources of security. Further work needs to be conducted to determine whether various child-care parameters, such as center care, number of substitute caregivers, and group size, differently affect an infant's ability to deal with separation and to form secondary attachments to nonparental adults.

Our point is that attachment theory provides a suggestive framework around which applied research can be organized. Although currently the gap between the theory and practical problems is immense, numerous bridging opportunities are available. While the issues of whether repeated daily separations affect the children's tie to the mother need further study, the inverse, that is, whether the pre-existing attachment tie affects adjustment to day-care and interactions with peers or caregivers, has received slim attention. A few recently completed studies have examined the relationship between the quality of the attachment bond and later social behaviours with peers. These studies indicate a relationship between secure attachment and subsequent social competence.

As part of a longitudinal study, securely attached children were found to display greater task persistence and longer periods of exploration at twenty-four months. These children were rated higher on scales of peer competence and ego strength at age three and a half and scored higher at ages four and five on measures of curiosity. In another sample, securely attached three-year-olds displayed more signs of peer competence than their anxiously attached peers. Even though secure attachment may promote social competence in laboratory settings or at later ages in school, it is unclear whether a similar relationship holds for younger children in day care where other factors such as the stress of separation might be expected to affect behaviour as well. Further, the implications for anxiously attached children's adjustment to day-care needs to be explored.

Investigations of individual differences in the quality of attachment might consider the process by which children use the substitute caregiver as a secure base as well as the quality of that relationship. Similar inquiries might also examine whether anxious secure attachment relationships with the mother are mirrored in the relationship with the caregiver. Apparently, children are able to sue substitute caregivers for security when under stress in new situations and many even do so with a stranger. Although there is a good deal of information on the conditions under which infants form secure attachment bonds to the mother, little is known about the formation and the nature of attachment bonds with new caregivers and the conditions under which these attachments optimally occur.

Early childhood educators have long struggled with the issue of initial adjustment periods and methods to bring the child about a sense of familiarity. Using a minimalist approach Schwatz and Wynn found that an initial visit to the center by the mother and child had little effect on later adjustment, but the visit was brief and exposure to the new adult was minimal. A maximalist approach would frame the issue somewhat differently. Suppose maternal presence in the center provides the child with a secure base to explore and become familiar with other children and adults. Suppose also that some of these individuals eventually become able to function as supports for the child when the mother leaves. A maximalist approach might attempt to identify the time span within which most children are able to form sufficiently robust secondary attachments to facilitate the transition. A teacher who has visited the child at home several times, a familiar peer, or a sibling may, separately or in combination, serve to smooth the transition period. Numerous other factors such as the level of cooperation and understanding between mother and caregiver, the mother's way of managing the separation or the warmth and skill of the caregiver probably contribute in some measure to ameloriating distress. Our point is simply that a theory of practice must identify controllable aspects of the environment which in various combinations make a difference for most children.

Arousal Theory

Children spend a substantial amount of time and energy exploring their environment. But this environment is not a neutral force. Some environments are relatively barren and offer little enticement. Others are excessively stimulating and overwhelm children rather than entice them. Although Berlyne's arousal theory of curiosity and exploration is less well developed than attachment theory, it provides a useful framework for considering the influence of the physical environment on child behaviour. If attachment theory implies that a secure base facilitates exploratory behaviour, arousal theory implies that some environments are more explorable than others. According to Berlyne, there are at least two types of exploratory behaviour, specific and diversive that differ in the way they are tied to environmental events. Specific exploration occurs when the individual is disturbed by a "lack of information, and is thus left prey to uncertainty and conflict". A lack of information occurs when the individual encounters stimulation that is novel, surprising, ambiguous, incongruous, complex, or in other ways too difficult to assimilate easily. Specific exploration supplies the "precise information" that the individual misses. Berlyne uses the term "curiosity" to describe the condition of discomfort that motivates specific exploration. By contrast, diversive exploration occurs when the environment is too familiar, too predictable, and too easy to assimilate. Under these conditions, individuals seek out stimulation to alleviate boredom. But sometimes stimulation is in excess; the environment is too novel, too ambiguous, too complex, or too unpredictable. Instead of eliciting approach and contact, these environments may elicit fear and withdrawal. The glue binding these behaviours is provided by the construct of arousal, a motivating state that can be too low, too high, or just right. When the individual's level of arousal departs from a comfortable optimum, the individual engages in exploration or avoidance until the optimum is restored.

Several studies have examined children's behaviour with materials varying in complexity. Two of these seem especially informative with respect to the physical characteristics of early childhood environments likely to sustain children's interest. In one study the investigators, constructed two play settings varying in complexity. The low-complexity setting consisted of two large trestles, one medium-sized trestle, a balance beam, four mats, a slide, a bench, and a chair. The high-complexity setting included all of the above and, in addition, a metal ladder and a rope spanning the two large trestles, five wooden panels and three ropes attached to each of the trestle, and two wooden boxes and four wooden cubes arranged underneath the trestles. Over a period of three consecutive weeks, two groups of ten children were exposed to each setting for fifteen minutes a day. The investigators asked, first, whether children would prefer the more complex setting to the less complex one and, second, whether this interest would be sustained over successive days. The results were relatively straightforward. The children showed a higher level of engagement with the more complex apparatus. Over the three-week period, their engagement with each type of apparatus dropped, but at the end of three weeks, the children still preferred the more complex apparatus. Clearly, with repeated exposure, children's interest in even attractive play equipment will diminish. There is also evidence that children's waning interests can be recharged. In one study, changing half the items in a toy set increased children's interest in the toys. Berlyne's theory and the findings that follow from it suggest that a theory of practice might need to include rules for producing complexity and variation in the classroom setting.

Properly speaking, Berlyne's theory is not a theory of development. There are no specific provisions in the theory for statements about developmental change either in the form of exploratory behaviour or in elements of the environments likely to attract children at different ages. However, the theory does suggest that as children encounter stimulation, their ability to process environmental information will improve. Older children are expected to prefer higher levels of novelty, and to be less likely to be fearful of new or complex events. However, for any particular event, preference, boredom, or avoidance will depend on the child's prior experiences. Unfortunately, the theory has not developed to the point of being able to identify in advance which events are likely to be more or less familiar or understood. However, the idea that children's response to such events will vary as a function of age is consistent with the evidence. For example, there is some evidence that young children may avoid excessive complexity. In one study, children were presented two-dimensional vinyl shapes varying in complexity according to the number of turns on the edges. In two-year-olds, exploratory behaviour increased from low to moderate levels of stimulus complexity but when declined. By contrast, in four-to seven-year-olds, exploratory behaviour reached its highest level with the most complex objects. The message of the study is that a level of complexity that encourages exploration in older children may discourage it in younger children. An activity that intrigues a four-year-old may overwhelm a two-year-old.

Theory of Exploratory Behaviour

According to arousal theorists, Len's aimless wandering can be interpreted as a response to boredom. The tussle with Jimmy offered a source of relief, except that it was not a permitted activity. The water table provided a pleasant level of novelty and the possibilities it offered sustained Len's interest for several days. In an attempt to refine arousal theory, Nunnally and Lemon proposed a sequential model of exploratory behaviour. according to this model, an interesting event produces heightened attention followed by specific exploration. The object is explored or manipulated until uncertainty concerning its physical properties is reduced.

Uncertainty reduction is followed by pretense or some other form of play identified with autistic thinking. Finally, boredom sets in, the individual sets off in search of stimulation, and the sequence repeats itself. The advantages of the Nunnally and Lemon model is that it introduces a role for play as distinct from exploration, but for the most part, the behavioural categories employed by arousal theorists are fairly global. Neither the stimulus properties that attract children's interest nor the behaviours they engage in have been sufficiently specified to offer more than a suggestive framework for a theory of practice.

In Berlyne's theory of exploratory behaviour, individuals seek out objects or experiences for their own sake rather than for rewards arbitrarily associated with such activity. According to this view, the motivation for activity is built into the activity itself. If intrinsic motivation were part of a theory of practice, emphasis would be more on the inherently appealing activities or materials practitioners might offer children than on systems of external rewards or inducements. In Berlyne's theory, intrinsic motivation is conceptualized as the alleviation of aversive states.

Theory of Mastery Motivation

For a more positive perspective, it is necessary to turn to White's notion of mastery motivation which owes much to the work of Piaget. Suppose an infant notices the movement of a toy parrot suspended above his crib. Soon after, the infant discovers that deliberate body movements will control the toy's movements. According to Berlyne, the moving parrot provokes the child's curiosity; he explores the parrot until sufficient information is gained and uncertainty is reduced. But this explanation does not account for the seeming goalorientedness of the behaviour. The baby's exploration is not haphazard and exploration is not a simple matter of visual or tactile contact. Rather, something special happens when the child discovers the contingency between his behaviour and an event. This discovery seems to have its own special reward. According to Piaget, the infant has a special capacity to detect such contingencies and to perceive them as causally connected. The child interprets the contingency as evidence of control and derives a feeling of efficacy from successful efforts to control the environment. According to this view, children not only are motivated to recognize a challenge when it is presented to them, but they also seek out optimally challenging situations.

Suppose children are presented a range of problems, some easy, some middling, and some hard. Which problems will children choose, and which will give them the most pleasure? Recent evidence suggests that children will choose moderately difficult problems, even when more difficult problems can be solved. Moreover, they derive more pleasure from mastering the moderately difficult challenges through the feelings of pleasure that come with mastery. These findings highlight what we already know; survival in a harsh world may enhance one's feeling of competence without necessarily bringing joy and pleasure. The evidence suggests that in a theory of practice, there may be a need for statements about the diversification of challenges and the child's freedom to choose those best matched to his or her ability. Unfortunately, the research has not clarified how the relation between ability and problem might be specified in advance. And although Piaget's theory has provided much of the basis for the concept of mastery, its structural account of development are challenging at different developmental levels.

Research on intrinsic motivation has yielded additional information of interest to a theory of practice. On the one hand, much of what children do is done because they derive intrinsic pleasure from activity, But on the other, adults often add external rewards in the form of approval, gold stars, or special treats. What happens when intrinsic and extrinsic rewards are mixed? Not surprisingly, the effect depends on the particular children involved. Suppose, for example, that preschool children are divided into two groups who have either a high or a low spontaneous interest in drawing. Also suppose that half the children in each interest group are offered a prize for drawing and the other half are not. Even though the experimental session is brief, rewarded children who initially had a high interest in drawing will, a week later, show less interest than high-interest children who received no extrinsic reward. Children who find an activity intrinsically challenging "turn off" when given prizes for doing what they ordinarily do for its own sake. Moreover, during the reward sessions, the quality of the children's drawings decrease, as if the intrinsic pleasure of combining lines and colours had been replaced by another source of excitement.

A strikingly different effect appeared in children who initially showed little spontaneous interest in drawing. A week after the reward session, these children demonstrated an increased interest in drawing during the free-play period. Changes in the behaviours of these children seemed to follow the rule that extrinsic reinforcement will increase the behaviour upon which it is contingent. But changes in the behaviour of the high-interest children suggest that this rule does not always apply.

According to Lepper et al., extrinsic reward may undermine children's intrinsic motivation because the basis of the activity changes from the intrinsic, "I do it because it's fun to make nice pictures" to the extrinsic, "I do it because it will get me a prize." The shift to extrinsic reward also leads to less complex, less creative, and less refined drawings, as if the introduction of external rewards also undermines the internal standard of excellence so essential to the pursuit of mastery.

A number of theoretical formulations have been developed to account for children's response to aspects of the environment such as novelty, complexity, or challenge. These formulations advance a common notion, namely, that much human activity is sustained by satisfactions inherent in an individual's transactions with the environment. These formulations also clarify differences in the way intrinsic motivation might be conceptualized. Arousal theory points to general features of the environment, whereas mastery theory points to the availability of developmentally appropriate problems.

The concept of mastery motivation is addressed to the general problem of why children acquire skills and learn to solve problems in the absence of social or appetitive pressure. But interesting things happen after a skill has been acquired. A young child learns to go down a slide with much effort; each steep step is slowly mounted, and during the first few trips, the child holds tightly and apprehensively to the sides. Within a few days, the same child goes down the slide in all sorts of complicated ways, rocking, clapping, kicking, singing, back-ways, belly-ways, head first, with a friend, a toy, or some combination of these. These ways of manoeuvring an inclined plane are repeated, elaborated, recombined, and varied. Piaget uses the term practice play to designate activities in which the child creates deliberate complications and seems to make things purposefully difficult. In a mastery activity under the control of a goal, means are marshaled in the service of an end. But in play, means are repeated, elaborated, and become a sources of interest in their own right.

Miller refers to these elaborations of means as "Galumphing". According to Miller, behaviour oriented toward ends becomes efficient and streamlined over time; the child can go up and down the slide with few unnecessary or wasted movements. But after mastery, what next?

Assimilation and Accomodation

Miller argues that pleasure comes neither from environmental challenge nor from arousal stimulated by a novel or unknown object. Rather, the pleasure comes from the child's control over arousal through the production of diversity, regardless of its particular form. Play involves a relative autonomy of means which implies a degree of autonomy for the player. Miller's notion of "galumphing" as a "patterned, voluntary elaboration or complication of process, where the pattern is not under the dominant control of goals" is entirely in keeping with Piaget's notion of play as assimilation. In Piagetian theory, assimilation refers to the process whereby the child imposes his own way of thinking on the world. Accommodation, by contrast, refers to the process whereby the child's organizations are adjusted to meet the world's demands.

In mastery activities, assimilation and accommodation operate synchronously—the child behaves according to what he understands; if the behaviour and goal is attained. In the example given earlier, the infant might smile at the parrot to make it move; if smiling does not work, some other behaviour will be tried until behaviours which reliably move the parrot are found. Assimilation refers to previously acquired action patterns brought to bear on the current problem; accommodation refers to the behavioural adjustments needed to solve the problem.

In play, assimilation dominates accommodation, there is asynchrony rather than synchrony. Action patterns are produced and varied without much regard to a particular goal. According to Piaget, "play proceeds by the relaxation of the effort at adaptation". The pleasure comes from a feeling of super-mastery, a"feeling of virtuosity or power". Play, then, represents a special type of challenge. It is not a type of challenge presented by the environment nor is it a type of challenge sought in the environment. Play represents challenge produced by the child, and as such it offers a special type of developmental opportunity. As one of the authors has noted elsewhere, pretend play illustrates this assimilative mode at a symbolic level. Symbolic play extends the sensory-motor play of an earlier period. Rather than actually going down the slide a hundred ways, the child may make a toy animal go down in ways that for the child would be physically impossible or even disastrous. The toy animal can hop down, leap down, or even fall down. The child can slide down hugging a "frightened" baby doll, turn the slide into a hill for cars, or initiate numerous other activities which transcend the literal meaning of a solid object on an inclined plane. Pretend play as assimilation also implies that means/ends relations have been temporarily severed. What at an earlier period were means are now meanings. During the sensory-motor period, going down the slide head-first was just that—a novel, challenging, slightly scary way of doing a familiar activity. Now the same behaviour might represent a down-hill ride on a sled, a plane coming in for a landing, or a trip to the moon. At an earlier level of development, the slide was a slide, the child was his real self, and the activity occurred in a world of tangible objects. Now, either the slide, the child, or any other feature of the environment can be transformed. According to Piaget, the special pleasure of symbolic play comes from the child's ability to manipulate the very meaning as well as means.

In discussing attachment theory, we noted that one of its values for teachers and parents is that it marks behaviours that reveal how children feel about people and social situations. The theory offers an interpretive framework within which behaviours such as smiles, eye to eye contact, and proximity along with their opposites—frowns, gaze avoidance and distance—hold privileged positions as indicators of children's affectional ties and feelings of comfort and security. In discussing theories of arousal and mastery, we argued that these formulations had more to say about the quality of children's environments than about the quality of their behaviour.

The notion of "galumphing", especially if placed in the context of Piagetian theory, returns us once again to behaviour. At a sensory-motor level of behaviour, play activities develop from activities with a single object to those involving combinations of two or more objects. The overall pattern of object behaviour changes as well. Between the ages of eighteen and twenty-four months, children contact more diverse elements of the environment, and as they do so, the tendency to get struck on one particular object diminishes.

Pretense, too, changes in systematic ways. Initially, the child produces the motions of sleeping without intending to sleep or the motions of eating without intending to eat. These activities seem to take place outside their customary context and are seen divorced from their customary functions of rest and nourishment. Over the next year and a half, these ephemeral gestures become elaborated and enriched. At first, a doll is simply an object to be touched, moved, or banged. Somewhat later, the doll is used as the recipient of food and eventually is made the recipient of a complex array of care-giving activities, it is put to bed, dressed, patted, and spanked. The child's voice quality might change to sound like a parent, gestures, clothing, and other element might combine to indicate that a role enactment is occurring.

At first, the objects used in pretense tend to be similar to the things used in the real life situations that pretend activities mimic. Gradually, the need for verisimilitude weakens and assorted objects can be used as substitutes in pretend enactments. Eventually, the child can create the semblance of a physical entity. Initially, pretend play is a solo activity. Adults may participate and organize it, but children under three years of age rarely share pretend sequences with one another except, perhaps, in brief, imitative, parallel exchanges. By two-and-a-half years of age, the beginning of sociodramatic play appear and, by the age of five years, what began as a few simple gestures encompasses intricate systems of reciprocal roles, ingenious improvisations of materials, increasingly coherent themes, and weaving plots. Sociodramatic play also demonstrates a systematic pattern of developmental changes. At first, children communicate primarily about their own roles. Later, they discuss others' roles and the activities that will be engaged in during the play. There are also changes in the types of role relationships enacted. At first, role relationships tend to be those in which the children have participated in real life, and only later do these encompass the role relationships observed in others. The social organization of the play changes as well. At three, children are more likely to engage in complementary role play in which differentiated roles are assigned, but in the play these roles are enacted independently. Older children are more likely to produce integrative role structures in which the activity of each player is tied to the activity of the others and the roles are constituted through reciprocal relationships between the players.

Information about the development of play behaviour and sensitive observation of behaviour provide clues to children's level of cognitive and social maturity. More important, this information can serve as the basis for attempts to enhance or elaborate the play. A major contribution to a theory of teaching practice can be found in Smilansky's detailed analysis of how teachers might proceed from a careful assessment of children's current level of play to a set of systematic strategies for enriching the thematic context of the play children's skills at using play techniques. Play is also enhanced by features of the physical environment. With respect to a theory of practice, several of these features are under the practitioner's control. Depending on the children's developmental level, realistic prop might be more supportive of play than abstract materials.

According to Nunnally and Lemon, novelty might enhance exploratory behaviour, but familiarity might enhance play. A play space protected from unpredictable intrusions, familiar peers, and unpressured time are other factors likely to enhance play. Further progress toward a theory of practice will require more intensive study of how teachers and others can create optimal conditions for play. As this issue is addressed, abstractions such as novelty or familiarity will require rules for their actual production, rules which then might yield examples of environmental variation currently unavailable to theories of development.

Conclusion

Developmental theory provides a rich course of information about the remarkable intricacies of human growth. Most certainly, respect for the child's special qualities is a necessary starting point for a theory of practice. But the relationship between a theory of development and a theory of practice maybe more intimate. Indeed, the relationship may be one of reciprocity and mutual dependence. Earlier in this chapter, we discussed three distinctively different development theories and the different issues they set out to address. Now, we offer some summary conclusions suggested by that discussion.

Initially, we characterized theories of practice as inherently maximalist, with the qualification that maximizing factors fall within the controllable domain of the practitioner. As Bronfenbrenner astutely noted, a theory of practice creates a demand for an ecological theory of human development. According to our analysis, such a theory will assume the maximalist orientation traditionally adopted by theories of practice and traditionally rejected by theories of development. Brofenbrenner's proposal in effect requires a massive revision of the form of developmental theory. Consider, for example, the way attachment theory has dealt with affectional relations. For numerous reasons, the focus of the theory has been consistently on the child's developing relationship with the particular person, who functions as the primary caregiver during the first year of life. In a theory of practice, this focus must expand. For a theory of parenting for example, the focus must shift to the parent's developing relationships with the child, and include the parent's perception of the social and material resources that impinge upon that relationship. Put another way a theory of parenting must consider the parent's perceptions of the child's perceptions of significant social and material resources. But such a theory must also consider the parent's perceptions of a broader domain, along with rules for mobilizing that domain to serve the best interests of the developing child as determined by the values held by the parent. At the heart of a theory of practice are statements about how controllable resources are to be obtained and allocated. These statements have enormous implications for an ecologically sensitive and valid theory of development. At one time, development theory rested almost exclusively on studies in which the experimental situation was rigged so as to demonstrate almost any possibility. These situations have been properly criticized as artificial, first, because they are likely to be perceived as ersatz even by children, and second, because they often bizarrely distort physical and social events. More recently, there has been a shift in emphasis from rigged to actual environments. But actual environments are inherently opaque because the rigging is obscure.

Attachment theory offers one illustration of the pressure of practice forcing maximalist expansion in a theory of development. Theories of exploration and play illustrate a different type of pressure. In the case of arousal theory, concept of complexity or novelty are too general to serve the needs if practiced without additional elaboration. In a theory of development, it is necessary to formulate rules for reducing the immense diversity and variability of the world into general categories; when applied, these rules transform particulars into potentially universal dimensions. These rules make it possible to define complexity as the number of moveable parts in a climbing apparatus or as the number of turns in a vinyl object. But in a theory of practice, universal dimensions must be transformed into particulars; the rules of practice are generative rather than reductive. These rules will be restricted to the particular domain of resources controlled by a given practitioner, but they will be stated so that within the domain an immense variety of concrete examples can be generated. If complexity and novelty are crucial physical dimensions governing the exploratory behaviour of children and if this behaviour is deemed a desirable goal for practice then a theory of practice must contain rules for generating environments that are appropriately complex or novel. The theory of mastery motivation illustrates another problem. To date, this theory has not taken full advantage of the development theory from which it was derived. The theory is unnecessarily overgeneralized, omitting the voluminous literature specifying qualitative changes in the nature of children's thinking. From the perspective of practice, this omission offers an instance in which development theory has not taken full advantage of its own potential. A proper theory of mastery requires evidence of the way in which children in the natural environment define and solve problems as a function of their level of cognitive development.

2
Curriculum Models

Since the advent of formal education for young children, curriculum models have appeared in one form or another. But focus upon the utility of early education curriculum models has sharpened considerably in recent years. Perhaps the most notable force in this sharpening process is the planned variation experiment first integrated into Project Follow through, later extended on a limited basis to Project Head Start. Selected educational authorities were encouraged to propose conceptual alternative for controlled application in educational settings for children of ages four to eight. The result was a widely ranging set of curricular activities and instructional strategies to operationalize preferred philosophies or theories of child development, learning, and education. Implicit in this thrust to develop, implement, and evaluate models were two fundamental assumptions : no one best way exists to educate all children in all social contexts, and different curriculum models are variously well suited for different children in different social contexts. This move to develop alternative curriculum models was consistent with the value of pluralism in education, conceivably to provide the citizenry with choices among legitimate and comparable educational designs. Serious students of early childhood education theory and practice will note many important questions about the alternative models ideals, three of which are addressed here.

The first question concerns model building—that is, which model characteristics or components are functional and relevant as a framework for developing curriculum models in the original sense? Once determined and used for model building, these characteristics or components should be further useful for the comparative analysis of alternative models. Such analysis normally will concern a specification of similarities and differences among models at theoretical-descriptive level. As for similarities, a prime issue is the extent to which models agree upon certain fundamentals eventhough these models may emerge from diverse theoretical wellsprings and represent "different roads to Rome". Authentication of similarities may result in the identification of a basic core of principles and conditions: to represent the best of educational thought about early childhood curricula, and to serve as the point of departure for the creation of new curriculum models. A parallel issue is the extent to which model rationales may differ in substance or design. From these differences will flow implications about children's educational welfare, cost to society, suitability to various social contexts, and so on. Differences among early educational curriculum models are certain to reflect value commitments about what is more or less important for young children and their families. Presumably, these differential commitments will affect educational practices and, in turn, educational outcomes. It is incumbent upon model builders clearly to identify these commitments at the theoretical-descriptive level so that analysts and consumers can determine distinctiveness.

A second major question about curriculum models goes beyond a conceptual analysis of similarities and differences at the theoretical-descriptive level. It investigates as to how clearly are these theoretical model similarities and differences revealed in actual educational practices? It is one thing to state distinctive curriculum components on paper; to validate such components by way of empirical observation is quite another. Validation requires a set of procedures for measuring model implementation, often referred to as process evaluation. Process evaluation involves an assessment of the presence and merit of program components antecedent to or theoretically functional for attaining model objectives.

The third major question about curriculum models is to what extent various models when implemented competently, are effective in producing their intended educational outcomes? This question usually draws attention first to any changes in children's behaviour and development that are associated with model implementation. But outcome assessment will often include the evaluation of changes among teachers, parents, and even community services that follow model implementation. In practice, curriculum model guidelines can vary markedly in criterion-based evaluation. This means that the acid test for model implementation is how well or how completely stated goals and methods of a given model as inherently worthy and evidence can be marshaled to demonstrate the model's capacity to "deliver", it may matter little how the favoured model compares to others. However, many consumers are understandably intrigued by questions about which models are more or less efficient and effective for achieving generic outcomes. This implicit competitive aspect of model development and implementation may be masked by the idea that different models are more or less effective for different outcomes. So the issue of comparative model effectiveness lingers on. A clear conception of model characteristics is relevant for several important tasks. Such characteristics can serve as analytical criteria useful for model selection. Those characteristics also provide a basis from which to plan model improvements and even create new models. An understanding of model characteristics is relevant to educational researchers. Many characteristics can be considered as independent variables to guide model implementation and impact research. Eventually, this research may provide a clearer picture of what model children whose needs and learning styles differ. In fact, research along these lines may disclose that some characteristics have little, if any, bearing on children's educational development while others are critical for this development.

Theoretical foundations for curriculum models typically reflect a mix of philosophical and psychological thought about educational aims. This mix will include value statements about the basic purpose(s) of education in concert with assumptions about children's learning and development. Thus,"should's" and "ought's" about education to promote the good life are focal. These statements of good usually link with convictions about what are the essential conditions of learning and development for instructional design. The interrelationships of educational ideology and psychological theory are at best complex and intricate.

At worst, these interrelationships are obscure, confusing, or conspicuously absent. Over time, however, certain bodies of consistent, integrated thought about philosophy and psychology have come to dominate curriculum models for early childhood education. These bodies of thought are identified by various labels, such as the behaviourist, dynamic, and constructivist approaches.

Model philosophies and educational aims are diverse, but much of their conceptual diversity can be reduced to a relative emphasis upon one or another of two broad goal orientations for children: to nurture general socialization or to achieve specific learnings, usually in the academic realm. Also associated with this emphasis are differences in interpretation of ideas about education as preparation for the future. One interpretation is a claim that young children's education should be designed on the basis of requisites for success in adult society. Children's momentary or transitory needs and interests are subservient to adult beliefs about what achievements and skills are essential for socio-economic self-sufficiency. Applied to early childhood curriculum models, this view includes support for "continuity in the educational enterprise as it currently exists".

A foremost priority is solving the problem of sequencing preschool educational demands to better prepare children for successive demands in the kindergarten and primary grades. This means that educational planning is essentially a "top down" experience. Broadly defined adult roles and values form the basis of formal K-12 span of educational requirements. Early childhood curricula, as preschool-kindergarten, are conceived to facilitate successful adaptation to existing primary programs, and so on. Although all formal educational programmes are to some extent "preparatory," the issue is one of degree or emphasis. Education as preparation for the future may too easily result in a "cold storage" concept of learning.

Should educators not be forced to justify the worth of learning experiences for children in terms of some projected scholastic or socioeconomic value? It is argued that such thinking diverts attention from young children's interests and unique learning thinking styles, especially as expressed in play. Instead, their uniqueness should be nurtured to stimulate balanced affective and cognitive development. Protagonists for a nurturance view of early education claim that the best insurance for successful adulthood is fully enriched, day-to-day, child-centered experience. From this, children will best develop a secure sense of competence and selfhood.

Curriculum planning begins with an analysis of children's developmental characteristics, consistent with their unique needs, interests, and modes of thinking a "bottom up" design. In this way, a strong foundation for subsequent growth and development is achieved.

Concomitantly, ideal early childhood education may promote both social and educational reform. This is because the educational system would accommodate *to* children instead of requiring the conformity dictated by top-down curriculum development. The philosophical difference in curriculum aims and purposes is paralleled in the fields of developmental psychology: a schism between proponents of "naturalistic, indigenous growth" theories of development and the "cultural competence" or "environmental determination" viewpoint. The schism aggravates contentions about desirable conditions of learning. These contentions, in turn, line to preferences about curriculum methods. Advocates of the natural growth or maturationsist view argue that the best education will be achieved by providing children with an enriched, permissive, and relatively informal environment. High value is placed upon children's need for creative expression.

Through such expression, self-development is best nurtured; developmental or maturational sequences provide whatever cues may be important for realizing individual growth potentials. In contrast, supporters of the "cultural competence" school emphasize more the shaping power of experience and necessity for social adaptation. Systematize and direct tuition thus figure more prominently in socialization practice and skill achievement.

Accordingly, the structure and continuity of environmental events will largely determine children's patterns of learning and development. This schism in thinking about the nature of human development has been adroitly couched in terms of context-free versus context-sensitive theories of development. Early childhood educators sympathetic to the universals of child development, especially stage-sequence interpretations from genetic psychology, will claim that basic principles of developmental education apply to all children. These principles should provided the basis for common educational experiences at successive age levels. Though differences in developmental level are carefully accounted for, differences associated with socioeconomic status, racial-ethnic identity, and other demographics do not figure strongly in thinking about goals or aims. From this it can be argued that development per se is the fundamental aim of education. Philosophies that are context-specific or context-sensitive will, in contrast, accentuate the role of cultural variables in promoting or impeding children's skills acquisition. Thus, educational aims may emerge from an analysis of any learning deficiencies allegedly rooted in social background experience.

Schism in education philosophy and psychological theory represent, of course, degrees of emphasis, and not conceptual dichotomies. Thus, curriculum model philosophy and aims can be viewed in relative position along a given continuum of thought. For example, the applied behaviour analysis approach leans more in the direction of a cultural-competence, context-sensitive viewpoint than do constructivist approaches, which have more in common with a natural growth, context-free position. Even, so pure applications of educational philosophy and developmental theory are not easily observed in everyday, practical experience.

Theoretically based differences can become a reality, however, as indicated by various model demonstration programs and the planned variation experiments within Projects Head start and Follow through. Among the clearest theory-based differences are extent of child-centeredness in educational planning, nature or type of learning sequences, account on basic academics, incentive systems, and explicitness in seeking affective outcomes. These differences are generally consistent with values and assumptions of alternative philosophies and theories. However, in the final analysis shorter-term objectives and methods for achieving them seem more vocally disputed among early childhood educators than are longer-range educational aims. In face, efforts to promote unification of purpose have been called for under the banner of social competence.

One's philosophical view of education and human development is the foremost model component from which statements about curriculum goals, content, and method will emanate. For a conceptual analysis of models, the issue for this component is twofold: comprehensiveness and internal consistency. A comprehensive, internally consistent statement will articulate the theoretical basis from which a model is conceived to clarify the logical interrelationships of philosophy and psychology. It will also clarify assumptions about educational purpose, conditions of human learning, and the nature of human development. It will further show how assumptions are integrated with other basic model components, especially curriculum content and methods. Coherence of philosophy and aims is a matter of both degree and kind.

Another major category of curriculum model components concerns policies and procedures for overall program administration or management. In contrast to philosophical discourse about education and child development, specific literature about administrative variables of early education models seems less extensive. Consequently, much information about this topic must be extrapolated from general educational administration literature. It is perhaps significant that specific administrative concerns are being addressed more and more by early childhood professionals. There seems to be no definitive consensus about how best to categorize administrative policy variables for the conceptual analysis of curriculum models. Some administrators prefer a human relations approach to administrative policy. Their focus is staff and community involvement for policy development and implementation. Other administrators work from a more technical orientation to management, dealing especially with the economics of a program, including fiscal policy and cost efficiency studies. Still others take an ecological stance, stressing the study of political, sociological, and legal forces that influence or dictate administrative decision making. Acknowledgment of different orientations need not distract attention from the point that administrative variables represent decision-making points about how best to insure the success of an educational program. Accordingly, it is convenient to group administrative policy variables into three interrelated categories upon which is superimposed a method for establishing program budget. These are policy about personnel, the physical setting for model implementation, and program evaluation. Personnel specifications for early education curriculum models include nature of the population to be served, identification of staff to deliver basic services, and community participation or involvement, especially parents or primary caregivers. Criteria should be present to define pupil eligibility for a given model or population characteristics useful for determining the suitability of a model. These criteria may include age, cultural-linguistic background, socioeconomic status, clinical health status, ethnicity, and even sex.

Some models claim their suitability for all children of a particular age group or developmental stage, regardless of cultural background. Others are designed specifically for special populations as, say a bilingual program for limited English-speaking children, in addition.

A pupil personal services policy should, address the following topics: health, safety, nutritional standards, individual pupil assessment practices, procedures for reporting pupil progress to parents, referral procedures for children with special problems, guarantees for children's rights and general ethical guidelines for program quality.

Program staff, a second major category for personnel policy considerations, concerns teachers, aides, administrators and supervisors, and adjunct service personnel. Minimal staff qualifications, hiring policies, in-service training provisions, staff evaluation procedures, staff pupil ratio designations, grouping practices, and extent of staff involvement in curriculum decision making are common sources of personnel staff variation. To illustrate, one sorely argued difference in early education staff function is the extent to which teachers are trained to implement a fixed or "teacher-proof" curriculum versus developing competence in the management of one that is more fluid. Flexible, informal standards or requirements for preserve credentials, staff training, selection, and evaluation will be influenced substantially by one's position on this issue.

A third major category of policy considerations deals with forms of community involvement in early education programs. These forms usually vary according to the age of the children. If a model's major thrust is home-based education, then parental involvement policies-including parent education-are of paramount importance.

Strategies for securing involvement can be described along a continuum from none-to-minimal to nearly complete parental control of an educational program. Some models are founded upon principles of parent involvement.

Others exclude direct parent participation. Either way, policies can be traced to a model's theoretical foundations and should generate testable assumptions about the relationship of parental involvement to children's developmental education. These policies may also extend to decision making about parent education. Inextricably bound to administrative considerations are physical setting requirements for model implementation. This calls for attention to space equipment needs and their arrangements, juxtaposed with health and safety standards. Existing programs carry remarkably in their degree to an ideal physical rationale.

Well-developed models often provide explicit graphics, as floor plans, to guide appropriate implementation. Minimum square footage for classroom and playground space may also be recommended. These considerations are significant in view of two broader issues about the physical environment for early education: first, the place where children's formalized early education is best conducted, and second, what effects physical space variables may have on children's behaviour. Space considerations are closely bound to time use as well. Time use—meaning allotments for specific learning activities—anticipates a forthcoming discussion about curriculum methods. But administrative policy issues are also involved in decision labour, full-or half-day programming, definition of a "school year," and so on. Incredible as it may seem, little is known about the effects of different time arrangements on children in formal educational programs.

The third and final major category of curriculum model administrative policy explored here involves provisions for ongoing program evaluation: determining the worth of integral model components and, ultimately, the model as a whole. These provisions can be classified into formative and summative evaluation tasks.

Formative evaluation-instrumental during the early stages of model development and implementation-addresses the extent and quality of intended services. In contrast, summative evaluation address the overall worth of a model program at some terminal or critical decision point. Program administrators may also find it desirable and even necessary in an increasingly economic minded society to apply principles of cost analysis to program evaluation. If so, summative model impact is studied in terms of cost efficiency, cost-benefit, cost utility, or cost effectiveness.

A cost-effectiveness approach will involve evaluation for the purpose of gaining maximum results for the lowest or most reasonable expenditure. Both formative and summative evaluation procedures demand careful attention to the selection of appropriate measurement and data-analysis techniques. Also important for this aspect of administrative policy are personnel qualification's authority, and responsibilities for evaluation.

Generally speaking, insiders familiar with the workings of the model have both an advantage and a vested interest in "trouble-shooting" their program and providing constructive feedback to other staff for program improvement. In contrast, qualified and disinterested external evaluation specialists are usually better situated to provide objective summative evaluation. In either case, administrative guidelines to justify the role definition and selection of evaluation personnel are at issue.

Administrative policies comprise a major category of curriculum model characteristics. These policies encompass practical decision making about personnel, physical facilities, and program evaluation. Ideally, policies are consistent with, if not determined directly by, overall model philosophy.

Any set of model administration policies must be accompanied by a master fiscal policy, usually to include cost-accounting procedures. Fiscal concerns will be model-specific though general principles for budgeting and accounting can apply. Interested readers may consult Candoli et al., for further information.

The joint issues of what and how best to educate young children have persisted unabated since the earliest days of formal educational thought. Neither issue is easily divorced from model philosophy and aims nor conveniently isolated from administrative policy decisions. For present purposes, however, content concerns the what of learning and its general arrangement in a curriculum: methods concerns presentation strategies—the how of curriculum delivery.

Model philosophy and content selection go hand in hand. For example, a model based upon a philosophy of essentialism will be defined in content by a selected body of knowledge to which all children are exposed, ecological variables notwithstanding. Key issues associated with this philosophical stance include justifying the essentials and determining valid means or securing their achievement. Fixed or uniform levels of mastery or minimum competence for children in advance of instruction are compatible with this position.

Content selection for a second model, in contrast, may spring from a moral imperative. This means that, to whatever extent possible, children should have freedom to exercise their own learning styles, choose their own content, and determine their own competence standards. Given this imperative, neither uniform content nor fixed ideas about pedagogy figure strongly in educational planning. Somewhere in between essentialism and the moral imperative for self-determined education may emerge a moderate, child-centered position to emphasize opportunity for content choices from among a varied but limited set of options. Emphasis vary even among moderate positions.

One longstanding content distinction in early education concerns learning for cognitive-intellectual achievement on the one hand and affective-social growth on the other. Cognitive-affective distinctions, of course, can easily strike a false or artificial dichotomy when, in truth, such leanings are highly interrelated. Yet, the distinction is important, especially for scrutiny of content priorities within a curriculum model. It is instructive to note that educational applications of integrated cognitive and social development theory have been proposed. A second, related distinction for curriculum model analysis is academic skills or subject matter proficiency versus intellectual content or cognitive skills proficiency.

A primarily academic emphasis concerns acquisition of predetermined factual material along traditional subject mater lines. Intellectual content, however, is concentrated more upon the heuristic of learning, general inquiry skills, elaboration skills, and problems-solving strategies.

Theoretically, a cognitive-intellectual skills approach is independent from academic content. If so, academic content is seen as a means to an end, not as an end in itself. It seems fair to say that uncertainty, if not confusion and wariness, pervades decision making about content for early childhood education. Research has not yet confirmed much about what program contents are best for successive levels of early education. Promising rationales for content selection have been proposed, but they are infrequently applied in practice. Perhaps the most basic content issue for educators to address, concerns a functional taxonomy for classifying educational content and objectives. To date, standard, consensual taxonomy permeates early childhood educational model building; nor is consensus likely in view of theoretical foundation differences among models.

Curriculum models for intellectually precocious children are frequently governed by Guliford's structure of intellect theory to emphasize figural, symbolic, semantic, and behavioural content. Still other taxonomies are used for educational planning and evaluation, despite nagging questions about their empirical validity.

The taxonomy issue prompts a further specification of three integral content components important for the conceptual analysis of curriculum models: scope, priorities, and structure. Scope refers to the breadth or variety of content and skill values built into a curriculum model. One model may incorporate content across a broad spectrum, such as aesthetics, cognitive intellectual skills, basic concept acquisition academics, and social-affective skills. Other models may emphasize fewer skills domains, even to exclude certain content areas such as academics or aesthetics. Closely related to scope are the relative priorities assigned to content within a curriculum model. One clear indicator of priorities is amount of time allocated for content exposure.

The variable time of exposure is critical for estimating children's opportunities for both acquisition and rehearsal or practice as well as practicing learnings. Exposure time can be operationalized in various ways, as, for example, by "time on task" or sheer duration of learning events. Either way, important links to curriculum methods surface here, especially pacing and intensity of stimulation. Multiple interactions between and among content and methods variables can thus be proposed for empirical study. Such interactions are particularly notable in the brouhaha surrounding basic language training and remediation for young children.

A third major content component variable is content organization or structure with accompanying rationales about sequencing content for different modes of instruction. Again, theoretical foundations are at least implicit in prescriptions for structuring content. One model, for example, may reflect armchair analysis of the structure of knowledge. Another may draw upon experimental task analysis procedures. Still another may base content organization and structure upon broad developmental sequences of cognition, as disclosed by longitudinal and cross-sectional research with children. However, it may be conceptualized, content structure provides another continuum insofar as analysis is concerned. At one extreme of this continuum are tightly organized, immutable content sequences prescribed for all children. At the other extreme are content structures supported by the moral imperative. These latter structures may be arbitrarily determined or conceivably, based upon comprehensive assessment of individual readiness for learning. There is some degree of consensus among theoreticians that much of human learning and development is hierarchical in nature. Consensus is lacking, however, about the precise nature of hierarchical learning and the conditions or forces that influence hierarchical progression. An issue is a basis for structuring educational content over time for most effective learning, retention, and transfer. Controversy along these lines seems most pointed in the extent to which model advocates believe that external organization of content and general learning activities is desirable or necessary for given learning outcomes.

Some additional content variables relevant to this discussion are continuity and stability or regularity in curriculum experience. To the extent that thematic content is introduced, built upon, sustained, and integrated during a given instructional day, one can speak of continuity. To illustrate, consider a teacher who introduces selected grammatical structures during formal language training and then integrates these same structures with other lessons later in the day, such as musical songs, poetry, and arithmetic story problems.

A common learning can thus be reinforced while simultaneously providing the occasion for generalization or transfer of learning. Stability refers to the extent to which a particular pattern of curriculum encounters recurs with predictable regularity, as daily, weekly, and so on. Model content high in stability will be revealed by specific curriculum routines.

A model may prescribe that each day opens with a group planning activity and closes with a group evaluation of things accomplished. The interim period would be filled with an established order of content-related activities. Presumably, stability is important for children as an aid to time perspective development, sequential thinking, and general emotional security. If so, curriculum stability may be more or less important, depending upon age and experiential background of the children involved. But a compulsive regularity, with few breaks from routine, conceivably could result in boredom and fatigue among some children. By the same token, insufficient regularity could breed anxiety and frustration among others. These ideas are relatively untested but appear together with other related hypotheses about the psychology of the open classroom.

A final content variable is how content and skills emphases are translated into program objectives. One feature of curriculum objectives readily culled from model analysis is the extent to which objective are explicit and operationalized for appropriate assessment.

In general, model objectives most suited to reliable measurement are specific, precise, and stated in terms of observable behaviour. The objective will state what a learner should be able to do, under what level of competency. A rich literature on the characteristics and application of behavioural objectives has accumulated together with many attendant issues about their utility and effects. Some content domains have been more amenable to behavioural phraseology than others.

Consequently, models may present varying degrees of specificity and precision across content domains. Models are far from uniform in their affinity for behavioural objectives and choice of measurement strategy. At the theoretical level, any set of content or skill objectives, however, operationalized, should flow consistently from the overall goals or global, long-range aims which are revealed in curriculum philosophy. Unfortunately, rationales for translating broad, general program goals into specific objectives for instructional design are obscure, if extant, in many contemporary models. The clarity, relevance, and appropriateness of curriculum content objectives surface as basic criteria for decisions about pupil progress assessment and model program evaluation. Still larger educational issues surface as well, including program accountability functions, how a curriculum model for young children may fit into broader developmental perspective, and measurement philosophy. As with curriculum content, methods are conceptualized described in many different ways. Standard designations of general methods come immediately to mind—tutorial, discussion, recitation, lecture, laboratory demonstrations—each of which has its own strengths and limitations insofar as establishing conditions for learning is concerned. More basic for conceptual analysis, however, is a set of methodological dimensions or processes that can be described as didactic versus prepared and group versus individual.

A didactic versus prepared methods dimension concerns the extent to which teachers engage in expository teaching in contrast to more indirect means for preparing or arranging the learning environment to facilitate children's active involvement and self-initiated discovery learning. At issue are the how's and why's of alternative teacher-learner role enactment, that is, role definition in relation to curriculum objectives.Likewise, the group versus individual dimension involves a relative preference for group-based activities common for all learners or the desires of individualized learning experiences. Group-based activity unusually emphasizes uniform presentation and teacher-controlled recitation strategies. Although group may range in size, adult-child interactions typically dominate with varying degrees of freedom for child-child interactions. Programs that emphasize individualized experiences can also present a wide range of adult-child interactions with considerable attention to tutorial relationships, self-pacing, varied-child materials, and ample peer interactions. In practice, model programs rarely show an exclusive preference for one or the other methodological format.

Dominant patterns of experience are common, however, and different combinations of methods may vary through time. Thus, there are model differences in pacing, wherein the frequency and rapidity of alternative individual-group and prepared-didactic experiences are salient concerns. Decisions about pacing various combinations of experience imply beliefs about what means are more or less suitable for what ends. For example, small-group activities may be preferred to promote children's cooperative behaviour;

individualized discovery methods may be introduced to promote autonomous problem solving, and so on. Such beliefs or preferences about means-end relations provide a rich source of research hypotheses for field research.

However basic the covering dimensions of didactic-prepared and group-individual methods are, additional variables further illustrate the methods substructure of curriculum models. For example, formal assessment strategies to determine children's program entry behaviour usually figure prominently in any diagnostic-prescriptive instructional design, regardless of whether the learning task in question are introduced at a group or at an individual level.

Motivational strategies also come into play. Curriculum models frequently differ in their emphasis upon activating and nurturing intrinsic motives or incentive systems that constitute extrinsic sources of motivation. The issue of relations between intrinsic motivation and extrinsic rewards has intensified in recent years, partly because of strong behaviouristic influences in early childhood education. Current research issues, by no means resolves to include the study of learn for learning's sake. A related motivational strategy variable under study is classroom goal structure: the relative emphasis placed upon cooperative and competitive activity as the antecedent to group versus individual rewards and recognition, respectively. A methods dimension closely tied with motivation psychology is the preferred style of teacher-child interaction to include corrective feedback strategies. Some research issues here are teacher's question-asking strategies and their effects, how best to deal with the wrong response, the role of different types and schedules of reinforcement for different kinds of learning, and nonverbal communications in teaching.

A second class of human interaction variables in model development concerns peer tutorial methods and cooperative team learning strategies. This class of variables reflects a growing research interest in the Learning Through Teaching movement.

Recent methods and results of various peer-tutoring and group-investigation strategies are reviewed by Sharan. Still another class of instructional methods important for model analysis includes procedures for facilitating retention and positive transfer of learning. As for enhancing retention, especially long-term effectiveness of learning, several instructional design variables are noteworthy: procedures for generating meaningfulness of children's new learning, assisting children it develop coding strategies for effective memory storage and retrieval, and appropriate practice and review tactics. In turn, securely reoriented learnings are a necessary, though insufficient, condition for positive transfer. By this is meant the extent to which school learnings facilitate later performance and learning, both in and out of the school context. It is tempting to argue that transfer is what school is all about. Theoretically, models designed to prepare children for successful adaptation to future schooling should show a strong commitment to vertical transfer; early, simpler learnings are purported to facilitate learning of later, more complex, and subordinate learnings.

Models that stress acquisition of problem-solving strategies or "learning how to learn" imply a bias for skills that serve children well in an unpredictable and changing world. In any case, methods to promote transfer will have in common a focus on rules or principles that have broad generality, varied application of these rules and principles and explicit procedures to establish a set to transfer, and so on.

A problem for model analysis is the extent to which a formal theory of transfer guides the process of instructional design. A final method component to be discussed here is the orchestration of instructional media and materials: how sensory equipment, audio-visual resources, simulation games, autotelic devices, kits, workbooks, and other resources are coordinated and used.

Variety in instructional media and materials is basic to any system of individualized instruction and enables a flowing of stimulation across different sensory modalities to maintain children's attention and reinforce learning. Appropriately scheduled, the novelty effect of various media theoretically can also sustain motivation for learning. It is important, of course, to distinguish among the mere presence of alternative media sources, their quality, how these sources are used, and their effects on educational development. Much has been learned about the impact of instructional media variables on learning that is useful to model builders. But with the possible exception of television studies, media research with preschool children seems to have lagged behind that of older learners.

Given young children's natural propensity for play, there seems to be a strong potential for games approaches to learning. These include physical activities to reinforce academic skills and group games for coordinated human development. Research possibilities seem especially promising for the media component of early childhood curriculum models.

The curriculum methods dimension of curriculum models can be defined in terms of certain basic criteria.

These criteria include the didactic-prepared, individual-group distinction as well as preassessment strategies, motivational procedures, interaction style, feedback procedures, provisions for transfer, and instructional resources.

Choice of instructional methods is tied directly to beliefs about the conditions of learning. That is, methods comprise means to manipulate the ways in which children receive, price's, and act upon information from the environment. Thus, any set of prescribed methods presumably will reflect hypotheses about what conditions are essential for learning efficiency and effectiveness.

From humanistic perspectives, education rhetoric supports the value of a warmly responsive, benevolent learning environment as best for young children. Humanists may call for the nurturant emotional climate primarily on moral grounds; but empirical data, such as a negative relationship between teacher's use of hostile criticism and children's achievement and attitudes towards school are also germane to this point. However passionate any rhetoric, the research issue here is how well an intended emotional climate occurs in model implementation.

Children themselves also contribute to classroom climate in several ways, the attitudes and expectancies they bring initially to the formal setting, their reinforcement that occurs in the classroom, and so on. In larger perspective, though curriculum models may be analyzed on conceptual grounds, independent of any social context, their implementation and effectiveness cannot. And both the implementation and the impact of a given model may vary with the context in which implementation occurs. Eventually, then, the validity of a model must be determined from the observation of real events. This prompts a shift from the conceptual blueprint stage of model analysis to issues and procedures of model implementations and impact evaluation research. The basic technical thrust for curriculum model evaluation is determining how, when, and from what sources information will be gathered and analyzed for decision-making purposes. Thus, evaluation contributes to decisions, certification and installation. Accordingly, a systematic approach to model evaluation will begin by clarifying the purpose of evaluation. Once the purpose is clarified, problem solving about suitable evaluation methodology follows.

Decisions about model program development and improvement, for example, call for the application of formative evaluation procedures. Decisions about program continuation or adoption will call for evidence of program impact or total effectiveness. Hence, summative evaluation procedures are necessary. Both kinds of procedures may be combined to promote understanding of basic psychological or social processes, depending upon the extent to which this kind of information is central to the evaluation effort. A specification of procedures for both formative and summative evaluation, or model implementation and impact evaluation, will comprise an evaluation design.The main components of an evaluation design are the conditions, schedule, and type of data collection and analysis, details of which are discussed elsewhere. Model impact or outcome evaluation has been dominated by applications of experimental and quasi-experimental research methods.

Although the feasibility of such methods is usually limited in field settings, these methods have earned an important place in educational evaluation. The literature on formative evaluation procedures is less extensive, but nonetheless important for students of curriculum models. Moreover, conceptual systems for determining the adequacy of comprehensive evaluation designs are noteworthy for study.

The merit of curriculum models typically has been assessed according to how clearly models produce desired or intended changes among children exposed to them. Support or opposition to a model then, is rallied on the basis of evidence about children's progress in academic achievement and other valued goal areas. However preoccupied evaluators have been with summative impact evaluation, a meaningful empirical test of any model clearly requires that certain basic assumptions be met. Firstly the stated outcomes are attainable through educational processes. This calls forth again the rationale by which realistic and worthwhile goals and objectives are selected, formulated, judged, and linked to instructional design. Secondly, valid, reliable measures are available to assess goal achievements. The assumption of technically respectable measurement has been difficult to meet fully in practice.

Satisfactory assessment of young children's educational progress poses peculiar challenges to evaluation. Not only have measurement strategies been limited in scope and technique, but evaluators have also tended to place ease of measurement above quality control. Evaluation has been heavily dependent upon the use of spurious testing procedures. Such problems and challenges to evaluation are discussed elsewhere as are the matters of measurement availability, construction, selection, and evaluation. Few will deny, however, that model impact data are only as valid as the procedures used to gather them. Associated issues for model outcome evaluation are determining what effects are worth assessing and how they shall be assessed. The third assumption for meaningful model impact evaluation is that a model is, in fact, implemented as prescribed or intended. The importance of this condition cannot be overemphasized.

A given model can easily be jeopardized on grounds of "no effects" or "poor results" in the absence of data about how adequately, completely, or competently it was implemented. The alleged early failure of Project Head Start illustrates this problem. That is, data from a limited range of generic, short-range measurements were taken virtually at face value to judge the effectiveness of compensatory intervention before any semblance of implementation quality could be determined. Premature and narrowly conceived evaluation seriously threatened Head Start's existence; and controversy about Head Start models impact has continued to persist still short of adequate implementation data. The Head Start object lesson among others, has contributed to a greater appreciation of process evaluation: assessing the merit of program variables antecedent to and presumably related in a causal way to program outcomes. Process variables encompass curriculum methods and materials, teacher personality or style, emotional climate, and characteristics of the physical environment.

In conventional experimental research parlance, process variables collectively constitute the "treatment," that is, the independent variable(s) to which subjects are exposed and upon which predictions about change are based. Process evaluation, then is, concerned with the problem of insuring that the treatment has occurred. The importance of this insurance for valid impact evaluation has already been stressed. But process evaluation is more and more valued for its own sake. For one thing, overall program quality is at issue. For another, process valuation is well suited to questions about what instructional methods and materials are best tailored to or most preferred by given program personnel. For still another, explicit process-outcome linkages are probably best understood through the careful examination and systematic manipulation of treatment variables. Process approaches to curriculum model evaluation depend heavily upon, but are not limited to, observational techniques. Consequently, a basic problem or process evaluation is of selecting or developing an appropriate system for taking and recording observational data.

Child development and early education researchers have provided a wealth of observational systems and procedures, many of which are aptly illustrated by curriculum model implementation and impact studies. Interview and questionnaire methods figure prominently in innovative approaches to determine the level of program implementation in specific educational settings. Systematic process evaluation procedures for measuring domains of instruction have also been proposed, the most detailed of which concern variations on the theme of mastery learning and prescriptive teaching. Arguments for integrating ethnographic techniques in the model research and evaluation activity have appeared with increasing frequency during the past several years as well. For evaluators who fear that use of such techniques undermines objectivity in evaluation research, strategies for dealing with the issue of subjectivity can be recommended. As progress in process evaluation continues, so does thinking about how to broaden the scope of impact evaluation for a better understanding of educational processes. One practice championed for this purpose is the multivariate analysis of model programs. Conventional evaluation practice has usually been limited to documenting average gains for groups of children involved in one or another model program. Multivariate analysis seeks to disclose interactions between child and program characteristics, that is, to determine which program characteristics are more or less important in accounting for variations in children's responses to programs. This sort of analysis has been slow in application to routine evaluation methodology as it figures prominently for questions about why some children may flourish in a given program while others may not. The more basic line of scholarly inquiry involved here, of course, is the increasingly popular aptitude-or trait-treatment interaction research.

Conceptually, however, this inquiry seems pertinent to solving problems about matching children to treatment, that is, finding the "best fit" between programs and their participants. A second, related idea for improved curriculum model evaluation concerns adaptations of longitudinal research methodology to better monitor long-term program effects on children, parents, and staff. Much of the impetus for this "cumulative impact" approach to evaluation emanates from exemplary programs, as the Perry Preschool Project, and the consortium for longitudinal studies.The push for standard longitudinal evaluation is, in part, a reaction to swarms of skeptics who question the values of early education. Broadly conceived longitudinal evaluation seems now recognized as essential for a more complete understanding of education and development.

Fundamental questions concerning type of intervention programs, duration and intensity of intervention, and amount of family involvement can all be dealt with at a more sophisticated level through longitudinal evaluation. Some authorities advocate that evaluation should be planned and conducted from a truly developmental perspective. Though cumulative, long-term impact is important from this perspective, more critical for ongoing evaluation are program quality which has a participant response to it. Qualitative change among both children and staff, especially in terms of realizing human potentials, becomes more central to evaluation than the conventional behavioural assessment of child outcomes. Still other authorities call for fundamental reformation in evaluation practice.

Among other things, reformation would require a softening of demands for technical purity in evaluation and greater commitment to progressive enlightenment, that is, a more complete understanding of program operations within their sociopolitical contexts. Relevance and credibility, not scientific quality, become principal standards from which evaluations are planned, executed, analyzed, and disseminated. Broadened perspectives on evaluation can often be clarified or enhanced by reference to one or another conceptual framework from which to chart essential evaluation tasks.

Thus, conceptual frameworks are available for planning formative-summative procedures, determining accountability to clientele, identifying deficiencies in staff training, determining the effectiveness of innovative programs and assessment, evaluating the context in which a model program may be implemented, evaluating unintended or unanticipated model outcomes, and other purposes. Such frameworks, usually called evaluation models, show still another use of the term "model." Use of an evaluation model appropriate to the various purposes of curriculum model evaluation is inherently sensible for any systematic, logical, and consistent approach to decision making about the worth of program process and outcomes. Among the more sensitive areas of decision making applied to early education is economics. Economic theory holds that continual investment in a given enterprise or opportunity is warranted insofar as that enterprise or opportunity shows or continues to yield "better returns" than alternatives would. In the context of early education, this theory guides a variety of cost-analysis procedures that concern measuring costs in relation to program effectiveness, efficiency, benefits to participants, and so on.

Methodological problems abound in this approach to evaluation; but impressive instances of cost analysis can be cited to indicate that the expense incurred by competently implemented model program may be compensated by long-term benefits to society. Interested readers should consult the technical literature for details. A final issue for curriculum model evaluation concerns the external validity of a model program, or the power of a model to produce similar effects across a wide variety of specific settings. Models are implemented in particular environmental contexts. Evaluation proceeds to validate their implementation, goal achievements, and even cost efficiency of effectiveness. But this documentation is insufficient to conclude that a given curriculum model will be equally effective under different environmental conditions and with different populations of consumers. There is a need for replicative evaluation research to better understand any intersite variation in model processes and outcomes. Needs, resources, personnel competencies, and support services are but a few potentially significant factors in intersite variation.

The project follow through evaluation is an ample precedent for showing that the same model may "work" better in some contexts than in others, even when instructional procedures are comparable across sites. Since much remains to be learned about such variation, caution against any premature generalization of model effects is advised. Models, even when refined to the point of high exportability, seem subject to subtle social forces. It appears that staff commitment to a model and the extent to which the values of a particular community are met through that model are among the most critical of these forces.

Comprehensive curriculum model evaluation will include both process and impact assessment in a longitudinal perspective with an eye toward reconciling cost with benefits to individuals and the larger society. Considerable progress has been made in the methodology for this purpose, a study of which is a requisite for genuine professionalism in early childhood education.

A curriculum model is an ideal conceptual structure for decision making about educational aims, administrative policies, curriculum content, and instructional methods. Educational philosophy and psychological theory combine to form the core of a comprehensive curriculum model. From those core are generated policy guidelines for the selection of curriculum goals and objectives.

Goals and objectives normally indicate degrees of emphasis upon education for cultural competence, naturalistic growth, and preparation for the future. At issue is a rationale or justification for taking any value stance about the functions of organized education for young children. Internally consistent administrative policies are also governed by theory in a thoroughly formulated curriculum model. Administrative policies have been classified into three interrelated categories. A first category—personnel specification—involves criteria for the target population of learners, program staff, and community involvement. Considerations about the physical setting or curriculum model development comprise a second category of administrative policy. The third is program evaluation policy. This category calls for decisions about formative-summative evaluation and may be juxtaposed with cost-accounting procedures. Curriculum content and method were discussed in terms of distinctions among academic skills, cognitive-intellectual development, and effective growth. The issue of a functional taxonomy for defining content emphasis was highlighted along with decision points about content priorities and the organization of content sequences. Arrangements for continuity-stability in content delivery and the issue of operational statements of curriculum model objectives were also discussed. Method variables in curriculum modes were examined in relation to two interlocking dimensions: didactic versus prepared, and group versus individual methods. Implications of these choices were framed against strategies, procedures for securing retention and transfer of learning, and the use of instructional media and materials.

Origin of Infant and Nursery Schools in India

In the early part of the twentieth century, most of the kindergartens were started by the missionaries. But the pre-school movement in India took a definite shape under the leadership of Mrs Annie Besant and Rabindra Nath Tagore. The Indian movement in the field of pre-school education owes much to Annie Besant and Tagore in the early part of the 20th century.

There were a few private enterprises in South India, who looked to "New Educational Movement" of Europe for a social change through education but the actual movement in India on a national scale was started by Annie Besant and Tagore. At that period, there were three types of institutions in the field of pre-school education in India: (a) Institutions run by Theosophists; (b) Special type of schools for children of rich families run by Maharajas: (c) Schools and Centres in Gujarat and Maharashtra, run by private individuals. Other developments which took place in the pre-school movement in India were opening of Shishu Vihar Mandal at Yeotmal in Maharashtra and Centre of Cosmic Education at Allahabad in 1951, Happy Education Society at Delhi, Nai Taim Sangh at Wardha, Balniketan Sang at Indore in 1941 and the Association Montessori International in India.

In 1944 the Central Advisory Board of Education (CABE) gave concrete suggestions for the reorganisation of pre-school education in India. The CABE Report recommended that we should make a provision of 1,000,000 free places in many schools or classes for children in the age group of 3 to 6 years.

The Sargent Report suggested "free atttractive pre-school education by the State in order to pay attention to a very impressionable, plastic and educationally potent period of child's life.

The pre-basic education of children under 7 years, which was termed as pre-basic education, according to Gandhiji, should be conducted in cooperation with parents and community.

The first pre-basic education school, established under Kasturba Memorial Trust, started functioning in July 1945 at Sevagram, under the guidance of Smt

Shanta Narulkar. Owing to more urgent calls on the national resources since 1947, it was not possible to plan any comprehensive development for the education of children of pre-school age until 1951, when Indian Council for Child Education was formed with Smt Sarladevi Sarabhai as its President.

The Ministry of Education, Government of India, in their report on Progress of Education in India 1947-52, remarked:

> Pre-primary education was for the most part confined to urban areas and has been the responsibility of parents. The policy of the govt in this respect has been that of assistance and encouragement. There has been a sudden expansion of this education in the middle of the quinquennium due partly to Madam Montessori's stay in India: but mainly due to organised efforts and ability of certain private bodies.

Though the need for pre-school education was stressed but no definite financial provision was made for this purpose, in the First Five Year Plan. All India Education Conference on the problems of Child Education held at Indore in 1955 remarked.

> It is also surprising that neither the First Five Year Plan nor Community Development Projects mention anything about the need for pre-primary education nor do they make any provision for the purpose. Obviously the importance of this subject has escaped the attention of the planners.

Eventhough, as a part of the first Five Year Plan the Central Government set up a Central Social Welfare

Board with the object especially of assisting voluntary agencies in organising welfare programmes for women and children. The CSWB assisted 2128 institutions of which 691 were child welfare institutions. But in the First Five Year Plan, out of Rs 169 crores provided for the development of education, no allocation was made for the pre-school education.

In the Second Plan the Planning Commission made a provision for child welfare and education. This was done on the recommendation of the Child Care Committee which was appointed by the Central Social Welfare Board. Out of Rs 307 crores provided for education during the second plan no special provision was made for the pre-school stage. Assuming 3 to 6 years as the normal age range for nursery schools or classes, there were over 40 million children in this age group in 1960-61.

The Government formally recognised the need for pre-school education, only during the Third Five Year Plan. The Planning commission had asked the Central Social Welfare Board to appoint an expert committee to survey and report on child care in the country. For the first time, pre-school education was recognised by the Government of India as the base of national system of education, and thus a national policy was to be formulated for the cause of pre-school education. The report of the expert committee, set up by the CSWB, is a landmark in the history of pre-school education as for the first time its recommendation to the government covered the "total child", including education, health, nutrition and recreation. The committee pointed out that pre-schools should be self-sufficient and should be started by the voluntary agencies. Balwadis should be started both for rural and urban areas. These shoulu be run by the Community development departments and Central

Social Welfare Boards. As a result of these efforts the total number of Pre-school Child Care Centres was estimated to be 3,500, with an enrolment of about 14.5 lakhs which was 35 per cent of the total population of children between 3-5 years. This, according to Ranjit Bhai, was "a very bright account of people's response in the interest of child education". In 1961 there were about 5000 Balwadis with an enrolment of about 3,00,000 children. Of these about 2,500 were assisted by the Central and State Social Welfare Boards. By the end of the Third Plan the number of Balwadis organised by these Boards rose to 5761.

The Third Plan provided for the setting up of six training centres for Bal Sevikas. In the programmes for education Rs 3 crores were allotted for child welfare and allied schemes at the Centre and about Rs 1 crore in the States in addition to resources available under the community development and social welfare programmes. Schemes that were formulated by the Ministry of Education included improvement of the existing Balwadis, opening of new Balwadis, expansion of training programmes for Bal Sevikas and a number of other projects in which education, health and welfare services were integrated. Regarding the enrolment of children in pre-schools and Balwadis upto the end of Third Plan, Iredale points out.

> The All India picture is more difficult to colour in any detail partly because of diversity of the agencies running both the schools and' the teacher training programmes. Between 1951 and 1966 the known enrolment in mainly urban pre-primary schools in the country rose from 28,000 to 250,00, while in 1966 the number of children enrolled in Balwadis was claimed to be 600,000.

It was suggested in the draft of the Fourth Five Year Plan that "in the field of pre-school education, government effort will be confined mainly to certain strategic areas such as training of teachers, evolving suitable teaching techniques, production of teaching materials and teachers' guides. In the Social Welfare sector, however, there will be a small provision for the opening of Balwadis, both in rural and urban areas." Children below 6 constitute nearly 17 per cent of the total population of India and 15 million are being added every year. In the last two years of the Fourth Plan, services for 1 million additional children belonging to weaker sections were to be launched. In addition to this training of personnel through new types of training programmes were to be launched. Therefore, Fourth Plan period was marked by these developments in pre-school education. For example, a national seminar on the pre-school child, organised at Madras jointly by the International Children's Centre, Paris, and Indian Council for Child Welfare, discussed three broad aspects of early childhood education, namely, health and nutrition objectives, educational and social objectives. In 1970, the sixth meeting of the IAPE was held. During this year, the pre-primary teacher education curriculum was developed by the NCERT. In 1971 the NCERT set up the Department of Pre-primary and Primary education at its National Institute of Education and special attention was paid to teacher preparation. More literature was produced for the pre-school level.

Seventh meeting of the IAPE in 1972, published its report on 'Relating Pre-School to Primary School'. A national seminar on 'An Integrated Approach to the Pre-school Child' was also organised at Bangalore in 1972. During this year the NCERT also published its report on 'Pre-primary institutions: Their Supervision'. The concept of supervision at the pre-school state has been discussed in this report. The evaluation instruments and directions for their use in making assessment of a pre-school were also included in this report.

The draft report on Fifth Year Plan recognised the importance of pre-school education. The facilities of pre-schools were however, limited as is pointed out in the report:

> The facilities available at present, are, however, limited to a number of privately run schools in urban areas and few thousand Balwadis and Anganwadis run under government auspicis in social welfare sector. While it may be difficult to provide pre-school education facilities of any sophistication, the situation demands that some effort of an elementary kind be made immediately. It is, therefore, envisaged in the Fifth Plan that children's Play Centres for the age group 3-6 may be attached to selected primary schools. In addition to these centres, private agencies will further assist in the strategic areas of teacher training, preparation of teacher guides and promotion of research for evolving methods of pre-school education suited to our condition.

The Fifth Plan had the rural, tribal and slum areas as its target for child welfare. The Plan aimed at providing integrated services—health, welfare, education, nutrition and family planning—as bases to promote child welfare. During this Plan, 13 million children in the age group of 0 to 6 years were to be covered by extending integrated services to 18 per cent of the total children in the weakest section of Indian society. In the Fifth Plan

Rs 25 crores were provided for the educational component and Rs 75 crore for the social welfare plan. A National Policy Resolution for children was issued in 1974. As a result of this a National Children's Board was constituted. The Integrated Child Development Scheme was introduced in 33 experimental areas which provided supplementary nutrition, immunization, health check, referral services, nutrition, health education and Non-Formal education to children in the age group 0 to 6 years. Further, 117 ICDE experimental projects were introduced during 1978-80. The focal point of the ICDS projects provided services through Anganwadis which were run by a local voluntary worker who was assisted by a helper. The work of Anganwadi workers was to be supervised by a Mukhya Sevika.

For the first time the 'early childhood education' has been used in place of 'pre-school education' as the former is intended to be more broad-based and covers the entire period of crucial development upto 5 years. Special attention is to be paid to the children of under-privileged groups. The Sixth plan report says: "This early childhood stage is the period of maximum learning and intellectual developments of the child and hence of great potential educational significance. The present pre-school child care programmes are limited to the distribution of food supplements and routine health cover; these contribute very little to the personality development of the child, especially to its intellectual, social and emotional growth. The concept of learning and development through play and joyful activities should be articulated, across age group, through an all round programme which should be comprehensive in scope, integrated in nature and reinforced over long time. Organisation of a creche for children in the 0-3 years age group and/or a Balwadi for 3-6 age group, with provision for educational toys, play equipment, learning materials and books for children's reading would be appropriate for this purpose."

The Sixth Plan provides an outlay of Rs 2524 crore for development of education and culture. Out of this Rs 905.37 crores, 35.87% of the total outlay, have been allotted for the early childhood education which is the highest amount ever allotted for this purpose.

Though education has been a state subject, yet the policies regarding pre-school education have been mostly framed and implemented by the Central level agencies like Central Social Welfare Board. In most of the States the Director of Social Welfare controls the pre-schools through Bai Sevikas and Mukhya Sevikas. Of late there are some more developments. There is perhaps some justification in entrusting the responsibility of pre-school education to the Social welfare departments. Pre-school education is viewed as a part of child and family welfare schemes. But for the education component of the pre-school programmes, especially in the matter of teacher preparation, the State Institute of Education are laying prominent role. For example, SIEs of Maharashtra, Rajasthan, Madhya Pradesh and of other states have started working in the field of pre-school education. In Maharashtra a course has been drawn up combining the training for teachers for pre-primary and primary schools. In Rajasthan, Balwadis are functioning under the guidance of SIE. In Madhya Pradesh, the SIE has developed teacher training course on the pattern suggested by the National Council for Teacher Education.

The private sector in India has played a significant role for the spread of pre-school education. They stepped up their activities after the visit of Madam Montessori to India. Many Montessori and Nursery schools as well as training centres were started.

There are several national and international level organisations working in the fields of pre-school education. The names of national level organisations are given below:

(i) *Central Social Welfare Board:* The CSWB organises activities of pre-school through its State Departments of Social Welfare. These activities are organised as part of the family and child welfare schemes and are organised under three heads: health, nutrition education and social welfare services. The State Departments/Boards of Social Welfare organise 'Balwadis'. The 'Balwadis' are day-care-centres. In the towns there are nursery schools, whereas in the villages rural Balwadis are run. The CSWB gets funds from the Central Government on the recommendation of the Planning Commission. It also appoints national committees to examine various issues pertaining to the child education and welfare schemes. Some time ago the CSWB appointed an expert committee to survey and report on child care in the country.

(ii) *Indian Council for Child Welfare*: The ICCW organises programmes of child welfare. It also helps in running the Balwadis and Bai Sevika Training Centres. It collaborates with the International Children's Centre, Paris and the United Nations Children's Fund in organising programmes of educational, social and nutritional nature.

(iii) *NCERT*: The National Council of Educational Research and Training has been actively associated with the development of pre-school education in India. The department of pre-primary and primary education was set up in 1969. The department collaborated with other state and national level agencies and prepared courses of studies for the pre-schools and training of school teachers. The two teacher training courses prepared by the NCERT in collaboration with the National Council for Teacher Education are B.Ed courses. The NCERT has also undertaken research projects for the developmental norms of Indian children in the age group 2½ to 5. The department of pre-primary and primary education was re-oraganised by the NCERT in 1975 and a separate Child Study Unit has since been set up. The CSU has brought out many useful publications on pre-school education and has also set up Children's Media Laboratory.

(iv) *Indian Association of Pre-school Education*: The IAPE was formed in 1964. Since then it has been actively engaged in promoting the cause of pre-school education. It has brought out several publications. In addition to this, the IAPE teachers give suggestions and recommendations on the various aspects of pre-school education.

(v) *Other Organisations*: All India Women's Conference, Guild of Service, Madras, Indian Red Cross, Bharat Sewak Samaj, All India Balkan-Ki-Bari, Bal Niketan Sang, Kishore Dal, Nutan Bal Sikshan Sangh, Bombay, Children's Education Societies in Gujarat Karnataka, Delhi and Association Montessori International in India which organises Montessori schools, teachers training programmes, day-care-nurseries, pre-primary schools, Balwadis and child health centres.

(vi) *Education and Community Development Departments* in various States run Nursery Schools, Nursery Teachers' Training colleges and Pre-Basic Schools.

(vii) *Labour Welfare and Health Departments* in States organise creches, maternity centres, day care centres and health centres.

(viii) *Public Sector Undertakings* have set up pre-schools in different cities under their own educational authorities.

(ix) The various religious bodies have started pre-school along with the primary, secondary and higher secondary schools.

(x) The CARE operates its nutritional programmes in collaboration with different States.

(xi) *The University Department of Child Development* and home Science colleges also have training programmes, mostly for women, at the early childhood education level.

(xii) Some national level institutes like B.M. Institute of Child Development. Ahmedabad and Child Study Unit at the Tata Institute of Social Sciences, Bombay are also working for the cause of pre-school education.

3
Primary Curriculum

No education is possible without a set of values, and any education which purports to be value-free is likely to be based on hidden values of its own. Similarly, any approach to education which claims to be entirely derived from theories of development, or experience, or of curriculum is unlikely to be adequate. For either it is based on a fallacious argument, such as that: because education is related to development, therefore education ought to depend on development; or it is based on an argument derived from other and still more basic premises.

More explicitly, this means that decisions negotiated within groups are preferable to decisions imposed by superiors; that individual views should not be submerged by group views; and that no group should impose itself by any kind of force on any other group. Such a set of values is somewhat idealistic as well as being somewhat imprecise; but it does have meaning and is clearly distinguishable from authoritarian attitudes. This basic assumption is reinforced by two others. One of these is derived from the Judaic-Christian tradition. It implies a way of valuing people which can and indeed must transcend the democratic stance, but is regarded as fully compatible with it and adding something to it, something which at the least implies a kind of compassionate concern.

The remaining assumption is simply that all unbridled ideological positions are in themselves dangerous. At the least, they imply a claim to certainty; at the most, they lead people to claim powers over others that are quite incompatible with the first two assumptions.

Moreover, ideological programmes are almost always pretentious and fallacious, and when their feet of clay appear, their adherents are left adrift and bewildered. It will, of course, be claimed that this position is itself ideological; but that is not so within the meaning given here to ideology.

In 1983 there were political currents of both Right and Left which regard this type of democratic attitude as context-bound, described, blind to stark economic, political or social realities. That is why liberal and 'social-democratic' are often use as pejoratives far beyond their standpoint as outmoded or incapable of leading to a somewhat juster social order. Rather, we think it is one of the least unlikely means of attaining a somewhat juster social order. At the same time, we do not believe that any secular stance can in itself hold the key to social perfectibility.

First, the relative roles and importance of development and experience have to be judged. Development, in its three aspects can be taken as anything from a set of negative limitations, reluctantly acknowledged, to a source of guidance, uncritically accepted. Individual children do have some inbuilt programme, and each programme is different. This can be deduced from principles of heredity, but also from observation. An attempt to impose a uniform, or even a nonuniform, pattern of education that does not take serious account of developmental considerations violates any concept of democracy as it has been described here.

Experience can be taken as implying anything from the unpredictable partner of development in an interactive process to a tabula rasa from which heredity can be, for all practical purpose, expunged.

The second of the possibilities has some emotional appeal, but it is contrary to much of the evidence that arises from direct observation as well as from systematic study. The limits of experience which bring about undue emphasis on its potential can easily involve brash attempts to re-mould individuals and societies, disregarding both the evidence in favour of developmental factors and the strains and misfortunes resulting for individuals when those factors are disregarded. On the other hand, over-emphasis on the inevitability of some features of development can result in a belittling of the power of experience to effect any real change, so that those who are alleged to benefit from the developmental advantages drawn from their innate endowment may continue to do so. Thus, a democratic approach requires caution in the face of either extreme view of experience.

When primary education is considered in particular, development and experience both claim consideration. Both appear with more clarity than in secondary or tertiary education, where questions of content and organization so readily tend to supervene. Young children's development is so palpable; their experience so relatively uncomplicated. What is more, the mutual dependence of development and experience is shown with particular clarity.

The third element, curriculum, should thus be approached on the further assumption that there should be a balanced interaction between development and experience. However, that does not mean that there should be some precise Newtonian calculation of their relative importance. The balance refers not to a once-for-all weighting of their significance, but to a continuing process which gives the predominance not to one or the other, in particular situations, but which is directed in the long run to the best outcome for each individual child. It also implies a reassertion of the obvious but frequently overlooked truth that the interaction between development and experience begins before curriculum, continues alongside curriculum, and extends beyond curriculum. Moreover, curriculum, though it builds upon experience and constitutes that part of experience that falls within formal education, is still only a part of experience.

The role of curriculum considered in the rest of this book is that it is planned intervention in the interaction between development and experience. This is to be taken to mean that curricular experience is planned intervention between development and general experience. For the sake of simplicity, henceforth the nicety of meaning will be overlooked and 'experience' will denote 'general experience' while 'curriculum' will be used as a shorthand for 'curricular experience'. In other words, the relationship spelled out will be borne in mind while a simplified terminology is used.

If the terminology is kept simple, the relationships are far from simple. For there is an ongoing interaction between the development and curriculum, and between experience and curriculum, as well as between development and experience. The difference between curriculum and the other elements is the obvious one, that development and experience are continuous, whereas curriculum is substantially confined to the place and time of formal education. This does not mean that its importance is proportionately reduced. The pressures of society throw into relief what goes on in school; curriculum as a whole, unlike development or experience as a whole, is designed to make a positive impact on children; and curriculum is fashioned in such a way as to interact positively with development and experience and to maximise their value for children.

Among those who emphasise the importance of development in education stress, as Montessori did, most emphasize on the necessity of curriculum as a means of optimising development. Similarly, many of the ablest and most thoughtful advocates of experience in education, stress that curriculum is itself a major component of experience.

All of these circumstances represent social imperatives of one kind or another, and all present much the same curricular dilemma. If too little notice is taken of those circumstances, the curriculum may prove irrelevant or even unworkable; if too much notice is taken of them, it may act as a means of reinforcing the separateness of the local community from the wider society and even as an obstacle in the path of those who would like to transcend its barriers and to take part in the wider society. The social-imperatives approach does, therefore, make considerable demands upon any democratic approach to primary education. However, the positive importance of the forms and process approaches is greater.

The forms approach, in its stronger embodiment, makes claims almost irrespective of development and experience, claims derived from a totally objective view of knowledge and endeavour. But in its more flexible form it looks upon curriculum as consisting of broad areas of understanding and endeavour which have emerged within the historic process in almost all societies, certainly within those which today have established systems of formal education. This more flexible version of the forms approach does not make elaborate claims for the individual forms, nor for their precise definition, but it does assert that they are fundamentally distinct ways of understanding and endeavour, the omission of any one of which would impoverish education. This is a little less forceful than the argument based on initiation or on civic need, but it does imply that personal development and the expansion of experience require some exposure to all of them. Moreover, there is a sense in which they can claim to be themselves a part of the structure of development and experience.

However, the main emphasis has to be laid on the third approach to curriculum, the process approach. This is because if the purpose is to uphold individuals and their autonomous fulfilment, then what matters is how they discover understanding and endeavour for themselves. To combine this with a flexible version of the forms is not a contradiction. The particular acts of co-operative learning and endeavour involved in the various elements in the curriculum can, and should, be based on ways of discovery that are related to development and experience.

The choice of curricular areas, or indeed to the possible range of problems and activities within them, cannot be left entirely to an arbitrary process of discovery which, in practice, is often devoid of purposive sequence and structure or of the expertise needed to guide, interpret and stimulate that discovery. In other words, at the level of micro-planning of individual episodes of learning, the process approach makes strong demands: at the level of macro-planning of curriculum, it requires interaction with forms, and to some extent with social imperatives. There is one further important consideration: In the preceding discussion there was some danger of regarding the curriculum as static, or at any rate of giving priority to the curriculum as it appears at the later primary stage.

But primary education has to be considered as a whole, and begins at a chronological age when, on any showing, development and experience preclude the clear differentiation of the curriculum into forms. To begin with, it must be much more of a totality. Differentiation into separate kinds of activity is itself a part of the curriculum process at the primary stage. More than that, it is something that forms part of guided discovery. For this reason the emphasis on the process approach to curriculum at the primary stage, is further strengthened. Whatever augments might be applied in secondary or even in later primary education: the primary curriculum as a whole has to take account of what happens at the very start. Hitherto some of the characteristics of a worthwhile primary curriculum have been indicated: its relation to development and experience, its prime but not exclusive dependence on the process model, and its modification according to age. It has already been defined as a balanced intervention in the interaction between development and experience, with the proviso that the interaction takes place between all three elements. What is needed now, before the discussion is taken further, is a more succinct term for the kind of curriculum that is to be elaborated. If we are to speak of an enabling curriculum, then it is necessary to say what it enables, and why it enables more than in case if it were not introduced.

It must prove additional equipment that arises through development beyond the powers of the human organism as such development that can arise only through the stimulus of a systematic process of construction of reality strengthened by awareness of widely accepted forms of understanding and endeavour. It must also provide opportunities for the expansion and reflective scrutiny of experience, within a social context that ensures that development and experience are social as well as individual. Beyond this, it must also enable each individual to become a person with an emerging set of values and ideals.

Development and experience do not necessarily imply this, so if it is a desirable goal it must fall to the enabling curriculum to promote it. Of course, the emerging set of values and ideals must itself reflect the general present purposes a democratic one, designed to function within the various contexts that have been considered.

A curriculum designed to operate within a quite different framework of values might also be termed 'enabling', but if this were to apply where only a forms approach, or a social-imperatives approach, was adopted, then its enablement would be much more limited in scope. It would be less productive, and less democratic, in its interaction with development and experience in general. Even so, an enabling curriculum envisages two further outcomes.

First, it does not simply condition development and experience, within however congenial a context. Based as it is on chosen values, it also enables choices to be made. Choices have to be made in any life situation, and choices made in the light of development and of experience are usually more widely made than those made, as it were, at random. An enabling curriculum is intended to go beyond this again. It is intended to reveal more clearly the conditions within which choices have to be made, and the influences which bear upon the chooser. Having stripped off much of the surrounding opacity, it leaves the chooser and the choice face to face. Then, the chooser depends on the emerging set of values and ideals. For it is the ultimate strength, as well as the perversity, of personal autonomy that choices must eventually be made without dictation. In a democratic ideology, autonomy and not automation must be the intention, and the curriculum must enable but not compel. The most that enabling curriculum can do is to leave the doors and the options open: this it should do, and it is great deal to do.

Secondly, an enabling curriculum must enable acceptance. This may seem to contradict the enablement of choice, but in fact it places choice in perspective. It is not false humility or social quietism, but a recognition that, in our existential situation, individuals must accept limitations, not least in themselves. It sets into perspective the aim often suggested for education, that all children should be capable. For such an aim can be achieved only if it includes the power of acceptance of limitations, constraints, frustrations, disappointments, betrayals, accidents, illnesses, disasters and deaths. It may be unfashionable to emphasise this, but a curriculum that has nothing to say to these experiences, in the fact of which development usually also remains silent, is a disabling mockery. Too often, primary education has been envisaged for an unreal world created by wishful-thinking adults who prefer to sweep the unpleasant and the tragic, vicariously, under the carpet while claiming that in doing so they are 'protecting' children. A truly enabling curriculum has to enable those who meet it in the interaction between development and experience to accept reality in all its ugliness as well as all its beauty and potential. Before the argument is taken further, it would be useful to indicate how this enabling curriculum relates to some terms which are more familiar in discussions of the primary curriculum. One of these is progressive. The enabling approach has much in common with the manifestation of progressive education, whose opponents might well assume that it is little more than a variant on that theme. But the usual contention of advocates of progressive education is that it should be more self-consciously linked with children's active learning and also with a mildly socialist orientation generally. The commitment of an enabling approach to forms of understanding might also be viewed with some suspicion. Much the same might be true of the term child-centred.

An enabling curriculum is intended to be more than child-centred. It takes account also of differences in social situation, and here again the acceptance of forms of understanding may act as a mark of distinction between an enabling and a child-centred approach. At first these distinctions may seem trivial and tedious, but they do in fact embody quite an important distinction between the typical embodiment of educational reformism and what is recommended here. For in the enabling curriculum the process approach has the principal, but not the only place.

In the remainder of this book an attempt will be made to use a consistent terminology about the enabling curriculum, even if it sometimes involves a tendency to be repetitive. There will certainly be objections to this enabling curriculum, especially perhaps from those who are sincerely convinced of the primary of forms of understanding and endeavour as such, and of the predominant significance of subjects and disciplines.

Almost as many objections could be raised by those who, from whatever point of view, accord first place to social imperatives. There will also be others, of a philosophical cast of mind, who will contend that this enabling curriculum may not in fact do the enabling that is expected of it, and that other types of curriculum might in fact be found to do the enabling at least as well, or even better. They may maintain that it represents just the kind of wishful and soft-centred extrapolation from selected research findings and from edited experience that has plagued English primary education ever since Plowden, modified only by a touch of existentialist pessimism. Still others will cavil at the mixture of forms and process that is advocated, and may wish to substitute something more sturdy and homogeneous; this position might be adopted by Blenkin and Kelly with their radical empiricist model, or by Egan with his essentially developmental approach, or by those such as Kirby who adhere more closely to the child-centred tradition. Much that is advocated in this enabling curriculum corresponds to the central tenets of one or more of these approaches, so that they are more likely to criticise it for lack of clarity and homogeneity—a curricular fudge-and-mudge, an embodiment of Richard's 'liberal pragmatism'—than to regard it as embodying that spirit of reaction.

Certainly, it would gain if upheld by empirical verification, which would be a lengthy and complex business. In default of such confirmation, it is presented as a relatively appropriate way of intervening beneficially in the interaction between development and experience. What is more, it tallies with much that Richards calls for in his advocacy of a well-grounded, 'fine-grained' curriculum consistency.

An enabling curriculum is bound to require a distinctive approach from teachers: not necessarily greater demands, but a willingness to think in terms of the development and experience of individual children,to plan curriculum as intervention, and to consider equipping children for choice and for acceptance. It is not only necessary for teachers to consider curriculum in the light of children's development and experience. They have also to take account of their own development and experience. They too are on a series of curves of development, physical, intellectual and social/emotional, which powerfully affect their own powers and procedure.

Inevitably, different teachers are at different points on those curves. Even in primary schools the youngest teachers are nearer in chronological age to their youngest pupils than they are to their oldest colleagues. In the extreme case they may be at the pinnacle of achievement in a sport which is only a memory and a clutch of trophies to their colleague in the next classroom. In intellectual terms the younger staff may retain a flexibility of mind that acts as a counterpoint to the accumulated wisdom of the older staff. In personal terms heads nearing the end of their careers may well think of the youngest staff as, professionally, their children or even their grandchildren. Their own sons and daughters may well be considerably older than their youngest colleagues. Quite apart from these age-differences, individual teachers change as time passes. Their patterns of relationships with colleagues and children undergo modifications as they become less physically vigorous but more generally mature, and it requires regular vigilance to ensure that an individual teacher remains aware of these changes and of their consequences. Through consistent cultivation of awareness of their own development, they become more sensitive to develop-mental considerations among children.

It is equally important for teachers to appreciate the significance of their own experience. In one sense this is always recognized: there is general respect for 'experienced' teachers both in selection for posts of responsibility and in recruitment for teacher education. At the same time there is widespread suspicion about teachers' lack of experience of life in general. In considering an enabling curriculum, teachers need to be aware of both these characteristics, and also to build on their experience of children to extend their own understanding of development and experience in children. In fact, any teacher gains in experience simply by dint of working with children, and gains in quality of experience by reacting sensitively to the development and experience of children.

The appraisal and assessment of pupils, one activity which will shortly be discussed, is a process which becomes both easier and more accurate because it has been done before, though at the same time there is a risk that the teacher, either through personal development or experience, may alter the norm of assessment without being aware of doing so. Also, with the passage of time, there may be real differences between, say, 6-year-olds in 1980 and 6-year-olds in 1985. The difficult point to grasp and to bear regularly in mind is that the entire teaching-learning complex—pupils, teachers, curriculum, and cultural context, is changing all the time. None of us can stop the world. There is another form of experience that has also to be borne in mind. Professional training was a very different matter when the older teachers were in college. The sequence of professional experience that, in England

and Wales, leads from an ordinary B.Ed. or an open university degree to an honours degree, or a diploma, and then perhaps an M.Ed., or from a degree and Post-graduate Certificate in Education (PGCE) on to the same path, is very different from the two or three year certificate course which was formerly considered adequate and self-contained, requiring only occasional supplementation with a refresher course or two as - in a significant phrase—'post-experience' training. To teachers from the more recent patterns of training, the expectation of professional growth is much more inbuilt. Thus, teachers at different points on their curves of development will not only have different extents and kinds of experience. They are likely also to be differently equipped to understand and take account of the development and experience of children. This is bound to affect their general readiness to consider curriculum as planned intervention in the interaction between development and experience, though many individuals in both patterns of professional training will stand out as exceptions. When we think of how teachers as a whole figure in relation to an enabling curriculum, a number of considerations present themselves. Some of the most prominent are

- Are some teachers more suited than others to develop an enabling curriculum?
- What kinds of equipment do teachers need in order to develop it?
- What changes in teachers' role are implied if it is to be developed?
- What cooperation can teachers look for among adults in developing it?

– What are the implications for the initial and in-service education of teachers if an enabling curriculum is to be developed?

The first issue is as complex as it is important, and the literature relevant to it is immense. For a long time it was thought that research might reveal which people were likely to become good teachers of any kind, until it became evident that there were many kinds of persons, and there was no simple definition of good teaching, even though it is fairly easy to recognise at least some forms of bad teaching.

More recently, attention has come to be focused on particular styles of teaching or particular principles of procedure, and also on the social origins and experience of particular teachers and their congruence with particular categories of children. To take this last point first, there is some reason to think that the most appropriate teacher to understand and enable working class children, or rural children, would be a teacher from their own background; and similarly for other situations. In fact, there is little consistent evidence to that effect.

Similar considerations apply to the processes of pedagogy. These are skills that can be taught and learned in teacher education, as Stones has advocated. They are related to individual acts of teaching and learning that can figure in any structure of curriculum, and can improve teaching within it. This being so, they are important in any teacher education, including preparation for an enabling curriculum. But they are not strictly linked to that curriculum.

The two principal studies of infant schools in England do not show a consistent pattern of evidence on this theme, though they do indicate its potential importance. Bennett's study was of course directly focused on teaching styles, this time in junior schools, and in the interaction between variables analysed in his study there was a distinct advance in knowledge about the effect of a range of teaching styles. However, the main dependent variable was an objective measurement of attainment, which is rather a different matter from the implementation of a particular pattern of curriculum. The Oracle team at Leicester carried this type of analysis a stage further, bringing out the interactions between styles of teaching and styles of learning, but here too the measure selected was attainment. The most directly relevant findings of the Oracle studies in relation to an enabling curriculum were probably those concerning the outcomes of class teaching. For it was demonstrated that the class-teaching pattern allowed more direct pupil-teacher interaction than was possible through 'individual monitoring' of pupils working on their own, so that, paradoxically, a curriculum that aims to cater for individual needs may do so more effectively when some teaching, particularly of subject-areas depending on sequential skill and concept formation, is done collectively. This is not to be taken as an inflexible paradigm across the curriculum. In the Oracle studies particular attention was paid to language and mathematical and scientific skills, and it could well be that a combination of individual and group study would be more suitable for some topic work in the social subjects.

Again, there is probably a legitimate contrast between the teaching of skills in art and craft and of those required in music. In addition, any individual teacher is likely to find a particular mix of styles most appropriate for himself or herself. The criterion of appropriateness here may be more than measurable efficiency, for it could be maintained, for example, that the social experience derived from group work, suitably and sensitively handled, is more important than any outcome measured in terms of performance alone. It is possible here only to hint at some of the implications of Bennett's studies and the Oracle publications for an enabling curriculum in primary education: and to emphasise the point that they have both made, namely, that these issues are more complex than protagonists of either 'traditional' or 'progressive' opinions have always allowed. In general terms, then, it appears that the social origins of teachers and their actual pedagogic acts are not directly associated with any particular approach to curriculum. Teaching styles may have some relevance, though it is more a question of finding the right mix than of opting for any one style.

There still remains the possibility that teachers' personalities, motivations, characters or values might have a direct relationship with the development of an enabling curriculum. It is still more difficult to appeal to research findings for this purpose. Ashton's study of aims in primary education provides a baseline for any such investigation, but its main thrust is the relationship between particular categories of teacher, values and emphasis in curriculum and other variables. If anything, it would indicate that teachers who are younger and equipped with a more sophisticated professional preparation would be likely to look more favourably on a process approach.

Bassey's survey within one county portrays graphically what teachers in primary schools actually do, but does not penetrate beyond this. Neither of these studies would claim to indicate more than trends to which there are many exceptions, or to postulate that opinion as measured at the time of their studies is not liable to alteration. Indeed Ashton has explicitly pointed out what changes may be taking place. Beyond this it would probably be legitimate to say that teachers with authoritarian tendencies, or with a penchant for hierarchical organisation, for dogmatic statements and enforced compliance, would not be well suited to implement an enabling curriculum; but then they would not want to.

Difficulties would arise only if somebody else, applying their own methods to a different value-position, said that they had to. Such a situation is not unknown in primary education, and indeed it may be worsened if it results from an innovation introduced brusquely and without adequate consultation. For the real necessity in the development of an enabling curriculum is the commitment of the teachers concerned to a value-system consonant with its implications. In most other respects the qualities, that make good teachers in a forms-of-understanding approach or a social-imperatives approach are likely to make good teachers in a process approach. In teaching styles there may be some differences. In values and commitment, the difference is crucial.

On the assumption that suitable teachers are available in suitable numbers, it is next to necessary to consider what kinds of equipment they need in order to implement an enabling curriculum. For this purpose it may be useful to look at the five elements in the armour of primary teachers designated in the report of postgraduate certificate courses for teachers in primary and middle schools. They apply to primary teachers irrespective of their pattern of training.

The first of these is what may be broadly described as 'technique', that is, the indispensable skills of classroom organisation and procedure. The next two require more specific comment. One of these is curricular knowledge, which not only includes knowledge about the concept of curriculum as discussed, but also sufficient knowledge of an appropriate kind about the main components of any curriculum, including those which apply to an enabling curriculum. The sheer quality of expertise that is potentially required for one teacher to mediate the curriculum discussed in those chapters is daunting, and must in practice result, at least in the upper primary years, in some form of sharing of function. Even so, a team of teachers can only just manage to cover the range of expertise in skills and familiarisation that is necessary. It must be noted that this is not a range of knowledge, for a process approach does not basically require the transfer of knowledge from teachers to children. What is required is a way of transmitting skills and concepts and attitudes. There are procedures appropriate to mathematics, to science, to art, to PE and to each other aspect of curriculum, and these are not mere concessions to the forms-of-understanding approach. The sharpening of perceptions itself depends on disciplined observation and deduction.

No enthusiasm for discovery will in itself lead a teacher for example to recognise the relationship between rock type, soil and vegetation, or to place a local building in the social totality of its historic period, or to know how to evaluate the quality of significance of a child's artistic or musical invention. And if the teacher is unaware, then the quality of the curricular experience for the child is thereby diminished. It would be unrealistic to imagine that any but the most exceptional of teachers can do other than accumulate, through their own experience, some equipment of this kind and to share it with colleagues, learning meanwhile from them and from others. Alongside curricular knowledge must be reckoned professional knowledge. This is the necessary cornerstone of an enabling curriculum, for it is through professional knowledge that a teacher is able to analyse development, experience, and their relation to curriculum.

Since each child's development and experience is unique, it might seem at first sight logically necessary to design a special curriculum for each child as planned intervention in his particular development and experience, and to keep doing so as he and his experience continue to change. Plainly, that would be absurd; yet the only practicable alternative is to enact some kind of compromise which is reasonably on-target for a class, and then to monitor each individual's progress through the common experience. It is in fact justifiable to do this, since one facet of an enabling curriculum is that it shall have common features and enable children to grow up and live together. This compromise has then to be negotiated with a class in order to secure their continuing engagement at a reasonable level, a procedure that implies not surrender but constructive realism. If a teacher has an idea about the development and experience of a child, or the children living together in class, this implies also some notion about how learning takes place. It involves knowing how to assess progress in respect of curricular experience in different aspects of curriculum, and how to diagnose, in the process, what children are capable of doing next. This is a procedure often to be identified in practice, ranging from the infant teacher's: "Why don't you make me a big one, and don't forget his ears?" to the suggestion made to children in a junior or middle school: "You two go over there and try it again, and weight what is left over."

In a broad sense each new venture is then assessed in its turn, and eventually it becomes possible to build up a cumulative record such as Clift, Weiner and Wilson advocate. In each individual learning episode this requires sensitivity about the whole process, including awareness that in each child, in each aspect of the curriculum, the profiles both of performance and of engagement are likely to be irregular, and the relation between performance and engagement, unpredictable.

The skill needed to achieve this degree of sensitivity and awareness requires not only a grasp of the ways in which learning actually takes place, but a readiness to match the assessment to the learning. This is more straightforward to undertake in the sequential, skill-based aspects of curriculum, such as mathematical understanding, than in those whose structure is more open and problematical. The remaining two elements in a primary teacher's equipment are of a more personal nature. One is in fact the set of personal and interpersonal skills and qualities that are needed in a teacher when relating to children and indeed to other adults too. These skills and qualities include sensitive facility in matters such as the grouping of children, the possibilities of peer teaching, and indeed the organisational curriculum itself.

Partly these arise from professional knowledge and from personality and character and from a teacher's own experience including the sustained habit of self-analysis. In the complex and varied organisation of a class for different purposes, it demands almost a form of intuition, which the ablest of teachers of young children seem to show, but which is actually built up through prolonged insight into the development and experience of children. The remaining element, hinted at in the discussion of personal qualities, is that of constant critical appraisal of oneself, one's aims, and one's context and outcome of action. Provided that it does not become discouraging on the one hand, or a form of self-indulgence on the other, criticism of this kind leads to the continuous readjustments that a truly enabling curriculum requires.

Awareness of the hidden curriculum is particularly important here. The consequence of maintaining these five elements is that the role-complex of teachers becomes widened and the task itself of higher professional standing. In addition to the usual roles of instructor, classifier, socialiser, etc., and the more fully elaborated analyses presented by, Musgrove and Taylor, an enabling curriculum requires at least three others. One is that of the teacher as researcher, as advocated by Stenhouse. By the mastery of procedures of systematic observation and recording, even in the most rudimentary way that is all that time permits, a teacher is able to combine the use of professional knowledge with the demands of interpersonal relations and the need for critical appraisal.

Being research-minded does not mean putting on a metaphorical white coat and distancing oneself from children. It resembles far more the situation of the medical man whose research orientation sharpens his diagnosis and medication. Where it is possible, a whole range of new-wave techniques of observation and evaluation can be learned and applied, but it is the orientation, the attitude, that matters; that of learning from and in the teaching situation rather than taking oneself and one's knowledge and skills as an invariant datum. In one of his later papers Stenhouse linked the teacher's research role with that of the artist, thus imparting a new dimension to it.

The second additional role is that of team member. This is an almost inevitable consequence of the expansion of curricular and professional knowledge. It has already become obvious that no one teacher can master all the skills, concepts and procedures that are needed in an enabling curriculum. But if there is to be sharing, it does not take place automatically. For one thing there may not be an exact match between curricular needs and teacher competencies. There may be too many geographers and too few physical scientists; a gaggle of guitarist and no pianist. In that case, a team has to look for some kind of adjustment, which in effect means either dispensing with something important for the curriculum, or seeing that somebody develops an additional expertise. Readiness to take this role has not always been characteristic of primary teachers. What is more, the newly acquired expertise—or any other expertise for that matter—may be in the hands of a junior member of staff who has to learn the skill of advising much more established teachers, while they in turn have to learn the harder skill of being advised by a slip of a girl, or a young fellow not five minutes out of college, or however it may be put. Yet this is the implication of staff development of this kind. It involves a kind of professional status-inversion. but it is a necessary step towards the other role of curriculum consultant that is advocated for this reason in the HMI survey of 1978.

It is necessary to mention briefly the kinds of development that can take place within a school. Basically, these must be designed and implemented by the head of a school, together with a nucleus of enthusiastic colleagues who may or may not be among the senior members of staff. This is in itself a delicate operation, for it implies that the head must exercise a dual role, that of leader and also that of innovator. He or she must be equipped for both, and confident in an ability to discharge both. And the innovation is not only a curricular innovation, but rather an innovation in organisational climate and procedures intended to facilitate a continuing series of curricular innovations which themselves have implications for the wider curriculum. It involves getting senior and junior colleagues to accept a situation in which there will be continuing demands on professional knowledge, professional skills and curricular knowledge, and the possibility of increasing and threatening conflict in values between colleagues. Almost by definition it is a situation calculated to increase rather than to decrease uncertainty.

Dewey once spoke of the need to substitute security of procedure for security of belief; but this is a case where security of procedure is itself the casualty, until a new kind of procedure is substituted. In an age in which an emphasis on either development or experience is frequently blamed for every cognitive and moral defect in the body politic, a transition within a school to a new way of looking at curriculum is likely to be still more difficult. Yet without it, any serious attempt to rethink the primary curriculum in detail must be at risk. At best it will influence two or three members of staff, who will continue to support each other until one of them leaves, after which the whole process may well falter and fail. At worst, the whole process of curriculum changes may be frozen out at the start, the reason given being that it is high-sounding theoretical idea with no practical significance, whereupon everyone heaves a sigh of relief and goes on just as before.

If the school is a very small one, a different set of problems may arise. There is no doubt a considerable value in the small, familial institution, but the demands of curricular knowledge and professional knowledge fall disproportionately on small schools, and ironically it may happen that the very efforts needed in order to make an innovation effective will cause greater strains than in a larger school which is already better equipped in terms of range of expertise and personnel. In an age of declining school rolls in so many countries, the small-school problem is not itself declining, even when it is held at bay by amalgamations So this small-school problem is not likely to disappear. Meanwhile, there is even more bitter irony in the contrast that those countries with growing populations and greater numbers clamouring for primary education are just those which cannot yet afford to resource an enabling curriculum at all. Of course, in this as in most other forms of innovation, case-studies of successful initiatives provide the best evidence.

Even for this purpose it is necessary to provide some effective support. The twin aspect of the researcher role, that of closer observation of children and that of enterprising experiments with formal and wider curriculum, both call for professional support beyond the resources of individual schools. Fortunately, they can be supplied by different agencies. This indicates the patterns of in-service provision that are required.

The first is concerned with the refinement of professional skills. This could well be entrusted to two kinds of agencies. One is the personnel skilled in this field that are to be found in universities, polytechnics and colleges of higher education. The practical difficulty in such matters is always that of deploying the resources of time, manpower, and money in a mutually satisfactory way. At the same time there is a different problem, that of rendering outside experts and school staff mutually acceptable. There is always the danger that both 'sides', at their own stages of professional development and experience, will stereotype the other, the personnel from higher education tending to think of the school staff as context-bound and perhaps lacking in perspective, while the staff regale each other with despairing comments about the jargon-ridden approach of their counterparts, and perhaps with lurid conjectures about how they would manage the most troublesome of the 9-year-old classes. Yet this too is a phase that can be transcended by experience based on a combined approach to curricular problems, provided that both 'sides' interact regularly with the children and genuinely value the development and experience of the other. The other potential agency is the advisory service of the local education authorities. Here too there is a role-problem, but it is rather a different one. There may still be some suspicion of those with a lack of demonstrable recent classroom experience, but it is sometimes overshadowed by the dual role of advisors, for they are also seen as inquisitors bent on facilitating accountability. Here too, collective experience can fairly soon reduce suspicions, but this requires time, which is often desperately short for both partners.

In view of the long and increasingly successful partnership that has been built up between parents and teachers, it is evident that the help of parents can be drawn upon in several ways. First, their own knowledge of their children and of their neighbours' children, especially at the infant stage, is a positive asset. If they can be persuaded that a curriculum is really intended to enable their children and not to subject them to some current fad, they can play a number of valuable roles. They and their extended families can figure also as experts in particular fields. Their development and experience can also be drawn on, and in the case of the unemployed and the retired, it may help to give significance to their own lives if they are invited to contribute from their expertise, their concerns and their memories. Families can also help particularly in the informal curriculum, when resources permit, by lending a hand in the planning and execution of journeys and visits which can make a powerful impact on the experience of children.

Finally, the involvement of families can have a direct outcome because it gives them dignity and significance in front of their children and their children's friends, and contributes to the organisational curriculum by presenting the school in relation to the community, and to the hidden curriculum by combating value-differences between home and school. Meanwhile there is another kind of support that may be required, in curricular knowledge itself. It is the more enterprising experts in different academic disciplines who can best help here: natural scientists, historians, geographers, social scientists—as well as those devoted to different kinds of artistic activity, and also the representatives of various aspects of political, economic, social and religious life. All of these could enrich the resources available to teachers, but it is difficult indeed to effect the necessary liaison. For one thing, unless their institution has been actively involved in the education of the young there is a lack of the basic mechanisms by which the experts can be brought together with the teachers.

Casual social acquaintances is one possible means of contact: team games, golf, chess and bridge have all been known to play a part in establishing such links, as have common membership of churches and of political parties, or simply chats over the garden fence. There may even be some positive virtue in what is just done 'for a pal', except that for each school such opportunities are left very much to chance. Even where they are effected, there can be problems.

The Schools Council Industry Project, with whose activities for younger children we have been involved, has often encountered the problem of how to persuade personnel managers and sales representatives that the style required in primary schools is rather different from their customary forms of discourse. Here again, however, there is scope for experience to bring the participants together, and be a part of the evolving role of heads to become facilitators of the participation of other adults in schools.

All of these suggestions may, of course, seem rather Utopian in terms both of resource allocation and of social reality. It requires a Plato or an Illich to envisage a troupe of scholars, research chemists, ballet dancers, car salesmen and representatives of British Raj holding themselves in readiness for a phone call from St Mary's of Acacia Avenue, even if they did know what to do when they arrived. In any case they can be released only occasionally for such purposes, however favourably they may regard them.

In addition there can be hidden conflicts, particularly where power and identity are under potential threat. An industrial enterprise is unlikely to open up its industrial relations to intrepid questioning from Sandra, aged 7 years, nor is a professional historian likely to welcome being asked to make a contribution to what he perceives as something perfunctorily and uncompre-hendingly termed Environmental Studies. Still less is a member of a local bureaucracy likely to submit to the sort of interrogation from primary pupils that he contrives to avoid in more public situations; and if this is done, it only gives a false and cosy impression of social realities.

All of these considerations have to be borne in mind by teachers and especially head teachers as they draw on the repertoire of potential support. They in turn constitute a form of professional experience whose acquisition is a challenge, which can result in a third addition to the role-complex of primary teachers, that of community relations facilitator. Alongside these developments there is a place for more systematic professional enhancement through courses for named qualifications. Open University degrees in Educational Studies are a case in point. Further, the analysis of development and of experience could figure valuably in Diploma, Phil and M.Ed. course, or their equivalents, which customarily include a component of more rigorous empirical study. Where honours B.Ed. courses are required to involve studies in education and one other discipline, as is often the case, this combination is particularly well suited to a case-study of a teacher's own class embarking on something new related to the student's other main discipline. However, it would be self-defeating if every teacher were to feel it obligatory to undertake such sustained study for a named qualification. This is only one way in which collective professional experience can be enhanced, and one that should be neither belittled nor given exaggerated importance in a teacher's career profile. The principal value to a school of having on its staff one or two members who are in disciplined study of this kind is that they can, and increasingly do, act as translators of educational scholarship and research and thus as a means of bringing their colleagues more effectively into the wider discourse of the teaching profession as a whole. This too involves the process of professional experience in which they personally may be open to the same suspicions that can attach to their mentors, but which they can learn to overcome. Incidentally, there is much to be said for introducing into courses of advanced study at least some guidance in the handling of these colleague relationships, as a necessary step towards the establishment of effective curriculum planning.

Schools in the present circumstances may manifest a situation in which the most senior members of the staff were trained in an age in which subsequent professional development was not regarded as important when compared with the virtues of experience, while the younger ones have been educated with the opposite assumption. It is this kind of situation that is caricatured in the story of the head who basked in the security of thirty years' experience, which his irreverent colleagues preferred to regard as one year's experience, repeated thirty times. This is where professional status-inversion may arise. Ironically, the more effective the programme of post-experience and advanced study, the greater the likelihood that this professional status-inversion will emerge. The course themselves should, therefore, also include some reference to coping strategies for this purpose.

In the longer run, however, the main determinant of change in schools is the pattern of initial teacher education. If the teaching profession is to be increasingly equipped with teachers capable of planning an enabling curriculum; as interaction between development and experience in the lives of children which can equip them for choice and acceptance; then it follows that their courses of initial training have to prepare them for this task. There is, of course, no need and no room for such considerations to be added to an already full programme.

Therefore, the existing programme has to be used, and if necessary modified, for this purpose. It is worthwhile to look briefly at the way in which the necessary competence in studies of development, experience and curriculum can be fostered, and to consider how far this might involve modifying the usual pattern of course.

Unlike teachers on post-experience courses, students in initial training are all at more or less the same point in professional development, and often in the same early-adult phase of general development too. They have thus reached a point at which it becomes possible to consider their own development with a little more insight and objectivity than is usually possible during Adolescence, and to learn to transcend any tendency to stereotype what they may have. They have also probably been able to observe the development of relatives and friends, to read more widely, and to begin to make valid generalisations from personal experience, to be set against the background of what they read in the professional literature. At the same time, and for similar reasons, they can also formulate opinions about their own experience and that of others, and to distinguish experience from development. This capacity can be fostered by general information about child development and social background. It is quite usual to include in a course of this kind some form of child study, and this appears a very suitable way of focusing attention on what development and experience mean in an individual child. It can also be enriched by some study of the child's cultural context, for as Bernstein insisted, teachers must first be acquainted with this, if they are to enable children to grow toward their own culture.

But a closer analysis of development and experience in relation to curriculum is also needed. This could be a separate requirement or a prescribed part of the basic exercise itself, with an obligation to consider the implications of development and experience in that child's life for his or her curriculum. It would then be interesting to match the student's interpretation of what is desirable with the actual curricular sequence encountered by the child, and to reflect on the outcome. So far, these requirements would involve only a slight modification in what is widespread practice at least in B.Ed. courses: the PGCE may allow less scope, but it should not therefore be assumed that this is impossible or unimportant.

Children in fiction and autobiography, carefully selected, can reveal the relationship between development, experience and curriculum vividly, and one or two seminars based on the comparison between dissimilar child careers could quite quickly bring out some of the main issues, which could be further examined through direct observation in the course of the work in schools which is likely to constitute an increasingly important part of B.Ed. and PGCE courses. Finally, due emphasis could be placed on the significance of development and experience in each piece of curriculum planning in which the students take part, individually or collectively, in concert with teachers or otherwise. Where it is possible to make some form of IT-INSET link, and thus to lay emphasis on the importance of development and experience simultaneously in the education of new and of experienced teachers, the advantages may be considerable. Attitudes in the collaborating schools may thus be changed at the time that the new teachers' attitudes are being formed, while the resources of the 'training institutions' could be more readily made available to the schools in these circumstances.

Curriculum is seen as planned intervention in the interaction of development with experience. Since every child's interaction is unique, it must therefore follow that every child's curriculum is unique, and that in a sense every child constructs his or her own curriculum. This is of course implicit in what has already been said about the self-curriculum, but the idea is worth pursuing further.

National curricula are of course made available to more than one class, to more than one school, in fact to a whole people. Yet whether the formal and wider curricula are devised for a class, a school or a people, and whatever variations they permit, still each individual constructs his or her own version of curriculum, and in the process evolves his or her own achieved version of the pupil's role. And these personal curricula differ from each other in a number of ways. The most obvious of these is performance, which depends quite substantially on development and experience as well as on the curriculum itself. Almost equally important is what may be called engagement, the extent to which children are motivated or enthused or bothered by curriculum. There is a distinction between these two. As the Oracle studies remind us some good performers are able to maintain their output without giving much of themselves or, in the present terms, engaging enthusiastically with the curriculum.

On the other hand, some children who engage vigorously with the curriculum simply do not perform well, like those adults who profess to like a subject while being hopeless at it. If this distinction is accepted, then a further point can be made. For if every individual child makes his or her own curriculum, then it is engagement as well as performance that is its true indication. In a curriculum with a process basis, one that emphasises skills and concepts rather than performance outputs, it becomes more defensible to emphasise the importance of engagement.

At first this may seem like saying that it is better to travel hopefully than to arrive, and if a forced choice has to be made, then it is better to travel hopefully, though everyone has to arrive somewhere too, and then to move on, and on again. More important for the present discussion is the close relationship that exists between engagement and experience. To put it directly, engagement is likely to be greater where experience is more closely aligned with the formal and wider curricula of a school. That being evident, it is now necessary to look at some of the same issues in the light of performance and engagement as they relate to the continuity of children's experience throughout primary education. Evidence of children's own view of the curriculum may be taken from three sources: descriptive writing about or for children, direct observations of children, and the results of empirical investigations that appear to throw some light on the question. The last of these categories, the outcome of empirical studies, does not in fact help very much. There has been quite a long record of investigations into the relative popularity of school subjects at the primary stage, but this kind of study does not reveal anything more informative about the actual nature of the work that proved popular, or about the relation of preference choices to either performance or engagement. It seems at first sight likely that the relation with engagement would be closer than that with performance, but there is little evidence on this. More could perhaps be inferred from a close and continuous case-study such as those by Nash or Armstrong, but this particular question has not usually figured in such studies. There is a wealth of information hidden in the memories of teachers, and tersely transcribed on record cards, which does show something of the relationship between performance and engagement. However, the categories are generally poorly defined, and in any case are not specifically considered in relation to experience. There is plenty of scope for something more systematic, as will be indicated, but at present the data are scanty.

Direct observation is scarcely less systematic than this. In the course of clarifying some of the ideas presented in this book, we have made a practice of checking ideas as they emerge against real children in various situations, and we hope that this precaution has in general held us back from making rash generalisations. Incidental observations of this sort can rank as evidence only in a negative, preventive sense, and it is in this way that they will be used. There is also a third kind of evidence, a kind less usually found in what we rate as professional writing about education.

The Formal Curriculum

Most children take their formal curriculum for granted, at least at the primary level. Development impels them to envisage primary education as an accepted process in which they are taking part, the process of being at school as part of growing up. Experience embodies their reaction. Necessarily, they think of the curriculum as being first and foremost the formal curriculum, within which they usually have little doubt about the importance of the basic skills and modes of communicating. For the rest, they are likely to envisage the curriculum in terms of subject titles rather than of topics or activities, though topics and activities themselves may come to be regarded as another kind of subject: 'We did a project about that'.

It is scarcely necessary to say that the enthusiasm of children for their work has little conscious relation to the curriculum theory on which it is based. Like their parents, children usually adopt quite a conventional view. They will respond to curriculum as it is, or as it changes, only if it seems in some way advantageous to do so. Fortunately of enthusiastic teachers, they do usually think it advantageous to work along with somebody who is vigorous and good fun and doesn't expect the impossible. Only years later will they be able to judge how enabling their curriculum has been. The significance of this can be taken a step further. Children themselves see some of the curriculum in terms of their growing powers: this was noted in the discussion of growth, health and movement, and it clearly applies also to the basic skills and to others such as handling a microcomputer. Much of the rest of the curriculum, however, is perceived throughout the primary years as a series of episodes to be lived through with good-humoured tolerance and with varying degrees of engagement, rather than as a series of skills, concepts and attitudes to be acquired. They are in a sense the passengers in the aircraft. Only the pilot, i.e., the teacher, has to master the route plan and the controls. The figure of speech is not quite appropriate, because now and again some of them do glimpse something of the purpose of it all, and it is an aim of primary education that they should gradually come to perceive that purpose and gain access, so to speak, to their own flight deck, as they learn to construct their self-curriculum. Meanwhile, the formal curriculum is likely to make differing impacts on differing groups of children. This is where the question of engagement becomes important.

For most children, for most of the time, the quality of engagement is not particularly high. Sometimes there is a burst of concentrated effort, especially among the younger children, but when social relations develop more richly as the children grow older, the social world of the classroom acts as a distractor to all but the most single-minded and the most socially neglected children. At the same time they may develop an effective skill in peer teaching, helping their friends either in official or in illicit ways. Indeed, one way of justifying ability and effort, and thus of avoiding ostracism, is to pass one's knowledge and skill unconditionally, thereby frustrating any competitive ethos that may be officially encouraged. Teachers who prefer a cooperative ethos can here work with the grain, but have to remember that as soon as this cooperation becomes official policy, the social situation is changed.

As a safety-valve, there must still be forms of co-operation that are officially discouraged but unofficially tolerated; and that then becomes a part of the organisational and hidden curricula. And needless to say there are other children in whose case it is a minor triumph for a teacher to persuade them to engage in any effort at all, even though they have considerable ability that occasionally shines through their protective armour.

The Wider Curriculum

To some the informal curriculum is where they come into their own. They are the stars of the teams and of the plays and clubs, the ones who stay behind after school and get to know the teachers in a more direct way, and it is incidents in the informal curriculum that they remember most vividly. These may include some who also shine in the formal curriculum, but the informal aspects are what appeal most to them, the ones within which their social relationships are forged. They have a particular developmental significance too, because these are so palpably matters which are appropriate for children of their age, with an evident potential for leading towards the next step. These are the activities in which their elder sister once excelled,that sister whose current preoccupation with her boyfriend is now made the subject of a mixture of mockery and awe, or in which their elder brother first learned to take the measure of school long before he became devoted to his motor-bike and his mates.

There is, in fact, a wider range of engagement in the informal curriculum, with consequences for the kind of performance that is found, according to the ways in which informal activities are perceived. Activities within the informal curriculum attract considerable attention in literary material. They range from those to whom it included elements of agony, as in Betjeman's *Summoned by Bells,* to those to whom it is a consuming passion. What is shared by the two extremes is a sense of the vividness and importance of informal activities, and in any enabling curriculum they must surely be prominent. For some children, indeed, they may provide the one moment of significance in primary education. Closely associated with the informal curriculum is the organisational curriculum, the messages conveyed by the school as a social organisation. Usually it is seen as a centrally important matter. Its 'taken-for-granted' nature seems accepted even by truants, and in works of fiction it is usually portrayed as something to be 'sent up' and treated with light-hearted and tolerant confidence when all is going well; as a menace when there is an important test or when it is time for transfer from one stage to the next; as an intrusive nuisance in moments of high drama within the children's social world; but as a very prompt help in times of real trouble or terror, when even the toughest surprise themselves and everyone else by crying too.

It is not just the order but the values of the school, the hidden curriculum, that are involved here. Sometimes it may engender opposition. Sometimes, however, it may express a deep concern for individuals and exemplify genuine social education in action. For example, in Tom Wakefield's *Forties Child* the author, recalling his wartime childhood, singles out the cuddling and comforting of a particularly revolting classmate by the teacher, and the challenge to accept the girl, smell and running nose and all, that the teacher directed to the author himself: 'I suppose Miss Craddock made us all a bit older—or something like that'. On the other hand, a latent attitude of racial prejudice can engender fierce resentment among children, though here it is necessary to remember that the prejudice may not lie entirely, or even mainly, with the teacher. Similar issues are, of course, raised when religious or class or gender differences are involved. It is scarcely necessary to say how important they can be in influencing individual children in the extent and nature of their engagement with the curriculum. To cite instances of literature that deal with any of these aspects of the hidden curriculum would be hazardous, since there are so many of them. But this in itself emphasises something of the widespread recognition of the importance of these issues. Here again, no enabling curriculum can be adequate unless it takes them sensitively into account. It was emphasised that children's experience, even their experience in school, is not confined to the formal and wider curriculum. There is always a part of experience that exists alongside the curriculum, and one of the latent functions of primary education is that it provides an arena within which this experience can be enacted.

One of the perennial messages from school stories over the past hundred years is that the secret life of children is powerfully influential in their experience and in interaction with their development. Here, more than within the curriculum, are concentrated the episodes which arouse their attention, their effort, their excitement and anger and grief. It is as if their wider experience swamps the curriculum from time to time, like flood water after a storm. This again is a common theme in literature.

As the plot thickens, teachers continue woodenly to implement the curriculum, especially the formal curriculum, like some shadowy back-cloth in a drama, occasionally shouting from back stage that someone is not attending, and then being fairly satisfied with an answer and fading out of experience again. In fact, this experience beyond the curriculum can be interpreted as a collective alternative self-curriculum, for over the years it involves learning, in the neighbourhood but more intensely in the playground, a succession of codes and adjustments and conventional learned responses through which children complement their development with collective experience. It is here that pecking-orders are established and unmade, that the alleged conventional wisdom of the adult world is challenged, and that the more popular and confident individuals make their first half-ashamed, half-amused bids for heterosexual recognition. The boundary between all this and curriculum is a real but invisible one. The ringing of a bell or the clapping of hands may be all that divides the one from the other; but everybody knows where the boundary is, and everybody except the most extreme advocates of pedagogic liberty assumes that it should be, more or less, there. This leaves unanswered the question whether the school should officially concern itself with what happens beyond that boundary. In one sense it must; there are regular appeals through the organisational curriculum when some little procession brings a casualty to the teacher. Yet, despite the existence of pastoral-care systems there may be a variety of views among the children, as well as the teachers, about how vigilant those teachers ought to be, and how far it is better to let them have their own, quite false, views about what is going on. It could be that willingness of individual children to engage in curriculum is related to what happens to them outside it.

In a boarding school, or elsewhere where social relations among children are concentrated in school with particular intensity, these issues are all the more cogent. Independent primary schools include a number of boarding schools and, while the term lasts, they are total institutions. That means that the wider curriculum occupies a very large part of life, but not all of it. There is still an area of autonomy within which social relations can be worked out with all the stark directness portrayed in school stories, such as Philip Toynbee's *A School in Private.* There, as in day schools, the impact on individuals has much to do with their family and social context, and it is easy to see this as a simple, clean form of socialisation that is a part of life. But this cannot be assumed. The seeds of disengagement with curriculum can be sown in the seedbed of non-curricular experience, for children who do not succeed in these relationships may learn to reject the whole context with which they are associated.

Hitherto the child's-eye view of the curriculum has been confined to what happens within the normal stream of events in normal schools. It is important to emphasise this. For in a sense there is no such thing as an ordinary school, or ordinary children. However much they may try to be ordinary so as not to be left out of the swim, they are in fact all different. Of course, every respectable theory of the primary curriculum says that they are all different, but so often leads to actual curriculum planning that assumes that they are all, in most important respects, alike.

The curriculum then comes to symbolise alikeness: this is what we do when we are all together and being alike, as distinct from what we do outside when we are all being different. Indeed, school itself often comes to symbolise the alikeness of society in its public guise. In a sense this is itself a valuable part of the organisational curriculum since it promotes social cohesion and security. Norms are more closely observed in the classroom. To cry, or swear, or be sick in class is on a par with such behaviour in church, though more immediately penalised. However, the limit of its value is reached at the point at which teachers slip into the habit of thinking that this classroom alikeness extends outside. As is often revealed in informal situations such as discos or school journeys, 'normal' children may turn out to be more enterprising, more aggressive, more original or more vulnerable than school suggests. The formal curriculum is thus revealed as a very special and protected kind of experience, and the enabling function of the wider curriculum is thus thrust into greater prominence. There does, however, often come a point at which the semblance of normality cannot be maintained, even within the formal curriculum. Engagement may become so minimal that performance is seriously impaired.

The children most prone to this disengagement are those with serious physical or mental handicaps. The sheer problem of managing themselves becomes significant, even when they are strongly encouraged to belittle their handicaps, and very much want to do so. This is a central problem of the social psychology of special education, one that acquires a further urgency when children with handicaps are educated alongside others, as the 1981 Education Act advises for England and Wales. Some light is thrown on this issue by autobiographical accounts. It is one that teachers are coming to recognise more generally, and it is impressive how much they can achieve, even when enabling is such an apparently formidable task, and how much it is appreciated when they do.

Presumably the extreme case of enablement is that of Anne Sullivan's handling of Helen Keller's multiple handicaps and their social consequence: but that was not in school. It is not easy to know how the least able children perceive the curriculum, except by inference, since they are the ones who find most difficulty in articulating their problems and are thus doubly disadvantaged. It seems likely that a personal, dependent, relationship with the teacher will be more prominent than any particular aspect of curriculum, and that therefore there is a form of engagement that can facilitate performance. Here too there is a dilemma, because the satisfaction of group membership, always rather fragile for the less bale, is sometimes difficult to reconcile with the need for some element of segregation so that the teacher can make the formal aspects of an enabling curriculum more personally relevant. The case of the emotionally disturbed children is still more difficult. Here the barrier to engagement lies precisely in the area of personal relationships. There may be some unfortunate element in the interaction of development with experience that renders curriculum as such, relatively impotent, and that also leaves the teacher encumbered with the problem of first coming to terms with this.

Severe cases are of course allocated to special institutional contexts, but the facilities simply do not exist for all emotionally disturbed children to be transferred from 'normal' schools, especially when it is considered more important that they should not be taken away from other children than be in the hands of specially trained teachers able, for example, to use the aesthetic aspect of curriculum diagnostically and therapeutically. In all these instances of children with special educational needs, their own perceptions of what curriculum is about will be heavily dependent on those special needs. At the worst it may be beyond a teacher's powers to devise for them the special curriculum that they can make their own. At the best, the need to do exactly that for them may encourage teachers to do likewise for all their pupils; but that requires outstanding quality. There is another category of children whose perceptions of curriculum in all its aspects are now becoming a matter of concern. These are the children from minority groups. Whose entire ambience in experience can dominate their pattern of engagement and thus, to a large extent, their performance also. Particular problems arise with children from strict and unusual family backgrounds who find a school's moves toolax and unstructured for their experience, or for those from permissive or structureless homes who regard school discipline with incredulity. Both set a real problem for the moral curriculum. In some sense their situation is not unlike that of the children with special educational needs: often, of course, they overlap with them.

However, the presence of ethnic minorities raises a different set of problems. The first of these, familiar to all who have worked in the field of multi-cultural education, is the danger of lumping all such groups together in a general stereotype such as 'non-native', 'immigrant', 'non-English-speaking' and within each group as marked individual differences as within 'normal' schools, despite apparent uniformities of dress. Yet to every one of these children, the curriculum has to be related to a distinctive pattern of development and experience.

Some ethnic groups do, in fact, show different average patterns of physical and social development when compared with the native children. All of them draw on different backgrounds of experience within which the concept of curriculum will itself occupy very different positions. For example, a Hong Kong Chinese family running a restaurant has clear expectations for, and from, its children in a way that a West Indian family headed by a unemployed second-generation immigrant may not. A whole study could be based on the different ways in which each group might envisage each of the six elements in the formal curriculum discussed, not to mention the three aspects of the wider curriculum. Moreover, any such conjecture, however true of the 'normal' members of these groups, is likely to be wide off the mark where individuals are concerned. Almost by definition, the aspects of the curriculum that are least familiar to all of them, and most difficult for them to engage with, are those most deeply embedded in the host culture, such as English history and English literature. Even this does not result in a uniform policy or a uniform response.

From one point of view, one that is clearly represented among some of the groups concerned, the learning of such initially alien content is itself the means of acquiring acceptance and of facilitating performance. The opposite point of view is that it should be rigorously excluded, and that in its place there should be some version of Black Studies or its equivalent in other cultures. Between these two comes the 'melting pot' view, in which everyone contributes from their own culture and the sum is better than its parts.

Clearly, it is not possible to follow more than one of these at once. What is less immediately clear is that to follow any of them involves substituting a social-imperatives approach for a process approach to curriculum and thereby perhaps aggravating the situation; since a social-imperatives approach draws attention to group differences, while a process approach places its emphasis on individual differences. It appears that much minority in-group opinion is in favour of a curriculum that takes account of groups consciousness as such, but then such views may come from individuals particularly prone to express them. Even if this is not the case and ethnic consciousness really is paramount in children's experience in a divided and prejudiced society, it still does not follow that the most effective curricular response is to be obtained by aligning the axis of the curriculum with that of the prejudice. In multi-cultural education many of the answers are still to be found. In finding them, the evidence from the children's patterns of engagement is still one of the most important considerations.

Similar considerations apply, though perhaps less starkly, to social class and community differences. Much the same also characterises the children's own reactions. There is a general realisation that children do disengage from the curriculum even in the primary years. It is less certain that this disengagement is mainly on account of social-class or community differences. There are middle-class rebels and working-class aspirants, and both are likely to be articulate enough to exemplify their attitudes in writing.

In almost every such case there is something in the immediate personal experience of the children or their families which proves decisive for their pattern of adjustment. Therefore, adaptation of the curriculum to ensure engagement, or for social-imperatives reasons, does not guarantee any one pattern of response. Although 'Nymphs and Shepherds' are remote from the experience of many children in most environments, it is not so easy to be sure what to put in their place. One final aspect of children's response must be remembered. The proportion of families who change house, and of children who perforce change schools, is considerable: between one-quarter and one-third, and more in some areas. For each of these there is a need for readjustment on each occasion, and sometimes there are many such occasions, for example, in the case of children of members of the armed services.

When children come from sharply contrasted cultural groups which are already in a minority position, the additional problems of horizontal transition may demand a higher price, especially when the school's formal and hidden curricula operate by means that the newcomer's own culture regards as meaningless, repressive, or simply wrong. Nevertheless, after a while they usually take such experiences in their stride, and gain in social maturity by doing so. Yet in the process they may lose beliefs and qualities that are not easily restored, while their intellectual development may be more seriously retarded than many people realise In their case the need for an enabling curriculum to intervene in the interaction between development and experience and to cultivate choice and acceptance is a very real and demanding one. There are other children who have to spend periods of their life in hospital, or ill at home, while still others absent themselves as truants or under family pressures.

Systematic studies have been made of such children and their education and these help to ensure that they remain represented in the professional culture of teachers: necessarily so, for there are some in most schools and most classes, and they remain recalcitrant exceptions to most neat schemes of curriculum planning. Like many other issues touched upon in the present study, this could constitute a whole important field of investigation in itself. What children think about their primary education is still only imperfectly known. Studies of the relative popularity of subjects or activities, contributions to newspaper competitions, and even close observation of children and teachers interaction in classrooms, do not fill in the whole picture.

Many teachers can supplement the written word from their own experience of schools and children, but even they do not plumb the whole of the pupil's perspectives; there is almost always some element of surprise when children vouchsafe their opinions more openly than in usual. There is always more to be found out about children, however well one knows them, and teachers realise this too. They may be encouraged by realising that they, as a professional group, do emerge from all of this welter of variegated evidence in a fairly favourable light; and sometimes children think the world of them.

School-based Curriculum Development

One of the problems faced by anyone attempting to understand school-based curriculum development as an idea is that it is used very much as a catch-all concept. For example, as illustrated by Mitson, it means something as substantial as groups of secondary school pupils, together with appropriate staff training and resources development; or it may be small-scale revision of a language programme in a primary school, such that described by Timms and Lees. The DES has stressed the significance of school-based approach, but two writers in particular have helped to sharpen the formulation of ideas about them. Eggleston's introduction to six case studies provides a useful starting-point. Although it is unclear whether Eggleston was describing school-based curriculum development or prescribing a particular way of doing it, four features of his definition are worth picking out:

1. *It is particularistic*: The curriculum-development activity is focused upon the diagnosed, or perceived, needs of the specific school or part of it.
2. *It is process-oriented*: In the terms of 'strategies for the curriculum' intended, the process by which these are developed is important in itself.
3. *It is participatory*: The appropriate style for developing the curriculum is cooperative, that is, staff working together to produce plans for change.
4. *It is preliminary*: The curriculum developed is to be seen as experimental, in the sense that it is open to evaluation and appraisal after its implementation.

One of the interesting things about this definition is the stress, not on the curriculum as such, but on the roles that teachers have to play in the process of its development, and the attitudes that are required to underpin it. This characteristic is also central to the analysis offered by another writer, Skilbeck. He identified three models of school-based curriculum development—the rational-deductive, the rational-interactive and the intuitive—and located them within differing politico-educational frameworks. The first operates in centrally directed educational systems, where the task of the school is to 'interpret central directives' and the role of the teacher is as a mere functionary in a bureaucratised educational service. The second emerges in mixed systems, such as those in England and Wales, which stress the active role of teachers in adapting the curriculum at school level within rather broad general outlines of national policy.

Teachers working within this kind of framework have a more complex role than in the rational-deductive model and have more demands made upon them; they 'have to act as course assessors, to help construct syllabuses, to select learning materials and to devise learning systems'. The third model stresses the individual teacher's decision-making and creativity, and leads to great diversity between teachers, between schools, and to inconsistency between 'normal policy and individual school programmes'. Although school-based curriculum development may share elements from all three, the rational-interactive model represents the style and values most appropriate to contemporary English schools, especially because of the stress put upon the range of roles expected of teachers, and the assumption that teachers have to negotiate the fine details of their roles by working in partnership with each other. Thus in this formulation also, school-based curriculum development is as much about changing roles and relationships among a school staff as it is about changing schemes of work or methods of teaching and learning. A second paper by Skilbeck offered a substantial analysis of the concept, rationale and aims of school-based curriculum development, and suggested a model for school use, with a commentary on the difficulties in implementing it. He identified a number of characteristics, including the idea of the curriculum as a set of experiences of value developed by the teacher and learner together from a close and sympathetic appraisal of the learner's needs and characteristics as a learner.

But, although Skilbeck identified the need for freedom for the teachers to define relevant learning experiences, he also noted the requirement for appropriate support systems, including national or regional curricular guidelines. This is an important point, not least to counteract the danger of a simplistic polarising of 'school-based' and 'non-school-based' approaches to curriculum development.

A major goal of school-based curriculum development in Skilbeck's terms is the continuous adaption by teachers of externally defined curricula into forms of educative experiences unique to the teacher and learner. We need a system for curriculum development that combines the advantages of national policy making, national centres for the production of materials and for research and development, with the flexibility, adaptability, and professionally satisfying features of local initiatives and creativity. Thus, school-based curriculum development is predicted upon the concept, admittedly idealised, of teachers who creatively reconstruct the curriculum within a recognised framework of local and national expectations; it is not predicted upon passive acceptance of external definitions of the curriculum, or the myth of the 'autonomous' school, existing independently of its political and economic context. Given the political development, outlined, of a national framework for the curriculum, the relevance of Skilbeck's model for teachers in England and Wales has increased considerably. Skilbeck's analysis enables us to add two further characteristics of school-based curriculum development to the four identified earlier. These concern the relationship between the school's curriculum and national or local guidelines, and the view taken of the role of the teacher. We can summarise these by saying that school-based curriculum development is:

1. *Framework adaptive*: Despite its particularistic focus, it need not run counter to national or local curriculum guidelines, but may on the contrary ride on them, if staff adapt them to suit their specific situation.

2. *Role extensive:* Issues acceptance by teachers of a wider role than that restricted to classroom performance and it consequently assumes change, or flexibility, in their existing roles.

The teacher role in curriculum development, discussed in the theoretical positions encapsulated above, is to do with what Keddie called the 'teacher-as-educationist' context. In her study of secondary school teachers, Keddie noted two different aspects of their activities: their role beliefs and practices in the context of their classrooms when instructing pupils; and their beliefs and practices elaborated in extra-classroom situations, when discussing educational ideas and principles with colleagues, and with outsiders such as advisors and parents.

Keddie's somewhat jaundiced view of the disparity of beliefs between the two contexts need not concern us here, but the distinction itself is very fruitful for analysing teachers' roles in school-based curriculum development. For most of their time, teachers in the Warwick inquiry were, as curriculum developers, operating in the educationalist context, that is to say, in situations where they were required to discuss educational policies and practices with their colleagues and other adults. This is a fairly novel role for teachers in primary schools, where traditionally it has been reserved for the headteacher, if anyone.

More commonly it has been allocated to the local-authority advisers or other educationists in courses located, and often focused, far from the contexts of the schools themselves. Eggleston and Skilbeck have provided a frame within which a fairly well-defined picture of school-based curriculum development can be held. It is dominated by process—by teachers collaborating in working groups as professionals to interpret general curricular assumptions into a specific curriculum practice suitable for their particular context. This process requires teachers to develop a role for themselves as educationalists in the sense that they will have to familiarise themselves with national and local curriculum documents, justify and articulate curricular objectives, implement and sustain innovation, and evaluate and account for it. Thus, the distinctive arena for school-based curriculum development is the staff-room rather than the class-room, and the distinctive discourse is concerned not only with the surface details of curriculum practice, but also with the assumptions underlying it.

The theoretical analyses discussed above are necessarily generalised, and need to be qualified somewhat in the light of the practice in the Warwick inquiry schools. Brief outlines of the programmes have already been provided, which suggest two characteristics that are perhaps distinctive to primary school curriculum development. They can be considered under two headings, namely gradualism and specialism. To dichotomise rather too simply, gradualism qualifies the idea of 'development', while specialism qualifies the idea of 'curriculum'.

By gradualism we mean three related features of the notion of development which stress the limited expectations that may be held for it. These three limitations may be thought of as the problematic, the unpredictable and the incremental qualities of curriculum development in primary schools.

The problematic nature of curriculum development derives from the fact that there is a conceptual difference between development and change. The latter is neutral and implies merely that practice has altered, not that it has been improved. 'Development', 'renewal' and probably 'innovation' imply not merely change, but change for the better. What counts as a change for the better in education is problematic.

An analogy with the practice of medicine may be helpful. If a doctor diagnoses, say, constipation in a patient and prescribes a change of diet as a remedy, there is not much professional or lay disagreement about what would constitute a change for the better in the patient's condition. Not being constipated is generally regarded as an improvement on being so. But the school curriculum is a more difficult area for diagnosis, with less sure a basis for agreement about what constitutes improvement. A curriculum where there has been, so to speak, little movement for a number of years is not necessarily in a worse condition than one in which there has been a great deal of it. One of the points that follows from this is that, although the term 'curriculum development' is widely used throughout the literature and in this book, in practice it cannot be shown in advance, and often it is not known even in retrospect, whether changes are actually developments.

At best it is commonly a matter of belief, intuition and professional judgement of those involved. Indeed, to return to Eggleston's emphasis on the process of development, it was quite striking to note how frequently the teachers in the Warwick inquiry reported that the major benefit, for them, of school-based development activities had been the experience of being involved in the process rather than, or in addition to, any changes in actual curriculum practice. It was as though they were hedging their bets on the curricular outcome of the initiatives.

Second, there is lack of predictability in outcome. Given the experimental approach characterised by Eggleston as 'discussion, planning, trial and evaluation', there is the built-in risk that the evaluation might show no tangible development in the desired direction. This seems to have been the case in the Oxfordshire Primary School reported in a case study for the Open University prepared by Clift. He reported a self-evaluation exercise by the school staff, lasting over a year, and involving at least seven in-school staff meetings, to prepare a review of the school's policy, provision and practices across a range of activities, including the curriculum. It appears to have been characterised by serious, professional involvement by the staff, and to have been efficiently and yet flexibly organised. It covered, among many other matters, problems or curricular aims and how they should be described, curricular practice, including the grouping of pupils and catering for individual differences, and the provision of curricular guidelines, and was carried out by effective teacher collaboration. The case study author reported in the postscript that the changes that followed this activity were:

(a) a new duplicator;

(b) a loss of a member of staff without replacement; and

(c) a new staff toilet.

It is perhaps very much to be hoped that, for these teachers, the process of their endeavours was valued at least as highly as products. But it does illustrate in an extreme way the uncertainty of school-based development—its almost chancy nature and the unpredictability of its outcomes. As Shipman writing about larger-scale curriculum development activities.

A third characteristic of the notion of development in the curriculum is incrementalism: that what is involved is not a fundamental change, but an extension of existing practices. The foundations of the school's curriculum are not being dug up and re-laid: the structure of the curriculum is being renovated a little, that is all. This kind of development cannot promise or deliver a dramatically different curriculum. It is not designed to do that, nor is it resourced adequately for it. The kind of sweeping changes in curricular aims and practices currently being promoted for the 14-19 year-olds, for example, could not easily be developed in the school-based mode precisely because they are predicted upon external intervention fundamentally to redefine curricular aims at least in the innovation period.

School-based curriculum development is a more modestly conceived activity, designed to build upon existing mainstream curricular practice, and predicated upon the assumption of a curricular framework about which there is already consensus, or which can be taken for granted. It is incremental, not radical, change in the curriculum, with slow, small-scale, almost routine, benefits, accruing over time from a school staff gradually building upon its collective strengths and, where possible, remedying weaknesses. There should be little of the heady rhetoric associated with large-scale national projects of the 1960s and early 1970s, not just because such rhetoric tends to lack credibility in the routine of school life, but because school-based approaches are designed to improve the normal curriculum, not graft abnormal practices on to it. Discussions with teachers in the Warwick inquiry illustrated the incremental quality in an interesting way, showing the mundane and highly pragmatic nature of what was involved. In School 1, a staff group met to review their curricular policy in social studies, and attempted to revise an existing scheme by constructing it around some basic concepts and skills, drawn partly from some School Councils curriculum materials and partly from their experience with the previous scheme. No grand claims were made, or were felt necessary to be made, about either the changes that might follow or the process itself. Many frameworks were tried in private and rejected; it was felt important to demonstrate that the content could be organized-conceptually. To test this we developed a matrix, setting four broad conceptual areas of Environmental Studies across four conceptual themes from 'Home and Family'. When we did this, we simply jotted down in the matrix what we thought would work, given what had worked before, and the overall conceptual scheme we were developing. And then we met and looked at what we'd written down and tried to sort it our from there.

Specialism

Specialism refers to the exploitation of expertise in a subject or, more accurately, in a curriculum area. This exploitation took a variety of forms in practice but three can be distinguished: specialist teaching, subject teaching and subject diffusion.

Specialist Teaching

This occurred in two cases, with teachers used to teach a number of classes and having no class responsibility themselves. The two cases provide ambivalent evidence, limited though it is, for the idea of specialist teaching as a basis for in-school development. Both teachers taught their subject to all the older children in the school, but none the less needed to influence the quality of work with the younger children, who were taught by class teachers. They exercised responsibility for raising the quality of work done throughout the school, though they also acknowledged a reduced impact upon the younger classes. They appear to have experienced little of the conflict and strain that other postholders felt, as reported. This was probably because teaching one subject and not having class responsibilities dramatically reduced the range of the other demands made upon specialists. On the other hand, the two teachers used as specialists tended to have involved their colleagues less in the process of curriculum development than did other postholders.

Subject Teaching

This occurred when teachers with specialist subject knowledge taught one or two other classes on a regular basis, while retaining a generalist class-teaching role with their own class. This occurred in two cases. A related version of subject teaching was when a teacher irregularly, and for limited specific purposes, taught alongside colleagues, or swapped classes, in order to teach a specialist topic or skill or to demonstrate a skill and show the quality of work that could be expected. This happened in three other cases.

Subject Diffusion

This occurred in all the programmes, when teachers with expertise were consulted by others who needed advice, or when they took a lead in curriculum planning and review groups. It was the main mechanism for spreading specialist knowledge from the post-holder to the other staff. It was what the Inspectorate meant when they talked of postholders' having an 'influence' on the work throughout a primary school. With organisational arrangements reflecting the class-teacher principle, even where some subject teaching occurred, this diffusion model was the dominant style of in-school development.

One of the heads explained the approach in the following terms:

> We had specialist teaching here some years ago, and given our staffing we could still use it much more than we do. But we've more or less abandoned it, except for French and our Remedial Specialist...There are two reasons. The main one is that the children here need a lot of structure and the class teacher provides that best of all...So the second reason follows once you've decided that. It is to use teachers who were specialists to lead curriculum review groups, and we've been doing that here for the

> last couple of years now...it doesn't always come off, but it's staff development as well as curriculum development.

The stress on the use of teacher specialism in the curriculum development programmes is largely explicable in terms of the political analysis. All the programmes, except for cases B and J, were focused on issues raised in the Primary Survey, which stressed the need to provide for greater progression and continuity, to cater for able children, to fill the gap in science, to extend advanced reading skills, and so on. Although it may not be a permanent characteristic of primary school curriculum development, it probably provides quite strong evidence of the impact of the survey, an impact followed up in two later surveys by HMI in which 'specialisation' and its contribution to curriculum development in first and middle schools were further examined.

External Influences

The objective raw indices of PTRs in primary schools have shown a progressive small improvement over the past decade, with the national primary mean PTR moving from 25.0:1 in 1973 to 21.8:1 in 1983. The rate has slowed down in the last three years, but the trend is still towards improvement. Moreover, the proportion of classes with over 30 pupils has also reduced, according to data released by Joseph. Both kinds of 'improvements' are partly created by falling rolls, which require some relatively small classes to be tolerated. There is considerable evidence that small improvements in PTR and/or class size are not associated with raised standards of attainment, and it is probable that the marginal changes in PTR and class size do not, of themselves, positively or adversely affect a school's potential for curriculum renewal. In a period of contraction, the range of skills and expertise within a staff group and the way they are deployed may be a more critical matter for curriculum development than PTR. The contraction in the school population may affect the potential of an individual school in two ways. It may push a school into competition—however unwillingly—for pupil numbers, or rather for parental esteem, with a neighbouring school with which it would previously have been seeking co-operation. In this context curriculum innovation which might be considered risky, is unlikely. More important, however, overall staff expertise may be affected, because the impact of falling rolls will lead to loss of flexibility in the ways that staff can be used, and sometimes to arbitrary loss of specialism. Even if staffing is reduced in line with pupil numbers, a school's ability to deploy teachers in ways that can effectively exploit their skills and expertise will become limited and, most crucially perhaps, the opportunities to free teachers for necessary curriculum development activities in school time will be lost. It is for this reason that some local authorities have developed what they refer to as 'curriculum-led' staffing policies.

Although there is a suspicion that such policies could be used primarily to decide that small schools are not viable, an interesting consequence of them is that the local authority has to make clear what its conception of an adequate primary school curriculum is, for curriculum-led staffing policies in effect move from a ratio as an index of staffing policy which emphasised the minimum number of classes that each type of primary school ought to be able to form if a satisfactory curriculum is to be available to pupils. Thus, in theory at least, staffing allocations, and curriculum-led staffing policies, can be seen as supporting school-based curriculum development. Precisely because, having broadly defined the curriculum provision thought to be appropriate, they highlight the need to identify, develop and exploit staff expertise in order to maintain and renew the local authority, conception of the primary school curriculum. This still obtains as a principle, even where teacher-redeployment strategies adopt criteria other than curricular specialism.

At the present time it is unclear whether decisions about which teachers should be redeployed are based on curricular demands, degree of seniority or local political pragmatism; probably all three are involved to differing degrees. There is no logical reason why redeployment of staff should in itself reduce curriculum development possibilities, assuming that the nettle of curriculum-led staffing priorities can be grasped. Put at its most basic this would mean that a teacher with essential specialist curricular expertise would not be redeployed simply because he or she might be the youngest, or the most vulnerable, or the least likely to cause a fuss, or a part-timer. Equally, it might mean that a teacher with expertise in a shortage area might work in two schools rather than, as is normal, only one,

In the recent past the real value of capitation resources allocated to schools has fallen quite substantially, and in some local authorities the reductions were regarded by HMI as endangering educational standards. Although it is a truism to say that such reduction adversely affects the potential of a school staff to improve their curricular provision, the effects will vary greatly according to the nature of the particular curriculum development programme.

There is a great difference in impact of resource expenditure upon a programme requiring for its introduction in a school—the purchase of new sets of materials and equipment and one requiring different applications of existing materials and approaches. It has been argued earlier that school-based approaches in primary schools tended to be developments of existing practices, and resource reductions may go some way towards explaining that feature. If so, it suggests that such reductions will influence the nature of school-based development, rather than stifle its growth entirely.

The objective experience of contraction may not necessarily be the most powerful constraint upon development; the ways in which such contraction is perceived subjectively by teachers may be a far more important determinant. Put crudely, curriculum development depends much more upon the ability of a staff to harness its collective energy and enthusiasm than upon marginal reductions in staffing, or even real reductions in resources. It is upon teacher morale that the progress of innovation hangs, and morale itself has been damaged by contraction.

In part, the impact of contraction has been cumulatively routine, with teachers coming in each morning to uncleaned rooms, dusty desks and other evidence of reduced expenditure, which has nothing directly to do with the curriculum, but which effectively eats away at teacher enthusiasm. But the dramatic impact is upon the teachers' perceptions of reduced career and promotion opportunities, which are real enough and may help to discourage innovation amongst career-minded teachers. This is, however, very much a two-edged sword.

Under an expanding system, teachers were sucked up into senior posts by a kind of capillary action and, having obtained their promotion, would demonstrate their merit afterwards. They would be given their special-responsibility allowances and then earn them. In a contracting system such promotion as there is will have to be earned in advance.

The impact of the external factors, even in a contracting system, upon a school's ability to develop its curriculum is not overwhelmingly and inevitably adverse. Perhaps the most optimistic element is that primary pupil rolls are expected to stabilise in the mid-1980s and arbitrary loss of specialist skills within a staff group will occur less often. A further issue in the next decade, currently being canvassed in some local authorities and nationally, is the idea that INSET could become part of the contractual obligation of teachers.

Internal Influences

For primary schools the internal factors pressing upon change are different. Two have been clearly identified; zones of authority and devolution of curricular decision making.

Zones of Authority

Zones of Authority were a focus of a study of primary schools by Taylor, Reid, Holley and Exon, who reported and analysed the views of primary school teachers on the 'operational' curriculum. i.e., the curriculum in practice in a school. They identified two separate zones of authority; the classroom and the school. In terms of perceived influence, the classroom was by far the stronger zone and, if generalisable, their findings suggest clear obstacles to the development of school-wide policies on the curriculum, for if teachers see their classrooms as the major arena for their control over the curriculum, any attempt to develop it from a different basis by locating the development in the arena of the whole school is likely to start from a position of relative weakness. Individual teachers may opt out, regard it as interference, or simply alter any school-wide policy in the privacy of their own classrooms, legitimising their behaviour by invoking autonomy. The issue is peculiarly strong in primary schools, which are hierarchically ungraded, and where a teacher leading a curriculum development activity is in a position of equality with his or her colleagues, even if he or she has superior expertise in a particular field.

Devolution of Decision-making

Recognised authority, in respect of the primary school curriculum, is nearly always perceived as residing in the office of the headteacher. There is a legal basis for this, but in an age when a broad liberal curriculum in mathematics, English, science, art, music, craft, physical education and social and moral understanding is expected to be offered to all children, the notion of the headteacher as an authority in all these fields is no longer credible, if it ever was. There is therefore a mismatch between authority and responsibility for the curriculum in primary schools, with teachers who are responsible for developing aspects of the curriculum in which they are the 'expert' having little in the way of formal authority ascribed to them, and the headteachers, who have the authority, lacking the expertise.

Lack of formal status is compounded for postholders by lack of informal recognition from their colleagues, according to HMI, who found few primary schools in which the postholders had a school-wide influence in their subject. It is disappointing to find that the great majority of teachers with posts of special responsibility have little influence at present on the work of other teachers. There are some practical implications of this comment for the primary school post-holder's workload, but the major issue concerns the attitudes of primary school staff toward curricular authority.

This brief review of the internal factors has been deliberately uncritical of them in order to report in summary form the prevailing view of the internal culture of primary schools. This internal culture is seen as structuring both teacher relationships in primary schools and teacher perceptions of curricular authority in classrooms and schools so as to provide a major constraint on postholder-led curriculum initiative development. A critical re-analysis of the relevant studies is provided which suggests that in some respects teacher relationships and teacher attitudes, although still a problem, are beginning to change. However, the view that attitudes and teacher relationships are critical to the success of school-based curriculum development, and probably more critical than the external resource and policy factors, was supported not simply by studies of English primary schools, but also by a report in which an international perspective on the school context was provided. The findings of this report are discussed below.

Creativity of the School: The cross-national study on the 'creativity' of schools carried out for OECD defined creativity much as school-based curriculum development has been defined as folows:

> A school's creativity is an awareness within the school of the problems it faces, a capacity to devise and adopt solutions whether initiated from outside or generated internally, and a willingness to evaluate their effectiveness.

A major interest of the study was the factors influencing school creativity, and two of these, which reflect the external/internal dichotomy above, were:

(a) administrative relationships between the school and outside institutions;

(b) organisation and relationships within the school.

The report offered three findings of particular relevance. It commented first on staffing/resources, second on school relationships, and third on teacher autonomy. The problems of stimulating innovation in systems where promotion was impossible or difficult were examined in the report. It raised doubts on economic grounds about the efficiency of substantially and contractually reducing teaching duties so that curriculum innovation could be sustained, although it accepted the usefulness of limited reduction for a particular specified purpose. Perhaps most interestingly it doubted the utility of limited reductions in class size as a way of enhancing the creativity of the school.

The report looked at the relationship between creativity and the internal organisation of the school. It identified four types of school organisation: authoritarian /bureaucratic, consultative, collegial, and full participatory. The collegial type is an organisation where decision-making is in the hands of the professional teaching staff, and the head acts as an executive. In consultative organisations, the power of decision-making remains with the head, but power is delegated and procedures for consulting teachers, students and parents are set up. These two organisational types were less likely to inhibit effective creativity than the other two.

The explanation for the greater effectiveness of these types is probably connected with the report's view that focusing upon the individual teacher was not the best way to induce change. The individual teacher working alone in his classroom is an inappropriate unit.

Rather, the small group of teachers with their group of students should be the basic unit of organisation. This is necessary both for interpersonal stimulation and essential mutual support. Such groups, which need not be stable over a long period, would be united by a common task but could be organised in many different ways. Of particular interest is the study's commentary on the problems associated with professional development in a collegial school which include the need to recognise the distinction between the practice of collective decision-making and the legal position of the hand.

Another point reflected uncertainty about teacher autonomy if collective decision-making was a prerequisite for creativity. In the literature on the creative school, there is a degree of ambivalence as to the autonomy of the teacher. It is often applauded as a necessary precondition of creativity, but the autonomy of the individual teacher is, in fact, under pressure in current developments. It is obviously important that the teacher should enjoy freedom from close supervision if he is to be encouraged to be creative. On the other hand, the creativity of the school as an organisation assumes a degree of collaboration that to some extent reduces the individual autonomy of the teacher. Since evidence on teacher satisfaction indicated that teachers value their autonomy very highly, there is the danger of a loss of satisfaction which needs careful consideration.

It is now possible to summarise the preceding argument by identifying three main features of school-based curriculum development in primary schools. First, it involves teachers in a more collaborative role with other teachers, working together to reconstruct, through informal discussion and critical appraisal, general curricular guidance into specific school-wide policy and practice. The process turns teachers into educationalists. Second, it involves teachers drawing upon the specialist expertise of curriculum postholders in order to improve existing practice and policy in a small-scale, gradualist fashion, with an openness to evaluation. Third, internal relationships as perceived by teachers, especially relationships resting upon authority in respect of the curriculum and classroom autonomy, are critical to the kind of developments being encouraged.

When summarised in the above way, school-based curriculum development can be seen to embody something more than advice about how change can occur—about mechanisms of change. It embodies a set of professional and moral values—what kinds of change should occur, and how they should be brought about. This point has been explored in a particularly sharp way by Henderson and Perry, who argue that curriculum development involves what is referred to as 'organisation development'. By this they mean three things. Firstly, the curriculum cannot be treated on its own, as a separate entity unrelated to the school as a whole, which is an integrated social system. Developing the curriculum means developing the school, especially the staff. Secondly, a static, mechanistic organisation is inappropriate for a changing society, which requires organisational structures and relationships that are dynamic, responsive and organic. Thirdly, development occurs through a 'process of education and re-education', in which all those involved, not just the senior staff, are themselves continually learning. The concept should not imply the responsibility for initiating and organising staff development belongs solely to the head and senior staff, that they alone are capable of determining what is best for staff. If the head and his senior lieutenants decide upon school needs and the kind of professional development necessary to meet them, this becomes another type of 'top-downwards' model. It is not appropriate to an organic social system, where development depends upon shared responsibility for mutually agreed goals, based on sensitive understanding of the needs of the system as a whole.

Although Henderson's and Perry's discussion is mainly concerned with the appropriateness of different organisational structures for effecting change in schools, it does highlight the moral dimensions of curriculum development, the idea that some ways of introducing change are better from a moral point of view, as well as from considerations of their effectiveness for bringing about change.

For school-based curriculum development in primary schools, two such value assumptions need to be articulated, even if briefly. They refer to two characteristics identified in the practice of the inquiry schools: collaboration and subject expertise. One useful way into the question of value assumptions is to ask what benefits would accrue to a school in which staff collaboration and subject expertise were key characteristics in the processes by which the curriculum was developed. There might be five such benefits—three concerned with staff collaboration and two with subject expertise—which are offered here as a kind of morale criterion reference list.

Staff Collaboration

(a) Curriculum policy and practice would be arrived at through collective discussion and decision-making.

(b) Initiative and responsibility for developing the curriculum would be devolved to relevant staff groups.

(c) Staff groups would be led and serviced by the postholder acting as 'educationalist'.

Subject expertise

(a) Greater continuity and consistency in the subject throughout the school would be practised.

(b) Class teachers would have enhanced respect for the postholder's expertise in his or her subject and increase their own confidence and competence in it.

When the benefits claimed for it are stated in this way, two value positions underlying school-based curriculum development can be confronted by teachers who engage in it.

The first position is fairly easily expressed. It is morally desirable that a curriculum policy and the school-wide practice that flows from it—the curriculum as experienced in the classroom by children—should be based as firmly as possible on specialised expertise. Consistency in curriculum practice is only valuable in so far as it is consistently right, not wrong. Similarly, increasing teachers' confidence in a subject, and increasing their respect for a postholder's expertise, are worth while only if such confidence and respect are justified.

The second value position is that decisions developed collaboratively, and taken collectively, are arrived at by a morally better process than those arrived at by other means. The position is derived from respect to be attached to teachers as people and professionals; decisions designed to affect the personal and professional life of teachers in school should be developed only through a process in which their responsibility and commitment are recognised and explicitly acknowledged. To avoid the process, inherently difficult as it will be, would be to treat teachers with something bordering on contempt.

As Hargreaves has hinted, that there is danger that a rhetoric of grass-roots democracy and participation might provide a distraction from the conventional exercise of undelegated authority both inside and outside the school. This is a constant danger in a profession that has been schooled to defer to authority as well as to exercise it. However, it will be lessened if the teachers involved in school-based approaches to the curriculum acknowledge and confront the values upon which it operates. If these values are to become palpable and authentic in the life of primary schools, curriculum postholders will play a central part. It is from them that expertise will have to come: they will literally, as well as formally, have a special responsibility for their subject. they will have to be, or become, the resident 'expert', responsive to other teachers' needs.

Thus school-based curriculum development raises fundamental questions of value for all the staff in a school—questions of the value to be placed on specialist expertise and group decision-making in the school, and the inherent challenge that both pose to conventional claims of classroom autonomy. The implications for the 'management' of curriculum development in primary schools were discussed, but for curriculum postholders they offer an interesting, challenging and possibly daunting extension to their professional life.

Control of Primary Curriculum

The problems that arose for those charged with managing the curriculum at the school level can be analysed in three discrete categories: curriculum time allocation, teacher expertise, and resources in primary schools.

The first reason for unmanageability is the apparently simple matter of time allocation: how much time is needed for each subject and for the whole curriculum. The problem has been commonly represented as the quart of the statutory orders and the pint pot of the teaching week. We say 'apparently simple' because, if you are sitting on a national committee inventing or revising the statutory curriculum, it must appear merely a mechanical matter. The second reason concerns the task demands on class teachers attempting to deliver the whole curriculum—most obviously the range and level of subject knowledge required, the pedagogical skills necessary, including differentiation, the sheer detail and number of Statements of Attainment, and techniques necessary for reliable assessment. The third reason concerns resources. As Alexander et al., pointed out, primary schools are staffed less favourably than secondary schools, even when the comparison is based on only Key Stage 3, yet the range and demand of their educational activities, and therefore their staffing needs, are almost identical. When Kelly ran a computer model of Stockport's curriculum led staffing, she found that it led to staffing needs that were more-or-less identical across the five to sixteen age range.

Time Allocation

One reason commonly given for this was that the statutory curriculum had been invented by means of committees of subject enthusiasts who were unable to consider how their subject had to fit into the whole curriculum. As Graham, the chairman and chief executive of the National Curriculum Council at the time, noted in what might be thought of as a Pilate-like distancing commentary: Eventual reform of the curriculum was inevitable the moment it was decided to introduce it subject by subject. The appointment of individual subject working groups guaranteed that zealots outnumbered cynics—always a dangerous thing—that no subject would be knowingly undersold. When the full enormity of the consequences became clear, complexity and over prescription became the cry of those who caused it. Nonetheless, if one had to err, it was a magnificent aberration. There was some truth in at least the first two of these sentences, but the extent of policy error was substantially greater than Graham and Tytler allow. First, at an early stage Ministers had worked on a broad view that the Education Reform Act would create a curricular framework in which the national prescription should cover substantially less than the whole curriculum. This was because Religious Education and other important curricular areas such as health education and moral development were conceived of as lying beyond national prescription. The consultative document suggested that in schools where there was 'good practice' the National Curriculum subjects would occupy 70-80 per cent of curriculum time. Angela Rumbold was quoted in Hansard as follows:

> As the legislation tries to set out the content of the curriculum...it is logical to suggest a time allocation for subjects within the school week or term. During the consultation period we discussed how to achieve what is required in the core and foundation subjects within a given time and whether the time allocated to them should be 60 per cent during the primary years.

Three implications arose for curriculum management from the notional time allocations. The most important is that they represented an error that was to have disastrous effects as the curriculum was implemented. The notional time for English and Mathematics combined, was dramatically lower than was conventionally provided by primary teachers, according to every study that had examined time allocations in the post-war period. A summary covering much of the relevant research in the last fifteen years showed that 50 per cent of time was typically given to English and Mathematics, excluding their application to other subjects. Empirically, the phenomenon of 50 per cent of time on these two subjects—what we might call the 'basic instinct' in the primary curriculum—is firmly established. Indeed, a study by Meyer et al., which is an examination of official elementary and primary curricula world-wide across this century until the late 1980s, argues that the phenomenon has been a global constant—irrespective of region, political economy or state of development.

The second point refers to the time available for the whole curriculum. It relates to 'evaporated time', a term coined in a professional development programme and used by Campbell and Neill to indicate time technically available for teaching but used for non-cognitive purposes such as supervising children changing for PE, moving them from one location in the school to another, lining up and clearing away. It is important because it is assumed to be available for teaching, but the studies referred to above that took account of this time by excluding it from teaching time, showed that something between 22 per cent of teaching time evaporates in this way, the amount depending upon the age of the pupils and the physical layout and size of the school and the methodology of time analysis. In general, younger pupils and those in open-plan settings experience more evaporated time. It occurs in small units of time in any one day, but in Campbell and Neill's research, based on time logs of over 3000 days from over 300 primary teachers, the average evaporated time per week was calculated at nearly two hours per week, equivalent to nearly 10 per cent of the teaching time available and equal to the notional time allocated for at least one of the non-basic subjects, in the National Curriculum.

A third point, made in the classroom observational studies is that subjects given large amounts of time are the ones in which lowest proportions of pupil time on task were observed. For example, Alexander's study showed pupils distracted for 21 per cent of time on an average in all curriculum areas with 26 per cent and 23 per cent of time spent in English and Mathematics, respectively distracted, but only 13 per cent and 10 per cent distraction in music and PE respectively. We cannot translate time formally allocated, directly into time spent by pupils on learning the subject. Moreover, as in all human activities, with the possible exception of sexual intercourse, the time spent does not necessarily reflect quality. Long hours spent on repetitive computation exercises do not necessarily mean challenging learning for bright pupils any more than do long hours spent by low-attaining pupils on tasks too difficult for them.

The conclusion from the research findings on time showed no general problem in primary classrooms about the adequacy of time being spent on teaching and learning the two basic subjects. Evidence after the introduction of the National Curriculum suggested that little had changed, with Campbell and Neill showing 51 per cent and 49 per cent of time devoted to the basics. The reasons for this state of affairs are three well-known ones. First, as Ashton's research showed, drawing on a national sample of 1500 primary teachers in the early 1970s, the highest curricular priority was given to the basic skills of Reading, Oracy, Mathematics and Writing. Art. PE, Music, Sex Education, Science and Technology and a second language were given low priority. A follow-up study by Ashton with a less representative sample at the end of the 1970s, showed, if anything, higher priority placed on Mathematics and formal language competence. Thus, commitment to the basics has always been at a premium in the professional culture. Second, parents and governors place highest curricular priority on the basics also, as Thomas's investigation of London schools showed, and the Government has required greater teacher accountability to parents and governors. Third, there has been a long tradition, stretching way back before 1988, of formal testing focused on reading, comprehension and mathematics, a tradition reinforced by National Curriculum assessment arrangements, though it is now slightly broadened by the inclusion of science in the core. Such testing washes back into curriculum priorities. The basic instinct is sustained and reinforced by the workplace culture in primary schools.

Thus, it becomes startingly clear that the National Curriculum in primary schools, introduced by a series of Secretaries of State who had constantly banged on about the need to get back to basics and to raise standards of literacy and numeracy, put in place policy guidance designed to reduce the time typically spent by primary teachers on the basics, and especially on English, where the astonishing reduction of about one-third of existing time was proposed. With respect to time allocations, the policy guidance outstripped the practice in the schools for liberality and breadth. It offered a fundamentally different concept and ideology of curriculum balance.

The guidance given to the working group devising the English curriculum was such as to encourage infant teachers to reduce the time they typically spent teaching children to read and write from about seven hours to little over four hours a week. No wonder there was widespread stress at Key Stage 1 with infant teachers accurately reporting that, against their own professional judgment, they were having to reduce the time on hearing children read in order to fit in everything else.

As if to confirm this interpretation of the general policy, the National Curriculum Council (NCC) issued guidance on planning the Key Stage 2 curriculum in which three presumably recommended case studies of school planning were provided: two of them (year 6 and 5 classes) suggested that the basics should be planned to occupy 41 per cent and 37.5 per cent of curriculum time respectively. The year 5 class plan was developed into a yearly programme in which Mathematics and English occupy 316 out of the 846 hours available, some 37 per cent of curriculum time in their terms. Schools are urged by the NCC to review the exercise, including reviewing whether the time allocations are appropriate.

In this context, it is interesting, but confusing, to see that in the summer update from the NCC, the curriculum planning in a coventry primary school was celebrated; it initially used a plan which involved only 40 per cent of time on basics, but after trilling, it changed to 50 per cent. There was thus built into the curriculum at national level a four-pronged problem for every primary school: too much planned prescription overall; too much content in the statutory orders for each subject: not enough flexibility to allow for evaporated time; a pretence or assumption that there would be more time available for the non-basics than there was in actuality.

Task Demands on Teachers

The task demands placed on class teachers by the National Curriculum have been analysed by Thomas, who shows that in the slimmed down curriculum, teachers at Key Stage 2 had to be familiar with about 500 statements of attainment, detailed and confusingly presented programmes of study, poorly defined cross-curricular themes and religious education. In addition they would have to posses subject knowledge in the ten subjects up to about Level 6, or to be able to differentiate the planning, teaching and assessment across at least 4 levels or the curriculum in each subject. To achieve all this they would need to be the curricular school equivalent of Albert Einstein. Marie Curie and Linford Christie rolled into one. The evidence about subject expertise sometimes takes a narrow view of the concept but the review of research by Bennett and Summers suggests that there are serious deficiencies in individual primary teachers' understandings, especially but not exclusively in the science and technology areas.

Graduate students training for primary teaching provide no greater reasons for being sanguine, if those studied by Bennett and Carre are typical. They brought with them to their PGCE courses misunderstandings of everyday phenomena, such as the energy in a sledge moving down a hill, the explanations for night and day, and basic arithmetic competencies such as expressing $18 as a percentage of $120.

Bennett and Carre's research used tests in Mathematics, English and Science based on National Curriculum levels 4, 5 and 6, and Assessment of Performance Unit (APU) tests. In some of these, the top 20 per cent of primary pupils scored higher than the average of the PGCE students. Technically, of course, the curriculum demands are placed on the whole school rather than the individual teacher, but in practice for the medium term further, most teachers will remain responsible for teaching most of the curriculum for the pupils in their class. Given the research findings, Alexander, Rose and Woodhead's assertion that, 'Teachers must possess the subject knowledge which the statutory orders require' sounds like a plea of desperation. A major management issue therefore becomes how the specialist expertise in the whole staff group can be deployed to extend the work of class teachers, with the overarching purpose that, as Richards argued, such deployment should 'support not undermine' the class teacher's role.

Resourcing of Primary Schools

Resource issues affect schools differentially, depending upon funding formulae, school size or pupil characteristics. There is however one key resource issue—the level of staffing. The disadvantage for primary schools of historic staffing allocations has been acknowledged for almost a decade, although the difficulty of translating the acknowledgment into staffing resources has been enormous, particularly since the acknowledgment occurred in a period of public expenditure restraint.

Nonetheless, if primary schools are to develop more specialist approaches to the curriculum, if class size should rarely exceed 30, and if teachers are to have some time free of class teaching in the school day; if, in short, the schools are to be enabled to implement the National Curriculum without stress and overload remaining a chronic feature of teachers' work, some improvement in the resourcing of schools is required. Acknowledgment is no longer enough. The funding formula at local level and the approval of schemes of devolved management at national level will need to be based on realistic assessment of the work activities now required of teachers in modern primary schools.

Management Implications

This stage of the argument is based on two assumptions about the relationship between a national quango and individual schools. National quangos are not good at details, and have little competence in respect of the curriculum organization of individual schools. For example, within the space of nine months the National Curriculum Council and the School Curriculum and Assessment Authority could not even agree on the simple technical matter of how many hours per year should be considered as available for instruction. Second, the National Curriculum was established by reference to the best practice in each subject. To be 'best' or even good at everything is not common in individual human beings or their institutions so that there was and is a certainty that virtually the schools would, to some degree, fail to meet the statutory requirements. He added that 'Schools in other countries commonly fail to meet the requirements of their national curricula'. If these two assumptions are confirmed, the first lessons for school management are that it is in the individual school, not a national agency, that will create a curriculum that can be made to work for the school concerned; and that concern to cover the whole curriculum will have to be tempered by consideration of quality and standards in pupils learning. This latter goal might be more readily arrived at by the school establishing its curricular priorities than by attempting to deliver every statutory prescription equally well. It was, after all, the quango charged with the inspection of schools that first made clear that coverage had been achieved only at the cost of depth in pupil learning.

To restore confidence in their own professional judgment, it may first be necessary for teachers to lose faith in the ability of the national agencies to manage the curriculum implementation process sensibly. Dependency on external forces is as counter productive for the whole school staff as it is for the head and is likely to reduce rather than increase empowerment and accountability. On this basis, six possible ways to move forward may be identified, though each will be contested by some teachers because of the value assumptions it contains.

In respect of time allocation, there is the possibility that much more of the teaching of English and Mathematics than currently might be planned, delivered and assessed through their application to other subjects. This is a position advocated for at least fifteen years by HMI, but has been found problematic in practice. The problem is not helped by the framing of the curriculum in single subjects, nor by the tendency for mathematics and English schemes to be subject-specific. It is a good example of how a staff would have to have confidence as HMI had, that standards in the basics would improve by their being applied to other subjects. Unfortunately, it may be easier for staff in schools where pupils already have high achievement to develop such confidence than for staff where pupils appear to need substantial amounts of time on basic skills.

Schools might consider the use of homework as part of their overall policy, especially perhaps at KS2. If there is shortage of time for English, part of the solution might be to cease to consider the pupils' curriculum time as synonymous with the time-tabled school day. Successful experience at SI1 with parental partnerships provides exemplars for developing similar approaches at KS2. Some opposition might be raised by those who would see such a systematic approach to homework as increasing the disadvantages of pupils who live in unsupportive families or physical conditions unconducive to doing homework. School-based provision for facilities for doing homework, while a contradiction in terms, might go some way to mitigating the difficulties, though at a cost in staff supervision time.

Another solution to the problem of curriculum time might be to extend the school day, week or year. This is clearly sensible for those schools who currently spend less than the minimum expected weekly hours on instruction. It will be opposed on grounds of workload and of inappropriateness in rural areas where pupils have to travel long distances.

A solution to teachers' lack of confidence and competence in subject expertise could be remedied by a greatly expanded in-service training programme along lines similar to the DES twenty-day courses. This is obviously true, assuming that the courses are effective, and that their effects are long-lived—an assumption that Bennett and Summer's review of research questions in part. However, the problem for primary schools is that extensions of In-service training programmes are also extensions of the times when teachers have to be away from school and their class, so that a substantial programme of In-service Training in the school day may have disadvantages for pupil learning where schools do not have access to good quality supply cover.

A second possibility lies in suggestions that schools should deploy their staff in ways that enable their subject expertise to be exploited more effectively to the benefit of the school as a whole, whether as specialists, semi-specialists or as coordinators. Again, within limits, this might offer gains to some schools, especially those with staffing allocations that permit some flexibility of deployment. For most schools, however there is almost no flexibility, and, as school size reduces, the range of subjects in which there is staff expertise also reduces.

A third possibility is that more use should be made of class texts in which the teachers can have confidence that the intellectual content is reliable, freeing them to concentrate more upon planning for how pupils may learn more effectively from the texts. There may be some reluctance in the profession to the purchase of texts for whole classes, since it is seen as at odds with concepts of good practice which stress learning from first hand experience, building on pupils' interests, and practical investigation.

4
Teacher Training

One of the clearest signs of the general lack of understanding of the importance of primary schools is the misunderstanding of the role of teachers in them. It is a universal problem. In many countries elementary teachers undergo a completely separate system of training, both shorter and less rigorous than that of their secondary counterparts, as if it were less demanding to teach younger children. Their very expertise as teachers is not rated as highly as the ability to know a particular subject well. This distinction between recognition of the importance of good teaching and expertise in one part of the curriculum is shared by the children themselves. By the time they leave primary school, children believe that it is only a preparation for the important events to come; that secondary school is more significant and that all education leads to the pursuit of qualifications for jobs.

The dominating difficulty in the purpose of primary schools is the fact that 'knowing' is rated more highly than 'teaching', despite the importance of the latter and its equally intimate connection with 'learning'. The distinct role of the primary school, often seen in terms of conveying essential skills—reading and writing and arithmetic—as well as the ability to mix in the society of others, it itself being eroded. We note the growing recognition of the part that parents can play. The primary teacher is therefore no longer seen as the only expert on whom the parent must wait so that the child can be instructed. Nor is the school any longer seen as the place where all the deficiencies of home can be compensated. The recognition of the more subtle skills of learning, through relationships and through motivation, through the home and pre-school experiences, means that the singular purpose of primary schools is less easily defined. The erosion of the traditional position of the primary school teacher also takes place at the point where children move on. There have been many experiments with middle schools, on the grounds that the transition from primary school to secondary school, from generalism to specialism, cannot be handled by the primary schools themselves.

From the Primary Survey of 1978 onwards the government has been concerned to make the primary teacher more of a specialist, playing the role of consultant to colleagues as well as handling the complexities of a large class. The training of primary school teachers is not only marked by the growing number of those who enter the profession after a specialized first degree followed by a postgraduate certificate, but the demand that all should have at least two years of a 'subject study'.

A simplified notion of the curriculum was first evident in the criteria laid down on teacher training, long before the national framework. On the one hand, the primary teacher is seen to be more dependent on, and answerable to, the parents and the community. On the other hand, the primary teacher is defined as a specialist, not as a specialist teacher, but as a specialist in a particular area of the curriculum. One of the reasons for this conflict in attitudes derives from the very image that primary schools have tended to project, whether they liked it or not.

For the 'general public' the virtues of primary schools have been associated with comfortable stability, where children's happiness has been deemed more important than their academic advance, as if the two were in opposition to each other. The desire to make children feel at home in strange circumstances, with other children, and to foster in them a sense of personal well-being, has given primary schools a particular ethos. The children themselves contrast their sense of the comfort of the primary school against that of the bustle and demands of the secondary. At best such a sense of security suggests that children's well-being is forested in a variety of ways, that they are free to explore ideas, to ask questions and fulfil their own talents. At worst, such emphasis on security can seem to outsiders as wasteful, not making enough demands and not matching appropriate tasks to the ability of children.

One of the abiding concerns in the educational system general is what Hargreaves calls the 'cult of individualism'. At the primary schools this can be projected as 'child centred' in the sense of a belief in the autonomy of the individual child and his innate ability to be creative and imaginative. The problem with such a view of children's own capacities is that it leads to the assumption that schools can do little to compensate for the problems of society or the child's home background. If a child is an autonomous learner it can be argued that each has to find his own way of learning, at the same time as adapting to the many rules of behaviour, both explicit and implied, that the school presents. This can be difficult for children.

If we observe children in a primary school, noting their experiences rather than being caught up in the demands of our own teaching, it is clear that from the child's point of view some of the impressions of school are not part of the school's intentions. It is impossible for schools to make everything explicit but there are many ambiguities for children. Despite the emphasis on achievement and concentration, children spend a significant proportion of the day waiting for things to happen. They are puzzled by the relationship between work and play. Play is constantly being redefined, as something which is a prelude to work, something which interferes with work, as a form of learning. Play is something done at particular times, and seldom if ever by teachers. Play is what young children do; work is done for the teacher.

Children begin to develop an attitude towards work which derives from these impressions, and begin to assume that it is those comparatively brief periods of 'work' that must matter. This also means that children accept that waiting for the next task to be presented to them is an essential part of school. Children wait while the classroom is organized, and sometimes look for things to do, volunteering help—'Shall I shut the door'?—or doing some covert reading or talking. Waiting includes keeping an eye on the teacher to be ready for that movement when she gives an instruction to which they have to pay attention. Children wait for tasks without questioning the purpose of what they are doing. The setting of tasks and the creation of order does not imply that the children are learning in every moment.

Given the extraordinarily difficult demands on primary school teachers, and given the traditionally bare resources devoted to one classroom and thirty children, it is not surprising that the experience of some children can be as seemingly purposeless as in the picture just given. But the real problem for the many creative and talented classteachers is to harness a sense of purpose both in individual children and in the schools as a whole. Primary teachers have not been helped by some of the mythologies about school. Many of the associations fostered by the Plowden report seem gratifying, but have not really enabled teachers to define their own sense of purpose. We know about the capacities of children, but cannot assume that their talents will reveal themselves the moment they are given the opportunity.

The Plowden report emphasized the need to nurture the personal growth of individual children rather than more formal aspects of learning, and directed attention away from the school to the child's own environment. But this was not a precise shift towards the involvement of parents, or towards planning specific ways in which those outside school could help children. Classrooms remained the same; they were only seen differently. Such optimism about childhood innocence meant that teachers were not supposed to be dogmatic about knowledge, and could not impose on the children. Instead they were to let children acquire knowledge from personal experience, and to create conditions in which they could do so. Such an account necessarily simplifies some of the arguments from the Plowden report but it does suggest that at the core of the report lay the belief that the role of the primary teacher was more to support than to direct. The teachers should provide a rich environment in which children would flourish of their own accord. The problem with such a Plowdenesque view of primary education is that it does not define the purpose or the role of the teachers, or, indeed, the nature of what the children are supposed to learn. The popularity of the Plowden report gave impetus to the idea that social and emotional development was more important than intellectual achievement. There was bound to be a reaction against such a perceived position, and this then led to a polarization of the views about the purpose of primary schools, especially in the early years. In simple terms schools are supposed either to provide a secure environment for learning or teach the children to do well academically. The desire to lay down a centralized curriculum, with objectives of achievement in terms of knowledge, which can be tested, is to be seen, since the 1978 Primary Survey, as an almost inevitable reaction. The wish to order what proportion of time should be spent on 'core' subjects and other parts of the curriculum is not just a determination to impose control but desire from outside to understand what goes on within the classroom. Individualized learning is subtle. It is easier for parents and others to understand progress in terms of subjects. Primary schools have not been helped in articulating their sense of purpose and distinctive ethos by these conflicts between different views of their role; whether they are concerned with the process of the developing child or with the outcomes of attainment as measured against pre-set criteria. There are many ways in which primary schools can be acknowledged for the importance of what they are doing, and be encouraged to develop the gifts of individual children, always acknowledging that their achievement could be much greater.

The sense of autonomy, or freedom from imposed constraints, can be used to advantage. At best, this means that teachers can take risks, can go beyond the idea of an allotted syllabus, and explore those questions that children most want to explore, the meaning of what they are doing and the meaning of their lives in relation to others. At worst, the autonomy of the schools can lead to a lack of enthusiasm, a satisfaction with keeping children happy, making sure that there is no disturbance in the secret enclosures of the classroom. The teacher in the traditional classroom, however, faces dangers as well as opportunities.

Ostensibly, freedom from outside constraints and outside contacts can mean that there is no need to explain or articulate what is going on. Teachers rarely see other's classrooms, or visit other schools. They are nearly always in their own classroom. They are not forced by colleagues to define or analyse what they are doing. Many of the most impressive teachers, sensitive to and responding to individual children's needs, are not given an opportunity to explain what they are doing. This is one of the reasons why there is so much misunderstanding about the demands and subtleties of their role.

One of the most creative uses of in-service courses is to enable teachers to work alongside others, to share their experiences and to define what they observe. There are, however, some outside pressures which might define the work of the primary school teacher more clearly, and might, ironically, lead to greater recognition of the importance of her role. The suggestion of the Task Group on Assessment and Testing that teachers should meet to discuss both their own and national criteria in relation to each other could lead to more awareness and communication about what children are learning, and how. Teacher appraisal is also a result of a developing concern for accountability and evaluation; firstly for institutions and then for individuals. It could mean little more than a diversion of resources into larger bureaucracies, with more inspectors rather than more teachers, but it could also lead to changes in which the complex skills of teaching are recognized by others.

Teachers have always been evaluated, whether at an anecdotal level or in formal interviews for promotion. But judgements will become more formally based on evidence. This will require some very complex changes, with people being trained on how to carry out 'clinical observation' and how to give advice. Formality in assessing the performance of the teacher also implies a commitment to staff development. Appraisal is not just a question of removing or chastening the weaker teacher, but after diagnosing what is weak, finding the means to rectify the weakness. New forms of teacher appraisal should lead to a greater concern for the professional development of teachers, and therefore a greater awareness of what it is that makes teachers successful.

When talking about 'values' it is easy to be vague, contradictory or abstract. But 'purposes' are often implicit, especially in primary schools, where the understanding of children's capacities for learning can be joined by an awareness of the intricate skills of teaching. All the subtle changes that are taking placed within the school community, from the greater involvement of parent to the demands of the national curriculum, will have an impact on the ways that teachers perform. There is a sense of inevitability about these changes because they are the result of conclusions reached from different points of view. The recognition of the role of parents in schools, for example, is shared for opposing political reasons. From one point of view the involvement of parents means an opening up of the school, a responsiveness to society. From another it means greater accountability to the clients and the community.

Teacher appraisal is seen by some as a means of making distinctions and demarcations between teachers, and removing any bad ones. By others it is seen as enhancing professional development. The role of a subject consultant might appear from one point of view the result of a standard and agreed curriculum. From another it is the manifestation of the natural enthusiasm of a teacher for her subject, whatever the subject, a specialism which conveys the excitement of the quality of learning for its own sake. Primary school teachers constantly need to redefine their purpose because of the ambiguities with which they are confronted, between the individual 'holistic' nature of learning and the imposition of a set curriculum leading to assessment. Relying on the assumption that children are innately gifted and merely need the right environment for their gifts to manifest themselves is no more helpful than defining the body of knowledge they must possess, according to criteria worked out by age. For there is much more to what a primary school teacher does than either minding children or directing what they should learn.The paradox for teachers is the fact that the more they define their professional role, as people able to help others make better use of knowledge, the less their status is likely to be understood. The position of teachers in some countries which possess an agreed curriculum seems more secure in the eyes of the general public. But it is in the more subtle understanding of the process of education that primary schools find their central role. As visible entities primary schools are easily recognized as distinct. But they are not uniform. There are many distinctions between the style of individual teachers and the sense of purpose in the school as a whole. The success or failure of children depends on the kinds of motivation shared by the staff and generated by them. It derives from a sense of purpose rather than a matter of what is added to the curriculum.

Teacher and the Ethos of the School

The term 'ethos' describes an aspect of school life, the reality and importance of which will be recognized by most people who have been involved in schooling. However, the 'reality' of the ethos of a school is essentially a social construction.

Ethos involves a climate that permeates and affects all aspects of the school. What then are the ingredients which together create this climate? Does the answer lie in the relationships between the people who work in the school, the head, the teachers, the children, ancillary staff and visitors? What influences do the physical surroundings, the material resources available, the school's location, the Local Education Authority, have on the school? Do wider factors such as the national economic and political situation or the prevailing social and educational ideologies also have significant effects? Perhaps one of the most influential pieces of research into the concept of 'ethos' was undertaken by Rutter et al., during the 1970s. This was a longitudinal study of 5485 children in the Inner London Educational Authority (ILEA) who were followed from their primary schools through five years of secondary schooling. They found that the differences in the schools' intakes could not explain the differences between outcomes when the children were fourteen. Schools with similar intakes seemed to produce very different results. The Rutter team put these differences in outcome down to differences in 'ethos' among the schools. More effective schools appear to be those which function as a coherent whole, with staff at all levels supporting each other and working towards shared academic and social goals. In such schools, senior staff give a clear lead and at the same time teachers feel views are represented. Thus, Rutter's work indicates that the ethos of a school is important because it is positively related to educational outcomes. Unfortunately Rutter's 'outcomes' do not necessarily define the purposes of schooling and some outcomes such as examination performance and rates of delinquency may have little relevance to the primary schools. Others may not be among the priorities even of secondary schools. The Rutter research did not explore process such as curriculum development or the willingness of the staff and head to innovate. In the more child-centred primary sector these may be more important aspects.

In a primary school the children themselves may have a greater effect on the 'ethos' of the school than Rutter suggests. However, despite these and other criticisms, Rutter found much evidence that some schools seem to have consistently better outcomes than others and this is largely a result of shared rules, standards and values of those within the school. The findings of Reynolds support the view that a positive climate is an important factor in school effectiveness. He found that the school's policy towards children is of central importance. A climate where children feel they are part of decision making, the school social structure, rather than being coerced, produces higher educational achievement. In such schools, teachers value and reward academic achievement and 'humanistic' activity. Attitudes to children are influential on academic achievement. In effective schools there is an assumption that the children are willing and able to learn and very few are 'written off'.

A criticism of these studies when applying their findings in the primary school context is that much of the work was undertaken in secondary schools. Outcomes that were measured in some cases seem 'mechanistic' and outside of the more 'romantic' primary tradition and concerns. However, there has been a more recent project looking at the effectiveness of 50 ILEA primary schools which discovered that some schools were more effective than others in promoting pupils' learning and development, and also in catering for particular groups of children such as boys or girls, and children from different social classes and ethnic groups. In the study, account was taken of variations in the pupils' background.

Factors Influencing Effectiveness of School

Twelve factors were found to influence the effectiveness of the school. The schools which produced a positive ethos had the following characteristics:

(a) *Purposeful leadership by the headteacher*: Headteachers were actively involved in the school's work, without exciting total control.

(b) *Involvement of the Deputy Head*: Headteachers shared and delegated some of their responsibilities.

(c) *Involvement of Teachers*: Teachers were involved in curriculum planning, guidelines development and decision making.

(d) *Consistency Among Teachers*: Teachers were consistent in the use of guidelines.

(e) *Structured Sessions*: Teachers organized pupils' work programmes and gave them plenty to do. Once work had been allocated, pupils were encouraged to work independently.

(f) *Intellectually Challenging Teaching*: Teachers used higher-order questions and statements, encouraging pupils to solve problems and use creative imagination.

(g) *Work-centred Environment*: Classrooms were busy and purposeful with teachers spending time discussing the content of work rather than routine issues.

(h) *Limited Focus Within Sessions*: Teachers concentrated on one or two curriculum areas in any session. All pupils were not, however, doing the same work and teachers geared the work to pupils' needs.

(i) *Maximum Communication Between Pupils and Teachers*: This was achieved by the teacher talking more often to the whole class or groups rather than to individuals.

(j) *Record Keeping*: Teachers kept good records of planning and assessment of pupils' personal, social and development work.

(k) *Parental Involvement*: Schools had an informal open-door policy with parents helping in the classroom and on visits and regular meetings organized to discuss pupils' progress. Parents were involved in pupil's' educational development.

(l) *Positive Climate*: The emphasis within the schools was on praise and encouragement rather than criticism and punishment. There was firm but fair classroom management with teachers having a positive attitude to their classes and taking an interest in all aspects of the children.

These factors cannot constitute a complete 'recipe' for promoting pupil learning but may provide a framework within which school effectiveness and its relationship to ethos may be considered.

Many of the factors identified in the ILEA study are similar to those found by earlier studies to contribute to the ethos of a school. This is important because effectiveness may require a different definition at primary level and the definitions may change alongside altering perceptions of the role of the primary school. At this level it may be necessary as Golby says, to ask new questions such as whether the school's purposes are in line with those of parents, pupils and society. It is not possible to assume that the conventional school curriculum is consistent with those purposes. Gray points out other questions that are relevant in the primary school context. For instance, measures of effectiveness can only be used with confidence if schools are stable from year to year and they enable educational practitioners to identify more effective schools. We need to know whether the effects of 'ethos' are greater or less at primary level. It is important to know how the 'ethos' of a school becomes established and whether, as Frances believes, process interacts with outcomes to produce a spiral effect, rather than a directly causal effect on outcomes.

Effective head-teachers are sympathetic, empathetic and accessible. Such head-teachers set clear aims for the school that are subject to negotiation within limits. The capacity to create cohesion and to support and encourage individuals is essential. This is likely to be enhanced by the head's own high standard of personal commitment and professional competence.

Simon identifies two leadership styles which may be adopted by head-teachers. The first involves the use of influence. Such headteachers seek to understand problems thoroughly in order to arrive at the right line of action. This involves an appeal to expertise and obtaining the consent of staff to proposed developments. The second involves the use of control, the exercise of authority to obtain the acquiescence of staff through a mixture of threat and persuasion.

Management that relies on control may divide staff and invite confrontation or passive resistance. Bolam and Pratt point out that controllers may adopt strategies that involve the use of incentives as well as sanctions. If compliance is forced it may result in low staff morale and lack of effort. Such a head-teacher is likely to lose the confidence of staff. Ballinger found that at the extreme such head-teachers may use autocratic strategies of lying, rigging agendas or altering information in order to deny or exclude opposing ideas.

School managements may be more or less focused on social satisfaction or task achievement. School managements which focus on neither may be described as impoverished. Those that focus on social satisfaction to the exclusion of task achievement may be described as 'Country Clubs', pleasant places to work at the expense of the social and emotional development of teachers and children. The ideal, of course, is to focus on both aspects.

Models of Organizational Health

Mile's model of 'organizational health' sought to identify dimensions of effective management. He grouped ten dimensions of organizational health under three main headings. Two of these, task-centred and maintenance needs, are closely related to those identified by Blake and Mouton but he adds a third, growth and changefulness. Miles's dimensions are as follows:

1. Task-centred
   (a) *Goal Focus*: goals should be clear, accepted, realistic and achievable.
   (b) *Optimal Power Equalization*: teachers motivated by feelings of involvement and competence.
   (c) *Communication Adequacy*: vertical and horizontal lines of communication should be open, easy and distortion free.
2. Maintenance Needs
   (a) *Cohesiveness*: clear sense of identity which is attractive to teachers.
   (b) *Morale*: well-being, laughter, lack of stress.
   (c) *Resource Utilization*: resources should be coordinated so that teachers are working hard, in jobs they suit but are not stressed.
3. Growth and Changefulness
   (a) *Innovativeness*: growth and development, increase in range of school's and teacher's activities.
   (b) *Autonomy*: staff respond to, but not be dictated to, by pressures from outside.
   (c) *Problem-solving Adequacy*: problems identified, solved and evaluated with minimum stress.
   (d) *Adaption*: strength and stability in order to allow for faster change.

A headteacher likely to foster organizational health might be described as democratic. However, Crick believes that democracy does not provide a good model for effective management. Its meaning is too uncertain.

It may mean majority rule, or the will of the staff, or 'one-person-one vote' or the pursuit of equality. It is not a suitable model for school management, where all decisions cannot be taken by the whole staff.

In a democracy, general interests may be taken into account but minority interests may be ignored. To manage well, headteachers may have to go against popular opinion and desirable goals may be mutually exclusive. Crick saw a political style of leadership as more appropriate, in which teachers' and childrens' interests are represented and communication is open but where the headteacher may take a wider view. Hoyle described the micropolitics of school management in which groups within the staff may cooperate to achieve a common goal. Such groupings may be *ad hoc* or formal and may be committed to preserving the *status quo*. Such groupings may lead to the 'dark underworld' of illegitimate micropolitics which include power broking and closed political processes. Marsh and Olsen describe how decisions may be made before consultation and negotiation and history 'rewritten' to make the process appear more rational. Handy describes how groups, whether legitimate or illegitimate, provide a psychological home for individuals by providing institutional and individual functions. Individual functions include the satisfaction of social needs, such as self-esteem, support and sharing. Institutional functions include management needs such as problem-solving, information collection and processing, co-ordination, commitment, negotiation and enquiry. Beneficial functioning of groups occurs where relations between individuals at all levels are good. Ideas are better evaluated and involvement is increased. This can lead to a positive cycle being established where greater productivity leads to more satisfaction, which in turn leads to still greater productivity. In this process

Richardson emphasized the importance of open and honest communication. This is only possible if the head-teacher communicates trust in the teachers' abilities to educate children. When this trust is built up teachers can risk exposing problems and revealing weaknesses and so develop their skills. A warm and accepting atmosphere is necessary before staff can examine what is good and bad in their school. The fostering of delusions, or suffocation of conflicting ideas beneath a veneer of politeness, will tend to mask problems. This can produce the problem of the preservation of harmony becoming an end in itself, resulting in a resistance to any change in the *status quo*.

Beeby pointed out the importance of an honest questioning and examination of behaviour and values that had to be taken for granted. Planning in education is not purely objective but involves value systems and attitudes. Having been implemented, change should be subject to criticism and feedback. This is only possible where teachers feel their interests are taken into account and there is communication between all levels of staff. An autocratic headteacher will invite confrontation or passive resistance. Such a head will be denied feedback from the teachers in the school and the opportunity to improve planning in the light of experience. The teachers are unlikely to experience support from the headteacher or the satisfaction of a task well done with the consequence of low morale. The headteacher's role within an effective school is thus very demanding and diffuse, in order to produce a climate where problems may be solved in cooperation.

Education takes place in a politicized context, with all its implications for accountability. In the context of the 1988 Education Reform Act, schools can no longer ignore the community in which they work. Parents will be closely involved in the management of schools and decisions over opting out. In addition schools will operate in a 'market place' where they must attract 'customers' and satisfy those they have already attracted. This is, however, not just a new phenomenon. Government reports from Plowden through to recent reports such as Warnock have emphasized the need for parental involvement in primary schools. This has led not only to a much greater openness but also to the development of tensions. The school has to become more explicit about its aims, and these may be challenged by parents who do not feel them to be in tune with their needs and purposes. Problems may become more acute with the publication of schools' assessment results. At the same time as schools are responding to parents' interests and needs, they are under pressure from government and local authority expectations. Those of central government have become very detailed and explicit and may conflict in some respect with its previous policies and philosophy of the Local Education Authority. The resolving of these tensions can lead to real progress, but in order for this to happen the pacing and timing of change needs careful consideration.

The problem which confronts schools and teachers is not in the first instance the truth or otherwise of the various criticisms, or the value or otherwise of the various initiatives but rather how to handle the volume of criticism and initiatives without damaging the morale of teachers which underpins the successful ethos of schools. There are, unfortunately, no simple solutions to these problems. Part of the answer may, however, lie in the work that teachers do together in defining a framework for the consideration of problems and issues.

Purposes of Teaching: As defined by Teachers

The ethos of a school is in large part determined by the values of those working within it. It therefore becomes necessary for teachers to discuss and analyse those values before priorities for action can properly be defined. It is important to define values within a school, because ethos is the expression of these values. There are questions which are fundamental to any such consideration. The first is the definition of the nature of teaching. It may not be assumed that all staff share the same view of what constitutes teaching. Fox discovered that teachers defined their purposes in teaching very differently. He grouped these definitions into four main categories:

1. *Transfer:* In this model teaching is seen as the; process of transferring knowledge from one person to another. The child is seen as an empty vessel and if knowledge fails to be transferred the problem tends to be seen as residing in the child.

2. *Shaping:* Teaching is the process of moulding children to a predetermined pattern. Children are taught skills and ways of behaving which are viewed as useful in themselves. The child's interests and motives are only important in so far as they interfere with the moulding process.

3. *Travelling:* In this model teaching is seen as a matter of guiding children through subject matter. The subject is viewed as an exciting and sometimes difficult terrain to be explored.

4. *Growing:* The focus of teaching is on the child's intellectual physical and emotional development. The teacher's job is to provide the situation and experience to assist the child in this development. This is a child-centred model, in which the subject

matter is important, not as an end in itself, but only in as much as it meets the child's needs and is in the child's interest.

Practical Implications of Purposes

Each of these models has important implications for teacher action and concern and hence for the ethos of the school. Many primary school staffs would define their purposes in terms of 'growing'. In this case there are important factors that arise and need to be discussed in order to develop a philosophy and action that will promote a positive ethos. A staff which has defined its values and developed a philosophy of teaching will need to consider the practical implications. Below we have outlined five aspects which may be considered.

1. *Evaluation and Record Keeping*: If each child's interests and needs are to be met these must be accurately determined, monitored and recorded. Reliance solely on the teacher's intuition and perception is likely to produce an inaccurate picture, and a more homogeneous one than exists in reality. Teachers will therefore need to share their knowledge of individual children and together devise methods of collecting data on individual children, for instance through observation schedules, checklists, analysing children's work, individual questioning and group discussion. Records of children's development, needs and interests will have to be constantly updated. In this the TGAT report may have provided a useful way forward—but not if teachers 'teach to the tests' in order to protect themselves from criticism and fail to use the results for diagnostic purposes to improve children's learning experiences and develop their teaching.

2. *Teaching and Learning Methods:* In order to meet the range of individual children's needs for intellectual, physical and emotional development, teachers may have to extend their range of teaching and learning methods. Many teachers rely on a relatively limited repertoire of teaching methods which are unlikely to suit the stage of development and learning style of each individual in their class, or even the different needs of any particular child meeting different subject matter or in various situations. there will therefore be a need for teachers to share expertise.

3. *Planning*: If the child rather than the subject matter is to be the focus of teaching, the planning of the curriculum purely in terms of subject matter will no longer be adequate. HMI suggest that the curriculum should also be analysed in terms of skills, attitudes, concepts and knowledge. There is concern that the emerging reports of the national curriculum subject working parties pay insufficient attention to attitudes. The national curriculum may help to ensure continuity and coherence within the subjects but teaching may become fragmented and opportunities to reinforce learning across its curriculum may be ignored. In addition, the needs of children who do not acquire skills, concepts and knowledge in a linear way will need to be met. Teachers will need support from each other to analyse what they are doing in order to maximize the benefits of the national curriculum and minimize its defects.

4. *Organization*: In order to meet the needs of individual children within the school, it is necessary that the staff group examines the way people, space and time are organized, including looking at them from the child's point of view. In many schools

routines have been built up that may interfere with the child's needs and interests. Space may need to be reorganized to allow a wider variety of children's activity to co-exist. Time should also be considered, both in terms of the 'class' day and the individual child's day. For instance, it is not uncommon for infant schools to 'work' in the morning and 'close' in the afternoon on the grounds that children are fresher in the morning. Assumptions such as this need questioning. What 'hidden' messages are being conveyed about the relative importance of different types of activity? Are the children's needs for changes in the pace of activity within sessions being met? When teachers examine the use of time as experienced by individual children they are often surprised. A child with learning difficulties may be in a class where a wide variety of activities take place, but day after day he works so painfully slowly that he never moves on from his written work.

5. *Relationship*: A definition of teaching which is concerned with children's intellectual, physical and emotional development, implies a consideration of the whole child. Children cannot be viewed as *tabulae rasae* when they come to school. This has implications for relationships within the community which the child comes from and especially with parents. A comparison of roles of the teacher and the parent will soon reveal much overlap. The parent and teacher will have much that is useful to offer each other. School staffs who adopt this model will have to analyse carefully their policy towards parents to discover if it is as open as possible and genuinely equal and two-way. Other schools are coming to realize the importance of partnerships

and parents after the Education Reform Act more painfully. There are, however, more important reasons for the involvement of parents than the Act. Without a developing relationship with parents, teachers will be less able to understand children's cultural background and treat them with the respect they merit. Through this understanding teachers can avoid simplistic labels and stereotypes, value minority customs and focus upon what cultures have in common rather than on differences and problems. The school's policy towards children will also need to be examined to ensure that all children's needs for social satisfaction and task achievement are met and special skills or talents nurtured. The actions of teachers will need to be analysed and questioned - for instance it may be necessary to examine the experience of education offered to girls and boys respectively or children from different cultural backgrounds.

The model presented here emphasizes words such as 'share', 'support', 'collaboration' and 'relationship'. This reflects the view that the development of ethos cannot be a 'top down' activity decided by a government or the head-teacher and implemented by the staff, but rather requires continual discussion and honest examination by everyone working in the school.

5
Primary Teacher Training

There are two main routes into primary teaching, the four year B.Ed. and the one year PGCE. The former is a post 'A' level undergraduate course and the latter, self-evidently, is taken by graduates in subjects which could equally well lead to other careers. Until recently the B.Ed. and its predecessor the Certificate in Education constituted the major routes into teaching, but because since 1972 successive governments have used this route as the tap to regulate teacher supply, the B.Ed./PGCE balance has now shifted. Thus, in 1963 19640 students started teacher's certificate courses, compared with a mere 3840 PGCE students, most of whom were intending secondary teachers. there followed a decade of expansion until by 1972 admissions were 37881 and 10365. Thereafter, delayed government panic about the declining birth-rate produced the devastating cuts of the 1970s, and the mergers and closures of many colleges, until by 1980, for the first time in the history of initial training, more students entered PGCE than B.Ed. courses. 1984-85 marked the start of a modest expansion of primary training, but one to be secured mainly through the PGCE. However, the B.Ed. will remain for the foreseeable future the majority route into primary teaching.

In the recent history of the 3-4 year route, four overlapping stages are clearly discernible, which are referred to as 'Certificate', 'B.Ed. Mark I', 'B.Ed. Mark II' and 'B.Ed. Mark III'. Firstly, the rise and decline of the teacher's certificate, which expanded from two to three years in 1960, was phased out during the 1970s and enshrined the basic structural elements which have dominated discussion about teacher education ever since. That structure is generally held to be a modified version of that recommended in the McNair Report way back in 1944 which in turn consolidated ideas which went back to the nineteenth century:

1. *Personal Education*: (a) one or more 'academic' or 'main' subjects;
2. *Professional Education*:

   (b) theory of education;

   (c) Curriculum or professional courses to equip the student with the content and method of the subjects he has to teach.

   (d) Teaching practice.

The second stage we can call B.Ed. Mark I. Following the Robbins Report B.Eds were introduced at great speed. These were essentially lengthened and converted into academic teacher's certificate courses. Because the course was now a degree rather than a certificate, it had to be academically respectable to the validating universities and comparable to other degree courses. This academic validity was seen to reside in the main subject and education theory, which were greatly strengthened, at the expense, it is now accepted, of professional studies and teaching practice. Following increasing criticism of this course, the James Report came up with a radical alternative model, which in pure form was not implemented, but its ideas provided the basis for B.Ed. Mark II. This was 'consecutive' and modular. Deferred student choice and flexibility were major aspirations; this was the era of the 'container revolution', of courses which students put together from a wide selection of units and modules, and which often meant that professional study and work in schools were deferred until the second or even the third of four years.

By the late 1970s, deferred choice, consecutive training and modularity were running into the logistical problems attendant upon contraction, for such courses had to be large to be viable. There were other criticisms chiefly revolving round the continued lack of sufficient professional emphasis, the perceived divorce of theory and practice and the split between subject and professional study. By now, moreover, the academic status of the B.Ed. was no longer an issue. A large number of institutions had transferred from university to CNAA validation and alternative notions of 'degree-worthiness' had begun to be explored. Mark III B.Eds lasted the full four years, were usually honours only, and included serious attempts to put professional concerns at the centre of the course and at last to break down the barrier between subject and professional study. But by that time, the early 1980s now, there were countervailing pressures. Successive HMI surveys, of primary and secondary schools had identified what were regarded as major weaknesses in serving teachers' professional expertise, above all in their curriculum knowledge. First HMI, then central government, then ACSET, the teacher education advisory body—less from conviction than recognition of the irresistibility of political dogma backed by landslide election success—and finally the DES again proposed that all B.Ed. students, whether primary or secondary, should spend half their course on main subject study in order to remedy these curricular deficiencies.

Courses are not disembodied artifacts but events and ideas which acquire their reality from particular institutional contexts. The majority of today's established primary teachers not only trained by the 2-3-4 year route but did so in a distinctive sort of institution, the college of education, which preserved a culture of remarkable homogeneity and historical persistence until the institutional reorganisations of the 1970s forced many of the surviving colleges into a usually reluctant alliance with mainstream higher education institutions.

While the PGCE was located mainly in the universities and until the rude advent of compulsory initial training, comprehensive schools and mixed ability teaching - prepared its students for grammar and public schools, the 3-4 year course reflected the requirements of a less prestigious tradition, that of secondary modern and primary schools. Thus, the two routes embodied and reinforced the mutual exclusiveness of the two central traditions in British education: minority/elitist/academic, and mass/elementary/utilitarian. Like primary schools, the colleges' origins were humble and impoverished. Like primary schools, they acquired a substantial contrary ideology—idealist, romantic, espousing values of self-actualization, individualism and student/child-centredness.

In most post-war teacher education courses the intending teacher's capacity to understand and relate to children has been seen as the virtually exclusive concern of two elements:

(a) *Academic*: courses in what until the 1960s were termed 'principles of education', subsequently the separate 'disciplines' of psychology and sociology of education, but more recently somewhat disguised within integrated, thematic education/professional courses;

(b) *Experiential*: teaching practice and other school-based activity.

This neat exclusivity of function is characteristic of initial teacher education as a whole. The dominant post-McNair model discussed earlier demarcates not merely 'personal' and 'professional' aspects of the training task but personal and professional course elements. Little or no overlap of function is envisaged or, in terms of academic territoriality, allowed. there is assumed to be an exact correspondence between professional attribute and course component so that each becomes the 'property' of a particular department or group of staff.

Psychology is relatively well-established in initial teacher education. The McNair Report's 'principles of education' included; physiology and physical education, psychology, 'great classical writers on education', history of the education system, and appreciation of the 'home circumstances of the pupils'. This approach lasted well into the 1960s: Taylor, Tibble, Browne and others record the dominance of the 'mother hen'—the education tutor dispensing a mixture of 'method', history of educational ideas and, above all, psychology. The 1960s witnessed the coming of age of the 'four disciplines' of education, but this strengthened the position in primary training, where the 'child development' course continued to rule supreme. Despite this relatively long-established pre-eminence in teacher education, it must be recalled that as an academic discipline, psychology is young, and sociology younger.

Through a combination of empirical research and theory-generation they seek to offer descriptions and explanations of individual and collective human behaviour which must be regarded as tentative, provisional and incomplete. Our first major reservation about this means of generating understanding of children is that the required sense of tentativeness and provisonality is too seldom conveyed to students. Theories and models are frequently put forward, or at least received by students, as unassailable truths about the real world, their status as such apparently confirmed by the strong positivistic orientation of a good deal of the research drawn upon and by the convenient tendency of such work to offer quantified findings. Wilson showed how in the very examination questions B.Ed. and PGCE students were required to answer presuming their tacit acceptance of a wide range of concepts and constructs. That claim is readily substantiated.

Psychology has sought to replace commonsense theories about mental processes with propositions derived from the application to human nature of the methods of the natural sciences. Pre-eminent in this methodology is the charting of observable behaviours. The 'introspective' method which seeks to uncover individuals' private knowledge, beliefs, attitudes, and so on, by eliciting these by word of mouth, is considered by the behaviourist majority to be inconsistent with the scientific claim. Thus, because by the canons of a particular methodology such data is deemed inaccessible, as the object of study it ceases to be of interest. This raises broader issues concerning the historical development of psychology—its origins in the philosophy of mind, the late 19th century rejection of mind in favour of 'scientific' study of the brain and the central nervous system, the consequent issue of the distinctiveness of psychology vis-a-vis neurology and physiology, and the continuity of the behaviourist/introspectionist debates.

Alternative perspectives on children which would complement the portrayal of the behaviourist psychologist —from literature, drama, philosophy and pre-eminently, everyday discourse—are explicitly rejected. Apart from its tendency to impoverish the teacher's professional development and classroom thought, this monopoly reveals the extent to which the view of teaching as science has pervaded academic and professional opinion, even including groups—like literature teachers and tutors— who might be expected to be more resistant. Perhaps, as academics so often do, they fail to make the connection between the claim that the arts offer unique and profound insights into the human condition and the obvious fact that teaching itself is nothing if not concerned with that condition.

The extent to which psychology of education courses directly reinforce the 'sequential developmentalism' element in primary ideology, which—drawing on King and others—provides a good example of several of the points above, particularly those concerning distortion in content and methodological oversimplification. The central theme or core of such courses has traditionally been a chronological treatment of child development. Here 'development' is conceived as a matrix with norms for ages and stages providing one axis and various categories of human development—'intellectual', 'social', 'emotional', 'moral', 'physical' etc.—as the other. This developmental matrix, open to fundamental criticism as it is, provides a basic, widely accepted structure for primary discourse, curriculum planning and pupil assessment: the firmly fixed reference points on an otherwise shifting and undifferentiated map.

The ages attached to stages postulated by Piaget are approximate, and that the inevitability of the sequence and the state-independent processes and mechanisms of cognitive development— equilibration, assimilation, accommodation—are more significant than any inferred chronology. Yet it is notable that in student essays, as in professional discourse and teachers, books and curriculum materials,the stages as such feature more prominently than the stage-independent theory, despite the fact that an understanding of the latter is essential to using the undoubted insights of Piagetian theory to promote or accelerate learning.

A Piagetian approach to HMI's concept of 'match', for example, would demand that children encounter learning tasks which are slightly, but not excessively, more complex than their present understanding, and that without this element of 'stretching' the disequilibration necessary for learning will not be produced. Where students or teachers perceived development in terms of states rather than processes they will tend to wait for learning to occur 'spontaneously' or 'naturally' rather than seek as teachers to advance it, on the grounds that the child has to be 'ready'.

Just as the dominance of developmentalism in everyday practice is matched by the dominance of the developmental 'matrix' in educational psychology courses, so the traditional fare of sociology of education courses corresponds strongly with another element in professional discourse, the family and home as the prime or even sole causes of the child's difficulties or failures at school. Until the early to mid-1970s, sociology of education courses were dominated by the issue of the effect of family and social-class factors on the child's attainment at school. Early studies of streaming pointed the way to the possibility that the school itself might be a contributory factor in the under-achievement of working-class children, but research on class-related socialisation practices, parental attitudes, language, and so on, tended to swamp such relatively slender evidence. Only with the 'new' sociology of education, with its two-pronged, ideologically committed concern to explore first the cultural loading of the school and its curriculum in favour of certain groups of pupils and, second, the nature of everyday classroom life, did alternatives to the family/home deficit model present themselves with much credibility.

A substantial literature concerning the effect of teacher expectations on pupil performance, teacher constructs and typifications, classroom interaction and teaching styles, now permits a more balanced appraisal of the relative impact of family and school, parents and teachers, on the child's educational career. Some of this work was referred. The shift, however, is recent, and everyday primary discourse, in as far as it is demarcated and to some extent controlled by senior members of the profession such as heads and advisers, still appears to display fairly unreserved affiliation to family/home theories. Certainly the confident professional assertions about 'good' and 'poor' parents and homes are part of the essential fabric of both staffroom discussion and pupil record cards. What will be worth monitoring is the extent to which the 'new' sociology of education produces a discernible shift in the way children's learning difficulties or lack of motivation are explained as students of the 1970s gain headships in the 1980s and 1990s and seek to influence their school's 'philosophies'.

Theories of child development and educability, it will be apparent, not only have ideological potential but need to be simplified, and perhaps even distorted, to achieve that potential. Thus Piagetian theory may be interpreted as confirming a doctrine of 'readiness' rather than as challenging the teacher's ingenuity to provide the child with appropriately structured and sequenced learning experiences.

Similarly, the complexity and tentativeness of, say, Bernstein's work on language and social structure may be ignored in preference for gross polarisations of 'restricted' and 'elaborated' codes which may confirm a student's or teacher's existing cultural stereotypes and prejudices. Both theories exemplified can be invoked to justify low expectations of children on the 'grounds' of age, or of social class.

In fact, much of the theoretical material regarded as indispensable in initial training is intrinsically extremely elusive and difficult to understand, let alone to apply, and especially so for the 18-21 year old with neither professional experience of schools and children nor a background of introductory study in the social sciences. However, its misinterpretation could be reduced or offset if the typificatory process which it appears to reinforce were itself the object of scrutiny on initial training courses. But it is a characteristic of mainstream education courses in initial training that, more recent sociology and social psychology perspective apart, they tend to devote little attention to the teacher as such. This particularly true of psychology of education courses: an examination of student texts and course syllabuses will reveal that most deal not so much with the psychology of education as with the psychology of the child, and that child's education is treated only in so far as it can be conceived independently of the person who is its chief architect, the teacher. The child emerges with an identity shaped by a combination of heredity and environment, having characteristics which are given and immutable. There is little or no psychological analysis of adults in general or teachers in particular; nor of the teacher's contribution to that classroom character of the child which serves as the basis for the teacher's appraisal of him or her. The child's actions are presented, if only by default, as independent of the teacher's. A conception of the child is encouraged which is somehow independent of the person, the teacher, who does the conceiving.

Understanding children is an attribute not of the object of that understanding but of the teacher who claims it. The teacher will perceive a child in a particular way not only because of the sort of person that child is but because of the sort of person the teacher is. And in the primary school, we remind ourselves, the class-teacher system ensures that a child is so perceived for educational purposes for a whole year by just one person: with that much at stake it seems indefensible for initial training courses to neglect the psychology of the teacher. Four shifts are indicated therefore.

First, the inclusion, as argued, of a substantial focus on teachers and their impact on those various aspects of the learner conventionally treated as independent of them.

Second, a deeper exploration of the ways individual behaviour—whether the child's or the teacher's —can be understood in the context of, and sometimes explained as a consequence of, interaction, possibly through the use of transactional analysis techniques applied in industrial psychology and psychotherapy, as well as interaction analysis schedules and theoretical perspectives of social psychology and interactionist/phenomenological sociology.

Third, a preparedness to explore the irrationality which frequently characterises human actions and interactions, not least in the classroom. The dominant psychological tradition in teacher education, as we have seen, takes the teacher's total rationality for granted and moreover imposes a sometimes over-tidy, predictive framework on the child.

Fourth, just as theoretical study of children in teacher education is required to be supported by work with children in classrooms, so teachers in classrooms and above all students themselves would need to be the object of practical study. If self-exploration is now included in the training of other professional groups whose job involves the management of people and relationships, it can surely be justified in the training of teachers.

Another major context a course provides for developing the student's understanding of children is school experience. Again, a historical perspective on this part of the course is helpful because its character and purposes have changed in recent years, though not as radically as some current advocates of 'school-based' courses would have us believe.

The McNair Report identified two main types of school experiences, practical training in schools and continuous teaching practice:

(i) *Practical training in schools*: To provide the concrete evidence, illustrations and examples to supplement and give point to the theoretical part of the student's training. The schools are his laboratory and the scene of his field studies. School practice of this sort should include comparatively discontinuous periods of teaching and observations in the schools, visits, minor investigations, and so on.

(ii) *Continuous teaching practice*: To provide a situation in which the student can experience what it is to be a teacher, that is, to become as far as possible a member of a school staff.

In 1979, a major review of school experience/teaching practice in all CNAA-validated B.Eds distinguished two main types, 'intermittent' and 'block', in almost exactly the same terms as McNair, but found the former a relative novelty in many institutions, something needing further development. It was indeed a novelty. Taylor's 1969 study of teacher education reported as the norm for both Certificate and Mark I B.Ed. courses block practices only, three in total, taking place in years 1, 2 and 3, with students given their final teaching practice grade at the beginning of year 3 and undertaking no more work in schools for a further five terms. This may seem, in retrospect, hard to defend but at the time the overriding concern of the universities—for the B.Eds academic respectability—was argument enough. This arrangement ensured that professional work, in general, and the pressures and anxieties of teaching practice, in particular, were not allowed to disturb the smooth flow of what was held to matter most in the final two years of the new degree, main subject study and theoretical studies in education. Thus, despite McNair, the history of developments in this part of the course shows three clear stages:

- *Stage I:* The nineteenth-century 'apprenticeship' model, or what in Britain is called 'sitting by Nellie' by some teacher educators: here the student acquires most of his/her teaching competence through close association with, and imitation of, an experienced practising teacher.
- *Stage II:* The 'teaching practice' model, where students acquire professional knowledge and skill in

the training institution, then apply or 'practise' these during extended periods in school, watched over by the experienced teacher whose class they take over, and visited once a week or so by their college/university tutor.

– *Stage III:* The 'school-based study' or 'school experience' model, where the school becomes not only a place to practise teaching, to demonstrate what one can do and to be assessed, but also a place to learn, to observe, to study and to experiment; to carry out specific tasks of observation, working with small groups of children, working alongside experienced teachers, undertaking small-scale inquiries, analysing at first hand how children develop, how they learn, the different styles of teaching used, how children respond to these, their impact on children's learning, and so on.

Whatever the espoused objective of school experience, students will gain some view of children simply by virtue of interacting with them. This applies equally when the acquisition of such experiential understanding is explicitly valued and when more limited objectives are pursued. The issue is not so much of the teacher educators' intentions as the dynamics of the situation in which the student is placed. The critical questions therefore relate to the treatment of the student's experiential understanding rather than the formal structure of school experience. To what extent and in what ways are the students encouraged to make explicit and explore the views of children and teaching they themselves evolve and encounter while in schools? What is the relationship between such views and those 'ready-made' characterisations offered in theoretical parts of the course? And what value is accorded to the different views, definitions and perspectives—theoretical and experiential—which the student acquires or meets?

Hitherto, however, even in courses committed to Stage III above, the everyday, experiential perspective has probably counted for less than it might. There are, of course, problems in explicating and communicating these understandings. Being to a considerable extent private and idiosyncratic, such knowledge is not readily expressed through the conceptual and linguistic structures currently on offer for public discourse about education. This may be a good example of the pervasive influence of behaviourist psychology on the initial training course as a whole.

There is no good reason why the distrust of introspective methods should influence a part of the course which makes no claim to psychological status. Still the urge to assert the 'scientific' character of teaching and teacher training may result in what are perceived as scientific methodological criteria being applied across the board without regard to their appositeness. In terms of such criteria the perspectives of individual teachers could be deemed inadmissible.

Moreover, difficulties in articulating and characterising such perspectives make for unflattering comparison with the apparent ease, sophistication and conceptual tidiness of academic modes of discourse. Everyday analysis, haltingly articulated, appears banal and brutish, a telling confirmation of the academic's disdain for 'mere' subjectivity, opinion and intuition.

In reality the reverse may well be the case: a complex, subtle conceptual perspective may not be readily amenable to expression in terms of the relatively crude public constructs offered by the existing, monopolistic modes of respectable educational theorising about such matters. Thus, for example, the general concept of 'typification' referred to at various points seems a potent one. What is less convincing is the claim that we can identify, in all their richness, diversity and paradox, exactly what a teacher's typifications and constructs are, using, for example, the relatively simplistic tool of repertory grid technique. Where then, lies the true banality: in the thinking and practice of teachers as such, or in the versions thereof offered by researchers and the procedures and models from which such versions are constructed? And what is being valued, depth of insight or sophistication of language? Fortunately, no simple answers to these questions are available. To provide them would be to compound the felony. But it can be suggested that the philosophical uncertainty surrounding the matter of how others' thoughts can be 'known' makes it inappropriate for teacher educators to accord such unequal status to 'academic' and 'everyday' versions of classroom reality. Take, for example, a course with a flexible 'workshop' concept of school experience, on which a student may be required, as now commonly happens, to come to 'understand' children's cognitive development by carrying out Piagetian tests in school. The rationale for this exercise is 'applying theory to practice's or put another way, demonstrating the validity of the theory, confirming the Piagetian model. However, since in replicating the test the student will also have to replicate the circumstances, the result is predictable. What the replication does is simply to illustrate the hypothesis, not confirm it. Indeed, possibly the last thing the psychology tutor concerned may want is genuine testing of the model.

We have then, two questionable assumptions endemic to teacher education and exemplified ever in Stage III 'progressive' models of school/course interaction,

First, that the academic model of human behaviour is qualitatively superior to the everyday. Less by virtue of its proven veracity than because of the context and manner in which it is generated and the language through which it is expressed. Second, that professional knowledge is acquired by making the idiosyncratically observed and experienced world 'fit' theoretical models of it; or, put another way, by theory verification rather than theory falsification.

The impact of this kind of covert epistemology extends well beyond the immediate circumstances of initial training and will affect or support the everyday predilections of the serving teacher in respect of both his knowledge of the child and his view of the child's knowledge of the world.

To make use of schools not merely as a context for practising executive skills but as a prime means for developing the student's capacities to observe, understand and relate to children is a *sine qua non* of teacher education. It has to be asked, however, whether the opportunities are fully exploited. This is only partly, as we have seen, a procedural matter; what needs closer attention is the teacher educators' and course validators' view of what this 'understanding' might mean.

At present, and certainly during the decade when today's primary teachers and heads trained, the interpretations, explanations and hypotheses of students and serving teachers have been under-valued and therefore insufficiently pursued and tested. And while a somewhat restricted canon of child-related theories has been, in comparison, over-exposed, it has been the exposure of obeisance, rather than critique.

There seem to be a number of ways the situation can be improved, of varying degrees of radicalism:

(a) the focus for 'understanding' can be broadened;

(b) better use can be made of existing education disciplines;

(c) additional sources of insight can be explored;

(d) 'everyday' modes of understanding can be more fully exploited;

(e) different conceptions of professional theory for teaching can be applied.

Students are the main concern in a course of initial training: The qualities, skills and knowledge which they are deemed to need are the course's *raison d'etre*. So in arguing that the course needs to focus more explicitly on the student and on the serving teacher, we are arguing for a specific kind of attention with which this self-evident concern is not to be confused.

Courses are premised on the importance of teachers' mastery of certain executive skills, their manifestation of particular personal qualities and their possession of certain kinds of knowledge. Pre-eminent among the latter is that academic knowledge about children which they may or may not make significant use of in practice. What by and large, are neglected are the many layers or facets beyond these generalised propositions which combine to create the particular ways individual students and teachers actually view, or 'understand', the children they teach in particular classroom settings: teachers' actual and tacit, as opposed to preferred or espoused or idealised, knowledge of children, and the biographies which produce this knowledge. Their subjective realities, as opposed to the quasi-objective ideas or the educational situation with which they are presented in training. Merely to offer to the student a set of propositions from psychological/sociological theory or research—'this is the way children are, this is what they are like, this is the reality to which your decisions must be addressed'—is to ignore, or at least to fail to acknowledge sufficiently, two basic arguments concerning children in classrooms.

First, regardless of generalised principles of child development, motivation, and so on, children are 'as they are' in classrooms, in part at least, because of the actions of the teacher; they respond, as in interaction all humans respond, to personality, to climate, to tacit or explicit signals, attitudes and expectations from a variety of sources, but chiefly, in the educational context, from the teacher.

Second, though individual children are viewed differently by each of those with whom they interact, and their self-concept indeed in part evolves from a consciousness of these various perceptions, in the educational context, the teacher's view of them is the most significant. It is the teacher who defines their abilities, their potential, their personality, their attainment and their attitudes, for the purposes of making curricular decisions, evaluations and predictions, and, as we have seen, in a way which is consistent with their ideology.

Such is the nature of the educational process, and the classroom power relationship, especially where young children are concerned, that the central assumption in child-centredness, of the child's autonomy, is not only fallacious but dangerously so. It can never be the case that on the one hand we have the child, about whom there is pre-existing objective knowledge, and on the other the teacher, who simply has to acquire that knowledge. The teacher's knowledge of the child is subjective, it is created by the teacher, its character is therefore as strongly conditional on the way the teacher is, as the way the child is.

The theme for initial training, which should complement 'understanding children' is 'understanding how teachers 'understand children'. And if it is indeed students understanding that we wish to promote rather than their capacity merely to parrot the prepositions and formulae of others, the source as well as the character of such 'understanding', on the basis of which students and teachers act, needs to be explored. This necessitates attention to the unique individual biographies of each student as well as to the more generalised analysis of the professional, historical and ideological situation of the particular groups of teachers offered. The outcome of this process should be to sensitise the student to the possibility of a much wider range of diagnoses and explanations.

The phrases 'self-analysis', 'self-awareness' or 'self-criticism' only partly encompass what is required because conventionally they are affectivity-oriented, referring primarily to attitudes, motivation and emotional response: self-analysis in the present sense has to include, in addition, attention to one's personal and professional epistemology—the nature of one's knowledge about the children one teaches, its validity,its source, its limitations, its influence, and so on.

The fact that introspective methods are unacceptable to some psychologists is worthy of debate in this context but is not grounds for rejecting the perspective we have defined. The course aims to train teachers, not professional psychologists, and if a perspective is helpful it should be included, methodological qualms notwithstanding. Thus the scope of understanding children in initial training needs to be broadened chiefly by taking in teachers' influence on both the children and their understanding of them. Equally important, and more easily enunciated, is the need to allow existing perspectives on children offered by psychology and sociology to be supplemented by alternatives from within those disciplines. We tried to show how currently taught models of child development may feed the complacency surrounding primary class teaching while different psychological traditions might provide a basis for a keener appraisal. Clearly, given our discussion of the complementary relationship between ideology, professional theory and practical situation, the introduction of less comfortable psychologies and sociologies might be resisted, but perhaps we can begin to accept that our comfort may well be secured at the expense of the quality of the child's education.

This shift has already begun in the sociology of education: the sociology of knowledge and of classrooms has provided the needed counterbalance to the family/home educability preoccupations of the 1950s and 1960s. We now need a 'new' psychology of education which more fairly represents the richness of mainstream psychology. The newer perspectives offer both alternative focuses and tools for analysis. Centre-stage are not only classroom processes and the interactions of teachers and children which feature in 'objective' study in the Flanders tradition, but also the meanings which the teachers and children themselves assign to those processes.

The underlying assumption here is that human actions can be properly understood only if one uncovers these meanings, since action is forged by the actor out of what he perceives, interprets and judges. The "objective" approach holds the danger of the observer substituting his view of the field of action for the view held by the actor. Equally important, we are presented with an alternative view of the self which might prompt us to look as closely at the child now, in the classroom, as at supposedly fixed and unalterable attributes like intelligence, personality and home background:

Social phenomenology examines events in their own terms and resists explanations in terms of wider social and economic forces. Sharp and Green's study of a 'progressive' primary school found this an unacceptably purist paradigm and injected a Marxist perspective so as to show how primary schooling both reflects and reinforces prevailing societal structures and ideologies. More determinist still, the notion of schooling in general, and curriculum in particular, as mechanisms of social control and cultural reproduction, is prominently represented in the work of Young and in the collection of papers edited for the Open University by Dale, Esland and MacDonald.

Moving back towards phenomenology, but representing in terms of historical origin a parallel rather than a related movement, and not asserting actors' total independence from societal structures and forces, symbolic interactionism gives prominence to actors' meanings but focuses especially upon the process whereby these are arrived at, often through 'negotiation'. Thus, in studying classrooms it becomes important to understand pupils' as well as teachers' definitions of the situation, and the extent to which the latter are not autonomous but are influenced by the former; at the same time the power differential in classrooms makes the impact of teachers' meanings on children and classroom life considerable. This perspective prominently informs the classic and comprehensive exploration of school interaction by Hargreaves and specific studies of primary classrooms like that of Berlak et al.

The study of infants' classrooms by King, to which we have made frequent reference, is eclectic: it is critical of phenomenological, interactionist and Marxist perspectives yet is also influenced by them. It belongs to the 'family' in so far as it is grounded in close and sustained observation which is interpreted by reference to actors' perceptions and explanations rather than observer preconceptions. At the same time, it places these in broader frameworks of ideology and social structure.

The other two disciplines in the educational studies pantheon are philosophy and history.

Philosophy of education—whether so defined or used thematically in an integrated course—tends to concern itself with broad non-contextualised questions about aims, the nature of knowledge, the justification for particular educational concepts and activities, the ethics of reward and punishment. Frequently it is conceived as a tool of encouraging a sharper, more reflexive and considered mode of analysis than the easy, instant judgement, as a basis for critique of teachers' and students' commonsense statements. This is undoubtedly necessary, but it is also the case that by such means, intentionally or unwittingly, is the status of academic thought preserved, for philosophical analysis ought equally to be applied to the statements, judgement and explanations offered by psychology and sociology of education: conceptual analysis should have no boundaries. Especially, a concern with epistemology ought not to start and finish with the school curriculum, but should encompass the knowledge and truth claims of the teacher training curriculum as well, the ways of making sense of and understanding children, teaching and learning which the initial training course expects the student to internalise and subsequently 'apply' in the classroom.

In other words, 'ways of knowing' about educational processes should be subjected to the same level of scrutiny as are the ways of knowing which constitute the school curriculum out there in the school. To fail to do this is to miss an opportunity to give the student a working understanding of epistemological issues; and it could be construed as hypothetical to subject to a critique the school curriculum, but not that of teacher education.

History of education courses have done little to remedy this. Courses in the educational system of England and Wales can still be as normative, functionalist, systemic and superficial as they were in the years following the McNair Report. They included resumes of the clauses of education acts and the recommendations of major reports, but rarely interpretations or explanation beyond a sort of sub 'O' level 'seven causes of the Boer War' variety. There was certainly little real delving into the pedagogy and curriculum experienced by previous generations of children and the justifications offered by teachers and others in support of these. 'Why do we view children like this?' 'Why do we define their educational needs in this way?'. These are questions as much historical as psychological, and the desire to ask them is surely a prerequisite for any teacher in a complex, changing, pluralist society. Teaching is constituted of ideas as well as action; indeed it is the putting into operation of ideas.

In a study, primary school teachers, at the start of a school year, were presented with information regarding their pupils. This information led the teachers to believe that some of their pupils were likely to become particularly prominent again during the school year ahead. In fact, the pupils thus identified as 'spurters' had been selected at random from each class. Any gains that were actually made, therefore, would be very unlikely to be the result of genuine extra potential, rather they would reflect the effects of a self-fulfilling prophecy.

This experimental manipulation of the teachers' expectations by Rosenthal and Jacobson enabled them to rule out simple prediction as a possible explanation of any link established between what the teachers expected and what actually happened. The results appeared to demonstrate that the expectations induced did indeed lead to higher levels of IQ in those children identified as spurters. In addition, at the end of the period of study, the teachers held generally more favourable attitudes towards the spurters than they did towards the other pupils. As the teachers could not remember by this stage which pupils had been identified as spurters and which had not, it seemed that they had genuinely developed a view of their class that had been determined by the bogus information that had been offered to them. In this study the information that had been provided by outsiders had been favourable towards the pupils that it concerned.

Under normal circumstances, Rosenthal and Jacobson assumed, teachers would form their own expectations concerning their pupils, and these could well be unfavourable. If the self fulfilling prophecy could operate to increase pupil performance with favourable expectations, as Rosenthal and Jacobson's study suggested, then it could also operate to depress performance if the expectations were unfavourable. If we also assume that teachers may not always form their own expectations on the basis of totally reliable and valid information, then we have to face the possibility that some pupils will be handicapped from the outset by the biasing effects of unfavourable (and possibly unjustified) teacher expectations.

A further study carried out by Rist at around the same time confirmed these fears. From an extended period of observation, Rist was able to investigate the ways in which a teacher's style of interaction with her pupils related to her early expectations for them. Rist's conclusion is a simple and in many respects a damning one. He took the view that children were effectively placed into different castes. These placements followed from early teacher judgements that seemed to have more to do with the clues available as to the children's socio-economic status (dress, cleanliness, manners, etc.) than their actual attainment or academic promise. Rist's data indicated that, having judged that a child had little potential, the teacher would then proceed to give him or her much less attention, and thereby make it very difficult for the child to prove the teacher wrong. Children placed in the lower groups on the basis of this apparently flimsy evidence generally stayed there.

The Pygmalion Study has been subjected to close scrutiny and careful criticism over the years. These reviews indicate that different samples and context yield different results and that it is therefore important to exercise care in coming to any general conclusions. The teacher expectancy effect apparently does not operate in all classrooms, with all teachers, at all times.

Nevertheless, there can now be little doubt that the effect can and does operate. Rosenthal himself has carried out a large-scale survey of research into the teacher expectancy effect, and has concluded that since his own Pygmalion Study there have been more than four hundred further studies that have demonstrated the existence of the effect. One individual study worthy of mention here was carried out by Crano and Mellon. By using data gathered over a number of years, they were able to test in a fairly direct manner the claim that expectations cause performance differences rather than simply predict them. The method they adopted enabled them to use the expectations that teachers had formed for themselves, rather than artificially inducing them as Rosenthal and Jacobson had done.

Crano and Mellon's results therefore have a greater likelihood of giving a valid picture of real classroom life. Their data show that expectations do have clear causal influence on pupil performance, particularly when the expectations are based on the teachers views of the social rather than the academic aspects of the pupil. That is, those pupils who are perceived as being well behaved, friendly, and pleasant to work with are the ones likely to benefit from positive expectations. Those perceived in the opposite way are those most likely to suffer.

Expectations relating to the actual academic ability of the pupil, while still important, were less likely to cause changes in pupil performance. In considering the processes likely to be involved in the teacher expectancy effect, this difference between the effects of social and academic expectations could well prove to be most important. What now remains to be done is the task of making clear just what is the nature of the process by which expectations are formed, transmitted and then acted upon. Several models of this exist. While these differ in detail they all share the same basic elements.

1. Expectations are formed from the information available to the teacher.
2. These expectations then lead to some systematic differences in teacher behaviour;
3. These differences are noted and responded to by the pupil, resulting in the pupil coming to match more closely the original expectation.

One characteristic of the research available to date is that it has centered on the teacher. The data available are therefore more complete with respect to Stages 1 and 2 than with respect to Stage 3. It is clear however, that each stage needs to operate in order for the effect to take place.

Teachers' expectations do seem to be influenced by the attractiveness of the pupil, the pupil's classroom conduct, the school's cumulative records concerning the pupil, and the pupil's race and social class. Perhaps surprisingly, given the current concern with gender differences in educational performance the gender of the pupil did not influence expectations, but there was some evidence to suggest a possible link between teacher expectation and the sex role behaviour of the pupil. Similarly, there was evidence suggestive of a possible effect of the teacher's experience with an older sibling, and the stereotyped views that a teacher may hold in respect to a particular name. It is immediately apparent that not all of these types of information will have a necessary connection with actual pupil ability. Their effect comes through the impact that they have upon the way in which the teacher responds to the pupil concerned. We still know relatively little about the sources of information that teachers actually do use in building up their expectations for individual pupils. In particular, it is clear that we need to know more about the ways in which the nature of the classroom conditions that the teacher works under has an effect upon the kind of expectations that are formed, and the degree to which these might persist over time.

The less advantageous a teacher's conditions of work may be, the more likely it is that relatively fixed expectations will be formed. The well-known work of Sharp and Green serves to illustrate these points. Under difficult working conditions teachers will have less time to reflect upon the developing abilities of each individual in their classes and will therefore be more likely to hold on to judgements arising from early impressions formed on the above types of clear, but not necessarily accurate, types of information. Other reviewers, such as Blease have suggested that we also need to look at the extent to which expectations are shared by several teachers in the same school. Expectations that are shared by many teachers are more likely to influence a pupil than those that are unique to an individual member of staff. The consistent adoption of a development viewpoint is also necessary. The pieces of information that may play a critical role in determining early expectations may be less important later in the school year. Information critical in the formation of expectations for young primary school children may not be relevant in the formation of expectations for young adults towards the end of their secondary schooling.

Further detailed examinations of natural classrooms over extended periods are needed. A further review by Harris and Rosenthal have examined evidence relevant to the second and third stages listed above. They draw together conscious evidence relevant to the differences in teacher behaviour that follow from differences in expectation, and the degree to which these differences in behaviour, in turn, relate to pupil performance. Teacher behaviour was shown by the Harris and Rosenthal analysis to vary in a number of respects. Further, these variations were associated with the teachers' prior expectations, and equally important, with the pupils' later performance levels, in particular variations in expectation which gave rise to differences in respect of : the amount of material that a teacher presented to a pupil; the degree of warmth and friendliness that is established in the relationship between the teacher and pupil (climate); the degree to which the teacher will attempt to elicit responses from the pupil through questioning (output); and the degree to which the teacher would supply the pupil with positive feedback through praise, acceptance of pupil's ideas, and so on (feedback). In each case, the pupil for whom the higher expectations existed received the most favourable treatment.

Harris and Rosenthal have continued their analysis to demonstrate the degree to which each of these four areas of variation in teacher behaviour is associated with variations in levels of pupil performance. Such links are indeed found, particularly for those areas of teacher behaviour referred to as climate, input, and output. This review of research, then, establishes some important links. It shows that if a teacher has varying expectations for the performance of his or her pupils, then there are likely to be predictable variations in that teacher's behaviour towards those pupils. The chain appears to be completed by the further demonstration that these differences in teacher behaviour are also associated with levels of pupil performance. The final step in the chain, and the least adequately researched, concerns the nature of the pupil response. Whatever effects teacher expectancies might have upon pupils, they will not take place by directly influencing pupil ability. Rather the effects are likely to occur by promoting changes in pupil motivation and self-concept, which in turn enhance performance levels.

Both self-concept and motivation have been extensively researched in general terms, but are only recently being subjected to detailed and systematic study within the context of the classroom. A promising line of investigation relates concern with motivational processes to the work of social psychologists in the field of attribution theory. Weiner has argued that the causes people believe to be responsible for their own (and others') successes and failures will determine the way in which they subsequently behave. Those who believe that their failures are caused by variable and, ideally, controllable causes are more likely to make a positive response to the failure, in attempting to overcome it, than are those who believe that the same degree of failure is caused by stable or uncontrollable factors.

A school environment that encourages the pupils within it to have confidence in their abilities, to increase effort, and to search for successful solutions when confronted with initial failure, will increasingly improve the motivation of those individuals. Recent research begins to show us how teacher behaviour can affect pupils' attributions. Two general points emerge from this literature. While the social aspects of the classroom are important, it is essential not to concentrate upon this at the expense of attention to the academic demands made on pupils.

One of the major factors linking teacher expectation with pupil performance is the varying amount of work that teachers set for different pupils. A pupil who is only asked to do a little is unlikely to achieve any more. Second, it is clear that an unduly competitive classroom environment will have a deleterious effect upon those pupils towards the bottom end of the attainment range. Relatively high levels of competition have the effect of emphasizing the degree to which ability is seen to be the main cause of success and failure. Failure under such conditions is likely to be most damaging to the least able.

Moves towards forms of assessment that play down the comparisons between pupils and highlight instead comparison between present and past performance by the same pupil are likely to help reduce teacher expectancy effects. The attitudes of the teacher will often be critical here. A teacher who accepts that some pupils have low and fixed levels of attainment is most likely to produce damaging expectancy effects. It is possible that our own culture produces the view that ability is a major determinant of success and failure.

There are three classes of consequences typically available to teachers which will be discussed in detail in this section. Our objective is to make clear to the reader the research basis underlying the conclusions to be drawn. The research strategies used in the majority of studies covered by this report share the following three features:

First, individuals are studied under specified experimental conditions, with the same individuals going through the various phases of the experiment. This approach leads more directly to knowledge of procedures which will work with individual children.

Second, the experimental procedure is often withdrawn after being introduced to show its effect more clearly. For example, when teacher praises more, task behaviour increases; when teacher praises less, task behaviour decreases.

Third, the behaviours to be changed are defined in terms of observables—events which the teacher can see and do something about. Reliability of observations is established before the experiment starts by checking the agreement between several observers. A review of field experimental research procedures may be found in Bijou, Peterson, and Ault. Studies by Becker and by Hall and their students have been conducted to assess the possibility of extending the findings on preschool children to the elementary school setting.

Combined Effects of Rules, Ignoring, and Praise

Becker, Madsen, Arnold, and Thomas chose two problem children from each of five elementary school classes. Categories of child behaviours were defined which disrupted learning or violated the teacher's rules. For example, gross motor behaviour was defined as getting out of seat, standing, running, skipping, jumping, and the like. Other disruptive behaviours included making noise with objects, aggression, orienting away from work, blurting out, talking to peers, and other off-task behaviour. Observers were trained to rate reliably the frequency of occurrence of these behaviours. Deviant behaviour was defined as any twenty-second interval in which one or more disruptive behaviours occurred. The children were rated for three twenty-minute sessions each week.

Observations of teacher behaviours were made to determine if the experimental program was being carried out effectively. After a five-week base line, the teachers began the experimental program which had three components. The teacher's rules for classroom behaviour were made explicit and repeated frequently. Teachers were also to show approval for appropriate behaviours and to ignore disruptive behaviours. If a child was hurting someone, the teacher could intervene as she saw fit. This rarely happened. The teachers were instructed to give praise for achievement, prosocial behaviour, and following the rules of the group. They were to praise students for such behaviours as concentrating on individual work, raising hand when appropriate, responding to questions, paying attention to directions, following directions, sitting at desk, studying, and sitting quietly. They were instructed to use variety and expression in their comments and to smile when delivering praise.

Teachers were to walk around the room during study time and give a pat on the back to children doing good job. The teachers were given daily feedback regarding their effectiveness in showing approval contingent on appropriate behaviour and in ignoring inappropriate behaviour. The percentage of intervals of deviant behaviour for the ten children dropped from 6.1 per cent of the time during base line to 29.2 per cent of the time during the experimental program when approval, ignoring deviant behaviour, and rules were introduced. T Don is a boy of average IQ who earlier as a fourth-grader had been recommended for placement as an educable retarded. He had a high frequency of moving about the room and talking during study time. He responded well to approval and his level of deviant behaviour fell from 40 per cent to 20 percent.

Dan, who was more than two years behind in reading, responded well to teacher attention only after tutoring in reading was begun. It was not enough to reinforce him for staying in his seat if he could get no measure of success from his academic work. Dan was considered by the school psychologist to be a severely disturbed only boy who required psychotherapy if he was going to be able to function in school.

Teacher had relied mainly on shouting to maintain order in an "unruly" class. The children engaged in much whistling, running about the room, yelling at other children, loud incessant talk, hitting, pushing, and shoving. The average level of deviant behaviour for the two boys fell from about 70 per cent to about 25 per cent, a drastic reduction. The teacher also reported many changes in other members of her class.

Hall, Lund, and Jackson reported a series of experiments further demonstrating the effects of teacher social reinforcement for study behaviour and withdrawal of attention of disruptive behaviours. For example, Robbie was a very disruptive boy who spent much of his time snapping rubber bands, talking and laughing with peers, and playing with toys from his pocket. He spent less than 25 per cent of work time actually working. During the base-line period, 55 per cent of the attention Robbie received followed nonstudy behaviour.

When off-task behaviour was ignored and good work behaviour praised, Robbie improved dramatically. In this classroom the teacher was signaled by the experimenter when to praise or otherwise give attention to study behaviour. This was done to help her learn to manage her own behaviour more efficiently. The reversal condition demonstrated the critical importance of the teacher's behaviour in maintaining Robbie's on-task behaviour.

Reinstatement of the reinforcement condition once again establishment good study behaviour. Following-up checks made during the fourteen weeks following the experimental conditions showed that the teacher was able to maintain good study behaviour without continued assistance. Similar positive findings were reported with other children and with other teachers. In a subsequent report, Hall et al., showed again the continuing importance of behaviours. Furthermore, he showed that teachers can reliably take data themselves on the children they are helping. By using a second person to check the reliability of observations, Hall found the percent of agreements ranging from 84 to 100 per cent. The implication is that teachers can be trained to monitor their own plans for helping children with behaviour problems.

Separate Effects of Rules, Ignoring Disruptive Behaviour, and Praise

Madsen, Becker and Thomas attempted to determine the relative effectiveness of the three components of the experimental program used in their first study. After base line, each of the three components of the experimental program were introduced separately. The rules phase of the experiment consisted of the teacher forming four or five rules for classroom behaviour and repeating them four to six times a day, e.g., "Sit quietly while working," "Walk," "Raise hand," and so-forth. The ignore phase of the experiment consisted of the teacher attempting not to respond to disruptive behaviours with scolding or reprimands. She was to act as if such behaviour had not happened. This part of the program was very difficult for the teacher to follow.

Finally, praise was added to rules and ignoring inappropriate behaviour. Appropriate behaviours incompatible with deviant inappropriate behaviours were to be given social approval. The teacher was to show approval of as many good behaviours as possible during the first few days. A prime rule was "Catch the children being good." Moreover, she was to give approval to improvements in behaviour in order to shape the child's behaviour. For example, a problem child who frequently wandered around the room would be given approval when found in his seat even if he was not working on a task.

As the time spent in his seat increased, the teacher would begin to praise him only when he was both seated and working on a task. In each case, the teacher would explicitly state the behaviours she approved, e.g., "Tommy is sitting nicely and working hard on his assignment." The results indicate that the introduction of rules alone was not effective in modifying behaviour. The procedures of ignoring inappropriate behaviour was difficult for the teacher to maintain. She would ignore for a while and then scold as the children got out of hand.

When praise for appropriate behaviour was added in conjunction with the ignoring of inappropriate behaviour, the latter behaviour fell from about a 70 per cent level to 30 per cent. Inappropriate behaviour returned to the base-line level when the teacher approximated her behaviour of the base-line period. Finally, when the experimental procedures were reinstated, the level of appropriate behaviour again fell. This correspondence between the experimental changes in teacher's behaviour and the level of inappropriate child behaviour points to the marked influence a teacher can have over classroom behaviour. These findings indicate that simply instructing children what to do is not enough. Reinforcement for following instructions is also necessary. A study by Schutte and Hopkins with five kindergarten children helps to show more clearly the contribution of instructions to classroom management. A list of ten instructions related to classroom routines was formed, such as "Pick up the toys," "Sit down," "Write your name on the paper," "Get out your mat," "Be quiet". These instructions were repeated daily for twenty days. The data recorded were the number of instructions followed each day. When instructions only were given, 60 per cent of the instructions were followed by the five children. When praise was added, following instructions increased to 78 per cent. A return to the instructions without praise led to a drop in following instructions to 69 per cent and the addition of praise led to an increase to 84 per cent. These findings are in keeping with laboratory-based findings on the discriminative control of behaviour.

Signals or instructions as discriminate stimuli become important because certain behaviour has been followed by reinforcers in their presence, but not in their absence. Such signal cannot stand alone and remain effective. They must at least periodically be supported by reinforcing consequences established by close association of neutral and evocative stimuli. If these methods alone were applied on the distant planet, the life span of Martians would not only be drastically shortened, but their brief period of survival would be expanded in prolonged and laborious efforts to master simple skills. The marked discrepancy between textbooks and social reality is largely attributable to the fact that certain critical conditions present in natural situations rarely, if ever, are reproduced in laboratory studies of learning. In laboratory investigations experimenters arrange comparatively benign environments in which errors do not create fatal consequences for the organism. By contrast, natural environments are loaded with potentially lethal consequences for those unfortunate enough to perform hazardous errors. For this reason, it would be exceedingly injudicious to rely on differential reinforcement of trial-and-error performances in teaching children to swim, adolescents to drive automobiles, medical students to conduct surgical operations, or adults to develop complex occupational and social competencies.

There are several reasons why modeling influences are heavily favoured in promoting everyday learning. Under circumstances in which mistakes are costly or dangerous, skillful performances can be established without needless errors by providing competent models who demonstrate the required activities. Some complex behaviours can be produced solely through the influence of models. If children had no opportunity to hear speech it would be virtually impossible to teach them the linguistic skills that constitute a language.

It is doubtful whether one could ever shape individual words by selective reinforcement of random vocalizations, let alone grammatical utterances. Where desired forms of behaviour can be conveyed only by social cues, modeling is an indispensable aspect of learning. Even in instances where it is possible to establish new response patterns through other means, the process of acquisition can be considerably shortened by providing appropriate models.

In social learning theory the phenomena ordinarily subsumed under the labels imitation and identification are designated as modeling. The latter term was adopted because modeling influences have much broader psychological effect than the simple response mimicry implied by the term imitation, and the distinguishing properties of identification are too diffuse, arbitrary, and empirically questionable either to clarify issues or to aid scientific inquiry.

6

Discusses the Effects of Modeling Influences in Detail

Children's Perception of Teachers

Children develop a clear idea of the contrast between primary schoolsand secondary schools by the time they are preparing to transfer from one to the other. The picture in their mind is a universal shorthand which they all share and which reflects the way in which the two sorts of schools are contrasted, not only in how they manage the curriculum and organize the school, but in the role of teachers. Primary school children share the view that secondary schools are more important, as well as bigger and more demanding:

In some ways the contrasts between primary schools and secondary schools are obvious. In primary schools children stay in one classroom, supervised by one teacher for the majority of the time. In secondary schools children go from class to class, to be taught by a variety of specialists. One result of this essential difference is that children associate primary schools with peacefulness rather than bustle, with calm rather than bullying and with close personal relationships rather than with impersonal rules. Such a clear view of the distinct and seemingly obvious role of the primary school implies an equally marked view of primary school teachers. By contrast with the secondary school specialist, they are assumed to know everything and to be helpful in everything. But there does not seem to be the same respect attached to such helpfulness as there is to the teacher who is only seen occasionally and who is associated with one specialist subject. The view of the secondary school teacher, by children anticipating the experience, is of someone who does not pay them close attention.

These teachers are seen to be 'strict' as well as distant, demanding more work as well as giving fewer explanations. These anticipations heighten children's perceptions of the primary school teacher. They share a view which seems consistent despite different teaching styles. Underlying the teacher's various roles, children feel that the primary teacher is there to help, and support, and is willing to listen and explain.

When children develop their sense of what makes a good teacher they often imply that the primary teachers stand, at best, for firmness of manner, ability to explain and friendliness. But as we will see, children do not necessarily respect those very qualities that they like. It is as if the very idea of the secondary school as a more fearful place, with bigger children, and bigger gangs, with more organized bullying, and with teachers so intent on their subject that they are indifferent to what takes place in the corridor, proved that it was more significant.

The very security that a primary school affords appears as being rather cosy to the children in their last year, as well as those in their first year at secondary school. The primary school is seen as altogether less demanding.

The primary school teacher, however, possesses particular opportunities because of the relationships which can be made. Many children respond to the idea of having the teacher as a friend.

However, children also accept that the relationship with the teacher has a professional basis. What they hope for from their classteacher is a sense of personal interest and encouragement. When children criticize the ethos of the primary school classroom, then or subsequently they single out how much depends on whether they get on with just one teacher, and how difficult it can be if they do not. In secondary school they do not feel they have to get on closely with any teacher. But the rewards of a good relationship with a primary school teacher are clear.

Children are also sensitive about whether they are liked or not; they want the teacher to 'look at you nicely' and to 'like everyone in the class'. With one or two exceptions they feel confident in their teacher because they feel understood and because they will not be rejected if they want help:

The teacher in the classroom creates a special relationship with both the class as a whole and with individual children. Within their classroom children feel a certain sense of security.

But whilst the classroom itself seems secure, it is placed in the context of the school as a whole, and this conveys a far more authoritarian image. The teacher within the classroom might strike up a special relationship with the children, but remains the teacher, who represents a particular status and clearly defined organization. For children, school represents a series of rules, a code of discipline and a hierarchical authority. Part of the security they feel derives from this sense of an imposed order. None of the children questions the need for rules. Indeed, they are adamant that on practical grounds, rules are not only necessary, but become more necessary as they grow older. Without rules, children imply, there would be chaos.

Children accept the authority of teachers because they see them as part of the edifice of the school, as a place where there needs to be strict control, and clear organization. Teachers need to accept this fact about their position, even if they find it puzzling that children feel so strongly about it. They do know that they can only develop close and friendly relationships within the context of such authority. Children do not like teachers to break down the barriers of their professional status too far. Indeed, children sense the distinction between their own private lives and the kind of working relationships they develop with teachers.

Children accept adult authority as more important than the authority of their peers, but they also accept the authority of their peers over that of adults who do not seem to them to justify, or carry out, the responsibility of authority. Teachers are therefore seen in a somewhat ambiguous light. At one level they are appreciated for their willingness to be friendly, to convey a sense of humour, and to take seriously the individual learning difficulties of children in their classroom. But this is within the context of their status, and their role within the authority of the school. Children's perceptions of what teachers should be like derive from a set of clearly formed normative values. They are based on expectations as much as experience and are shared consistently amongst them. Children feel that teachers should be authoritarian, that they should make decisions and that they should impose order and structure. These are, of course, not the only values that children perceive in teachers, and the ways in which teachers convey such characteristics varies greatly.

Nevertheless primary school teachers are seen as authoritative even if at a less exalted level than their secondary colleagues. Children respect the distance that they keep. They like to see consistency in teachers' behaviour, and this in itself implies a certain distance from children's individual needs. They do not like temporary teachers, partly because they do not know which rules have been negotiated and established. And children feel that they can get the better of teachers who become genuinely upset. One of the essential tasks of primary teachers, which they carry out with great sophistication, is the response to all the children in the classroom.

An experienced teacher knows instinctively whom to cajole, whom to ignore and whom to discipline when there is a sign of disorder in the classroom. But it seems that the teachers who are most closely aware of the needs of all the groups within the classroom are also those who have less highly defined authority in the children's eyes. Children appear not only to see the authoritarian teacher's role as ambiguous, as a tension between the need for control and the need for responsiveness, but develop such a tension in their personal attitudes to teachers strongly as ordinary people, outside their role. This is one reason why secondary school teachers have higher status in their eyes. It is, as if, the more the primary school teachers were appreciated for their openness and concern, the less closely they filled the prevailing sense of status.

Mitman, for example, found that teachers who showed concern for the slower, less gifted children were both flexible and more accurate in their assessment of children's individual abilities and needs. But these same teachers were also rated by the children as significantly lower in the quality of their teaching. It is as if quality of understanding and the ability to deliver information were not only separate, but somehow incompatible in children's eyes. Children's views of the authority of the teacher include the acceptance that part of their role is the suppression of disorder. They are seen not only to represent authority but to impose it. Children need 'people to supervise them' and the people who do that, of course, are teachers; 'teachers are always there to tell you off and that'. The problem with children's notions that they do not have any natural tendency to behave well is that they force teachers into a role which seems alien to the children's interests. Children assume that strict discipline is necessary but they also complain that there is not enough real knowledge of children and their work displayed by teachers. Whilst the children think that their own individual development is most important, the teachers rate staff cooperation as the highest priority. Children do not see much of the staff as a collective group, although they are assumed to be a coherent body, all fulfilling the same role. Instead, children are aware both of their own classteacher and the distinctions between one teacher and another.

Children's view of individual teachers are not normally so subjective. They are capable of giving a clear analysis of the teaching style, and more particularly, the teacher's attitude towards discipline. Teachers do not need reminding how acutely children observe them, and how children absorb clues from all the nuances of behaviour and language The very way in which children are spoken to reveals what the teacher is feeling and demanding, and children find it necessary to anticipate and guess what is being expected.

The better the children are at guessing what the teacher demands, the easier they find it to accommodate to the tasks that are set for them. This naturally means that some children are more adept at manipulating the circumstances to their own advantage than others. Part of the daily excitement of relationships between groups and the teacher in the primary classroom is the testing of the barrier, to see how far children can go in terms of independence or avoiding work, without causing the teachers to react. Pollard calls such children 'jokers': those who do not fit safely in the category of the obviously 'good' nor into the group which is definitely unco-operative.

The children who are best able to take advantage of the teacher are the 'brighter' ones, who both make use of the resulting freedom and make the teacher feel rewarded because they guess what is wanted. Some pupils, therefore, have more power than others over the teacher. Such power does not derive from increased demand, for in the teacher's busy day, there is a sense of relief when children are not insisting on too much help or too much work. If children were constantly demanding more, teachers could not always cope.

It is as if the circumstances of the classroom made it incumbent on all the children not to force the pace too much, to allow for a steady workload than in the end—suits both the children and the teacher. 'Brighter' children show their ability to manipulate, to guess what is wanted, and to please the teacher, even if they are not, or perhaps because they are not, working too hard. Many of these are girls. Boys and girls are aware of the distinction between teachers' attitudes toward them in the primary school, even if it is more apparent later.

Just as children assume that they are all naughty and need some form of discipline, so they notice that boys are more frequently told off, and that they need to be. Boys tend to initiate more interactions with teachers than do girls, and this means that girls receive, in return, less response from the teachers. But then boys also receive many more negative commands and reactions that have nothing to do with work than do girls. Boys accept this as a consequence of their different behaviour patterns.

Whilst children are aware of the developing difference between the sexes it is not something that figures in their attitudes towards teachers as much as in secondary school. Nor do children indicate that it matters to them whether the teacher is a man or a woman. The characteristics of the good teacher are not dependent on gender. When one boy remarks that he likes a 'man and a lady teacher but I prefer a man' it is a reflection of his attitude towards his home life: 'My Mum nags all the time... Ladies nag at home but at school'. The transmission of values, whether from the home, peer groups or school, is a complex matter. Teachers themselves use the way in which children see them, and their own roles, in a variety of ways. Whilst the ambiguity between their authority and their desire to help is at the heart of the way children respond to them, teachers find a variety of means to cajole children into working. They obviously succeed by taking on the attitudes and the policies of the school, standing for collective standards. But they can also withdraw from the institutional bias into a sense their own individual expertise, or their own stated expectations. They also recognize the ambiguity of their own role, just as the children experience it, as both part of a collective or group, and as an autonomous being.

But, however hard teachers try to explore different kinds of relationships, and however hard they strive to create in children a sense of their own autonomy, they are faced with children's perceptions of them as people who control events. Children therefore see praise for their work as recognition that it is 'correct' and that they have discovered the way to please the teacher. They also see criticism as referring to carelessness or lack of effort, as if the work set for them were tasks designed for practice rather than for originality. However hard teachers try, children will tend to interpret their 'open' questions which demand a variety of original responses as 'closed', assuming there is just one possible answer and that any other one is wrong.

Children seem to think they are learning a fixed body of knowledge. They see the teacher as the authority who knows what this is. It is not surprising that children transfer their awareness of what teachers actually intend in matters or organization and control, to the parallel circumstances of knowledge. Teachers use language in a distinctive way in the classroom, for instance with flippant remarks and insults, which are neither meant nor recognized as such and yet would be unusual if employed elsewhere. It is as if a different code were being used, like direct questions which demand nothing but 'closed' implicit responses. 'Could you open the door?' demands an active response, not a thoughtful consideration. 'Do you know the answer?' means 'Tell me'. Teachers' questions are perceived as purveying control and as far as the delivery of the curriculum is concerned, are assumed to be full of instructions. It is as if children assumed that the traffic of work were all one way; with them fulfilling whatever task the teacher wants, and asking the teacher only for help in carrying out that task. This is why it has been found that the teachers who actually ask most questions are least likely to receive questions back from the children.

Furthermore, a battery of questions, far from stimulating children into spontaneous comments or any other contributions, can actually inhibit them from work. And yet questions have an important role to play, despite the suspicions of children. For children also learn information best when they are asked about it, not just because questions are a form of testing but because children, through the teachers questions, see the information as falling into a structure that the teacher is conveying in a subtle manner. Questions are therefore not only seen as a means of conveying information but are used as a means of organizing information. There is one way in which children feel that teachers can help; one gift that is especially appreciated. This ability goes beyond being friendly. It is the willingness and capacity to explain.

Most children assume that at secondary school it will be up to them to 'work' it out, but that in primary school explanations are clearly presented:

This might be interpreted as a pupil's version of 'matching' but in fact children rate the desire to know and understand what they are doing so highly that it affects whatever work they are doing. They enjoy being challenged. They are willing to try new things but want to be able to get help, preferably from the teacher, although they also get help from their friends.

The willingness to be responsive to their individual needs seems to children to mark out the particular virtues of the primary school teacher. But the teacher is not only a responsive agent, waiting for clients behind the desk.

She is someone seen as active in promoting clarity, and is often juxtaposed against the image of the purely distant teacher concerned that children 'get on with it' themselves by picking up information from books.

The primary class is, after all, a collective enterprise, where children also help each other. they know that as a central organizer the teacher makes sure they all join in:

Girl: Instead of standing round the desk all the time and wasting time he reads out the answers. For marking, he gives us nice worksheets instead of using books all the time. He makes them up himself and that makes them better to do. He kind of puts them in his own words. It's easier as well.

Implicit in any analysis of work is the idea of the 'answer'; the correct response. This is true however the class is organized. The teacher needs to explain because the goal is to attain the right answer, or the right skill.

The teacher is seen to balance the needs of the individual with that of the whole class.

Children assume that the teacher's questions are directed towards helping them know the information, and organize the information. The kind of teacher talk that children appreciate is not the general introduction, that seems to keep them awaiting before they get on with the work, but the kind which is directed towards helping them understand how to do the set task. The teacher is there to help them learn the process of work, and not just the information. Children are interested in learning the skills of work, and lay stress on the pleasure of being able to do the work, whilst understanding what they are doing.

The sense of dependence on the teacher is not so much as a conveyor of information as an explainer of how to go about work. When children talk about the curriculum they appreciate the work which seems to them active and engaging. They make a clear distinction between lessons where they are able to work by themselves in an experimental fashion and what they dismiss as 'writing'.

One of the elements of the secondary school to which children look forward is the chance to do 'science' in a laboratory, with interesting experiments. What children do not like is 'doing the same things over and over again' or reading 'the same book so many times'. Interesting topics seem to the children to consist of activities, 'because you have to do things, like washing and cleaning and experiments'. Against this they feel that 'finding the answers is boring'. The sense of the skills of learning is clearly important to them.

Children are not afraid of having demands made on them. 'Easy' work is work they can understand. Once they know how to go about something they recognize the pleasure of doing so.

Children's pleasure in work derives from those moments when they understand the teacher's explanations and the task. The teacher is not just a responsive friendly person, but someone who is supposed to make their tasks interesting. Against the pleasure of doing work, like solving problems, children remember the many occasions when the work is undemanding, repetitive or obscure, so that they don't know how to go about it. There are many circumstances when children feel at a loss; not only when the teacher has not been clear, but when they feel held back by the lack of resources.

The bright child might be able to use the circumstances better, but this is often because he is not making too many demands. The child who does stand out can be difficult to contain within the usual practices of the classroom. Often the work of school seems to children to consist of nothing but routine.

Children are demanding clients. They want all the work geared to their individual needs, and yet derive security from being in the class, working together. They assume that the teacher will know the answers to questions and yet give them the means to find them out for themselves. They want to work to the teacher's formula and attain help from the teacher and yet learn a great deal from each other. They all say that they like to work with a friend for their mutual benefit. They all expect the teacher to be fair and to know what is going on in the social tensions of their own peer group. They expect the teacher to be responsive, and yet see hei as a distant authority.

Most difficult of all, children, in discussing the problems of school, say that the most important question is the friendliness or the distance of the teacher. And yet they also respect the most those teachers who seem to be most distant, most authoritative, and most associated with expertise in a particular subject. All this put primary teachers in an ambiguous position. Children see the complexity of their role. It is as if the attitudes towards primary schools generally prevalent in society were already being engendered in the children before they leave. They already see the secondary school as more 'important'; not only because of the examination system, and the assumption that schools are there to prepare them for jobs, but because the teachers are experts within their own classrooms, on particular areas of the curriculum. The very ability of primary school teachers to create a harmonious working atmosphere, and to deal with a variety of different subjects, is both admired by the children and seen as only a stage towards the real work they will be undertaking later, the one aspect of the role of the primary teacher that children never quite forget, is the individual attention, explanation and concern.

7
Parent's Role in Child Education

Investigations into parent-child exchanges have pointed differences in the abilities of parents to teach their children effectively. Maternal teaching styles varied widely from limited, reactive teaching to effective parental use of suggestions, instructions, modeling; and pointing out critical perceptual cues; emphasis being that a democratic home atmosphere as well as maternal acceleration of intellectual achievement was significantly associated with high achievement of children by the fifth grade.

Meticulous research by Hess and Shipman demonstrated differences in maternal teaching strategies of black mothers from different socioeconomic groups. The mothers were asked to teach their four-year-olds how to sort blocks by different attributes and how to create geometric designs with an Etch-A-Sketch toy. The children's task success and IQ could be predicted from maternal teaching behaviours. Low-social-class mothers offered predetermined solutions and few alternatives for consideration and choices.

A decade later, Bee and colleagues were even more specific in pointing out the social class differences in teaching strategies which support or impede problem-solving success. The middle-class mother tended to allow her child to work at his own pace. She offered many general structuring suggestions on how to search for a solution to the problem. She confirmed the child's correct actions so that he could acquire general methods to use in future problem-solving solutions. In contrast, the lower-class mother as a rule did not encourage the child to attend to the basic features of the problem. her suggestions were highly specific, did not emphasize strategies, and seldom required a reply from the child. By nonverbal intrusions into the child's attempts, she often deprived the child of the opportunity to solve the problem on his own.

Research within social class as well as across social class confirmed the crucial nature of family variables in relation to learning progress of children. Resnick found that the amount of conversation in the home, particularly talk, was directed toward the child's performance on tests. Yet, all families in his project were low-income. Wolf and Dave also related family process variables to child achievement. Another important research area helped to focus parent involvement efforts more broadly on the total development of the child. Parents are not only the first and most consistently available teachers of their young children, but they also provide the emotional base of security and the motivational roots that nourish exploratory curiosity. An infant well attached to a nurturant parent who is sensitive to infant cues and signals and who offers baby floor freedom to explore living space tends to be developmentally advanced.

Securely attached babies, when tested in toddlerhood, proved to be more persistent in solving problems. They had less temper and tended to use the parent as a resource to help them solve problems more often than poorly attached children. Thus, if parent involvement was to focus only on cognitive aspects of parental teaching, important emotional aspects that support learning might be neglected. The attachment literature suggests that loving attachment between tutor and child in the family situation sets the occasion for success in attending to learning problems and in consolidating learning experiences in order to solve problems. Even under adverse socioeconomic circumstances, many families give clues for ways in which parent involvement programs can work to support such efforts.

Swan and Stavros interviewed parents of low-income black five-and six-year-old children who were effective classroom learners. These children got along well with peers and teachers. They exhibited sustained, self-motivated learning styles. Parents described these children in a very positive and competent light. The parents fostered independence and encouraged the children to help in the home. They read to their children and talked about a wide range of topics.

Positive parenting dimensions were also pinpointed by Carew, Chan, and Halfar. Their naturalistic home observations revealed what family variables correlated with preschooler competence across social class. Honig provides a summary of positive parenting practices that enhance child competence.

Parent involvement became the indispensible ingredient for engendering optimal learning habits in children and for sustaining the accomplishments of enrichment programs. Some experts concluded that for teachers "to work with children alone is to invite failure and frustration". Others agreed with Chilman that basic income maintenance for poor people "must undergird any programme that seeks to deal effectively with poverty and disadvantaged parents and children". Chilman urged the need for individual counseling, supportive services, and participation in the school. The new thrust to involve parents resulted in federally mandated guidelines for adding a parent involvement component to already existing preschool programs such as Head Start. Whenever an agency provides day care for forty or more children, the Federal interagency guidelines state that there must be a policy advisory committee, the composition of which must include not less than 50 per cent parents or parent representatives. It is difficult to capture the richness of national effort. Gordon's analysis of specific programs suggests a way of listing conditions, variables, and parameters of a program in a column on the left side of a sheet. Program names are listed horizontally at the top of the page. An X can indicate the presence of that particular variable for a program. Such an array permits ready visual comparison of the qualities, comprehensiveness, and unique aspects of different programs.

The theory behind home visitation emphasizes the continuing impact that a parent can have as a support for and facilitator of the child's learning long after other program supports are terminated. Gordon pioneered the development of the home visitation model, and there are now well over 200 such programs in operation. Gordon envisaged that using trained para-professionals, costs could be curtailed and greater empathy and close rapport could be established between the worker and the low-income parents served. Such rapport would enhance the probability that the home visitor would be accepted as a model by the parents. In this project, the primary focus was on teaching the mother learning games during a weekly home visit. The games were based on Piagetian sensory-motor competencies, and a copy of a new game was left in the home weekly, so that the mother could try out the learning activities whenever she found time. Activities were ordered by area of competence, such as object-permanence games, and were graded by level of difficulty. Significantly higher general quotients for trained infants were found on the Griffith's Mental Development Scale for 127 trained versus eighty-four control infants. Trained infants also scored significantly higher on personal social skills; hand-eye coordination, and hearing and speech skills. Testing was done between one and two years of age. Lally has documented both the positive strengths and the pitfalls encountered.

Some of the problems encountered in training were:

1. Difficulty in getting abstract ideas communicated both from training staff to parent educators and from parent educators to mothers.

2. Missionary zeal at project commencement which turns to boredom or disillusionment as parents show reluctance to become involved with infants or as infants fail to show rapid intellectual growth.

3. Rigid use of the training materials without regard to whether an activity was far above or far below the level of the child's present functioning.

4. Reluctance to accept responsibilities for filling out weekly home visit forms and engage in other research data collection and record-keeping efforts.

5. Difficulty in accepting freedom to program own time and still be responsible for making all home visits.

6. Lack of patience with some families who did not cooperate.

7. Resentment that professionals would never understand all the hardships and difficulties that can happen in the field.

8. A desire to work directly with the infants rather than with the mothers.

These problems do not negate the valuable contribution to family involvement that the paraprofessionals made. Their insights into family difficulty and their ability to help some parents feel at ease with and accepting toward the project were often remarkable. Staff problems were dealt with in a variety of ways. Gordon's projects established the viability and vigour of the home visitation model and its unique effectiveness when family difficulty with transportation or family reluctance to venture out into "institutional" settings may effectively close out a family from receiving needed service. Home visitation has since become a widespread method of delivery of support for families with the goal of enhancing early development through work with the parent. Home visits may also serve as an adjunct to group services provided primarily for children, as in Head Start programs in many communities.

Through demonstration and practice, the visitors teach mothers at home how to provide facilitating sensori-motor experiences and language games for their infants. Particularly emphasized are ways in which parents can use daily interactions and caregiving situations with infants to create learning occasions and opportunities. Exercises and games appropriate to the level of development of the baby are taught each week; sample fact sheets describing the purpose of each new game and ways to carry out the game are left with mothers. The home visitor focuses on the parent as the important person to work with rather than the baby.

Educational programs for parents are often delivered as the integral component for a demonstration research project. The Ypsilanti-Carnegie Infant Education Project demonstrated that a Piagetian-based curriculum could be implemented in the home for low-income parents and their infants in order to enhance the mother's ability to optimize her infant's cognitive development. The goal of Levenstein's Verbal Interaction Project was to prevent educational disadvantage by aiding the two-year-old's early cognitive growth within the family. The mother-child home program was designed to strengthen parents in their conviction and know how to be verbally active teachers of their own toddlers. Levenstein has stressed the importance of training and supervision in the success of her home visitors who are called toy demonstrators. Her program is very cost-effective and securely places responsibility for the learning process with parents not project personnel. The toy demonstrator's role requires development of a warm relationship with the mother and child, demonstration of verbal stimulation techniques, and the development of maximum mother participation. The toy demonstrator visits each pair twice a week for a half-hour home session.

On the first visit each week she brings either a toy or a book which she uses as Verbal Interaction Stimulus material. She introduces the VISM to the child, encouraging it to talk by asking questions, listening to answers, and replying. At the same time, she draws the mother into the session by modeling verbal stimulation techniques, which the mother then imitates. She also encourages the mother to read and play with the child between home sessions. During the year, eleven toys and twelve books are brought to the home to stimulate the mother-child verbal interaction. The model program was run with professionals, and a mean IQ gain of about 17 points was found. The second year, trained paraprofessionals, recipients of the program themselves, were toy demonstrators. Mean IQ gain was 11 points. Replications show that "satisfactory IQ scores were retained by program graduates at least into first grade". At the end of a two-year program for replication, the treated children had a Stanford-Binet score of 104.8 and the control children scored 100.9. These replication results are not as per expectations the promise of the model program. Possibly because many more of the original families had fathers present in the home and were not on welfare.

When the home visitation model is used in connection with a research and demonstration project, the process generally includes assessment of family needs, planning, implementation—including role modeling by home visitors for parents on how to teach activities and follow-up procedures. Sometimes, a home visit includes several aspects. There may be a brief period of prescribed activities aimed at the target child in the family at the same time that the parent is taught a given lesson to be carried out with the child. There may be a period of group activities for other children in the home. Often, there is a period in which the home visitor discusses some of the family's needs as expressed by parents.

Child development information, including nutrition and health information is also given. Other information relative to family needs may be supplied, such as how to contact the nearest family planning clinic or how to find low-cost legal services. Forrester describes such a home visitation project, the DARCEE program at George Peabody College. In weekly visits, mothers were provided with the coping skills and assurance they needed to handle the job of being their preschool child's teacher at the end of a year of program participation. Sometimes, unless certain crucial fundamentals, such as establishing friendly, trusting relations are accomplished, the cognitive aspects of program may prove undeliverable.

In Adkin's program in Hawaii, home visitors were to deliver specific language or mathematics curricular lessons for parents to boost the learning of their children who were enrolled in preschool projects emphasizing such areas. Many mothers simply were not at home time and again, despite carefully made appointments. The parents assigned to one home visitor, however, were home and available. That worker had made sure that she always took time to listen to family problems and to develop a helpful and friendly relationship with the mothers she served. There is little sense in assessing the "impact" of a program when most home visits cannot be made. Only as they feel that they are cared about will many families begin to give back the active learning and participation desired. Weikart has pointed out that the home teacher is in a position of low power in the home and must adjust to the pre-eminent position of the parent in her or his own home. Certainly, not all classroom teachers will qualify as home teachers under these conditions.

Some home visitation projects are more concerned with provision of emotional support and the building of self confidence in families than they are with educational curricula. Van Doorninck reports on a project in which there was an attempt at a parametric variation of the intensity of supportive parent involvement efforts. Pregnant mothers were assigned randomly to one of three treatment groups: (1) routine services of the local health department clinics; (2) home visits weekly through the baby's first birthday by trained visitors; and (3) home visit plus invitations to parent group meetings held every two weeks during the same time period.

The purpose of the home visitor was "to provide support to parents, especially mothers, so as to help them cope with their own lives and enhance their abilities to care for their children" No significant treatment effects were found for measures such as maternal attachment, material perception of self- confidence as a mother, use of community helping service, or mother's educational efforts for herself. The project staff reported that about one-third of the full-treatment group seemed to have little or no overall benefit. They speculated that lack of hard data might be due to the overall excellent level of existing community health services for mothers. The project continued only during the first postnatal year and on the average no more than two home visits of 60 minute each were made per month. Few mothers attended parent group meetings more than a few times.

Sensory-motor tests of infant development rarely reflect rearing milieu differences before one year, the time at which this program was terminated. The lack of any specific educational goals may also be implied in the lack of "hard" effects found. Some families need long-term efforts of support before family involvement with project goals becomes visible. Parent involvement may take long commitment to some families. A clinical model which presents no outcome data but is characterized by an interesting theoretical rubric is the UCLA Material Behavior Progression Program. The initial emphasis is on enhancing the quality of mother-infant interaction. This goal requires constant assessment of the mother's feelings toward and skills with the baby.

The six levels of Maternal Behaviour Progression which the staff or team assists a mother to achieve are:

(1) mother enjoys infant; (2) mother is a sensitive observer of her infant; (3) mother engages in a quality and quantity of interaction with her infant that is mutually satisfying and provides opportunity for the development of attachment and the beginning of a system of communication; (4) mother demonstrates an awareness of materials, activities, and experiences suitable for the infant's current stage of development; (5) mother independently generates a wide range of developmentally appropriate experiences, (6) interesting to the infant and adaptive to changing needs.

Bromwich objects to parent intervention models that teach a mother how to play with baby. She feels that optimization of parenting can best be approached by enhancing the mother-infant relationship and quality of interaction at the basic level first and then building maternal confidence level by level. Thus, Bromwich combines clinical plus educational components in a progressive model that evolves as the parent shows signs of being ready for different aspects of this home visitation model. The emphasis on observation skills is fundamental to a parent program. They ensure project sensitivity to present level of parents understanding and parents' involvement. Many programs are designed to help child-abusing families with home visitation. Child abuse is epidemic at about 2,000 cases per day in the United States. Some projects use two home visitors-one to support the parents and be a parent friend and advocate and another to work on child development activities.

Fraiberg used a kitchen therapy intervention model to reach abusive mothers of infants. A skilled, highly trained therapist continues weekly with home visits to build a trusting, caring relation with the neglecting and/ or abusing parent. Only as the therapist reaches deeply into the earlier childhood experiences of the young mother do changes occur. As the young mother begins to feel with and for her baby, she may suddenly hear that her baby has been crying for twenty minutes in the living room; and she may run and pick and comfort the infant. The home visitation model has proved successful in clinical programs that deal with cases of disturbed parenting and failure-to-thrive babies. A succinct synopsis of a variety of such clinical infant programs, their research goals, and the assessment instruments they are currently using, has been published by the National Center for Clinical Infant Programs. Many state education departments have worked hard to help teachers of handicapped children look at parents as a sources of stimulation for the children. The most common approach is to have the parent educator come into the home and work with both mothers and their handicapped children. At the University of Wisconsin, counseling as well as practical guidance is provided for parents of blind infants.

The home visitor focuses on helping a parent establish a personal relationship with her blind infant and showing the parent how to interest her child in such activities as discovering, grasping objects, and crawling. At the Shield of David program in the Bronx, New York, a home visitor worked with the parent of a retarded two-and-a-half-year old on: (1) selecting a more varied diet; (2) suggesting exercises to use with her child on the playground; (3) toilet training; (4) how to associate articles of clothing with specific body parts; and (5) how to make contact with other children. Frost has commented that members of the family with a child at risk for developmental delay reinforce one another in caregiving attitudes and practices. To be successful, the parents must recognize and accept the child's problems. Helping the mother to learn positive caregiving practices may be less important for what it does for the handicapped child than what it does for the parent. Home-centered training for handicapped or retarded children does not divorce the child from his strongest emotional ties and his most diverse models the family members. Nor is there any problem of "transfer of training" from an institutional setting to the home. Frost reports that "researchers are still unsure about persisting effects of long-term intervention. Short-term effects are positive and significant." The Wisconsin Portage Project provides parents with activities for multihandicapped preschoolers.

Most of the families served live in rural areas so that the home visitation model is more feasible and useful. Parents are taught how to write a behavioral prescription and how to keep daily frequency records of behaviors being learned. They are taught what to teach, what to reinforce, and how to shape behaviors through the technique of initially providing and then "fading out" reinforcements. Each child is assigned individual weekly goals which can be achieved within the week regardless of severity of handicap. The parent is left with written materials and encouraged to carry out each activity several times daily and record what happens.

Levenstein has analyzed ethical problems of the home-based intervention model. Because home visitors are generally so strongly and lovingly committed to their work, it may be difficult for a family to think of a reason to resist participation. Also, the degree to which confidentiality about family matters as well as minimal intrusiveness into family privacy can be managed may be problematic.

Skill mismatch may occur when family lifestyles or problems require more knowledge and ability than a home visitor can provide. The right to worker acknowledgement of a need for further help or professional adjunct services may be a healthy item for a home-based program to keep in mind.

The most comprehensive home visitation model, Home Start, was launched as an alternative to provision of Head Start services through group child care. The objectives of the Home Start program are to strengthen parents' capacity for facilitating the development of other children and for direct supports not only for early childhood education but also for good nutrition, use of social services, budgeting, use of medical and dental facilities, creation of social networks for families,obtaining scarps and materials so parents can create toys and learning activities, and ways that household activities can be turned into learned games.

The home visitation component has served to create a secure base of mutually shared goals in a trusting atmosphere for branching out to other forms of family enrichment for children. Parents in the second year of the program participated daily in classroom activities with their children.

The reasons for the movement toward parent involvement are often based on the experiences of dedicated professionals trying to work exclusively with children. Poulton and Poulton found in a poor Yorkshire, England, community, for example, that after the first eighteen months, "a more important factor in early education than curricular design and approaches was the degree of understanding and preparation of parents as educators of their children".

More and more sophisticated ways were found to involve mothers and fathers in the education of their children. These children did better on the English PPVT after one year of such parent involvement. Unless the parents could be shown their educative role with their children, the Poultons found that there was little chance of maintaining any momentum gained through the children's early childhood education experiences. Introductory family visits were very important in establishing trust in a future partnership. Soon parents made arrangements to spend an afternoon once or twice a week at the preschool.

The Sumber Mobile Preschool Program in Syracuse, New York, is a program in which mothers serve as teachers in their own home with the supervision of a trained teacher. The local teacher chauffeurs a few children from the neighborhood surrounding the local elementary school to the home of a neighborhood mother.

Gradually, as toys, activities, concepts of numbers and counting, and taking turns, for example, are modeled by the supervisor, the home mother comes to take over more and more responsibility for teaching activities with the group of preschoolers who attend in her home for a half-day. Gordon and Guinagh's Back Yard Center program had a similar concept. Mothers in whose homes preschool activities occurred for a small group of children were employed as helpers to the backyard center directors. These directors themselves were paraprofessionals who had served earlier as teachers in Gordon's home visitation program.

Juniper Garden Preschool in Kansas City, Missouri, was a token-reinforcement preschool for culturally deprived four-year-olds. With the premise that, in the long run, more child progress could be achieved if parents of the children were involved, the staff began to provide lessons for mothers on how to teach their preschoolers. The thirty mothers chosen were characterized as from "upwardly mobile poverty families." Each mother was rewarded with dinner ware each week for coming to preschool with her child. Every day, each mother at first retired to a booth with materials to teach her child. Initial findings were that "the mothers were poor teachers. They used almost no praise or approval, and they showed little grasp of the technique of attacking complex problems by starting with its simplest form". Changes in the program were then introduced. The mothers were given instructions on how to start with the simplest tasks. They were to praise a child for each correct response, such as naming an object pictured. Mothers were then paired with children other than their own. Threats to children subsequently decreased. Teachers kept records of when a mother praised. They flashed a red light, mounted where the mother could see it. Mothers were asked to press a foot pedal whenever a child answered a question correctly. After a mother had learned how to praise another child, she again was allowed to work with her own child. Mothers also worked as classroom teachers.

In unstructured situations in the classroom, mothers found some difficulty in putting principles of positive reinforcement into practice. Staff continued work with the principle that mothers were to reinforce with attention only that behavior that they wanted the children to continue. From the beginning to the end of the program, the children's PPVT IQs rose from a mean of 69 to 87. One of the best known methods of involving parent in the education of their children is to invite them to parent group meetings, usually at a school which the child attends. Programs which involve parents of preschoolers in groups have sometimes opted for cognitive emphasis, for example, on teaching mothers how to improve children's language skills. Other parent groups have focused on:

- increasing parental self-awareness
- knowledge of ways to motivate children
- expression of parental needs
- home management skills
- making and learning to use inexpensive home learning materials
- increasing self-esteem in the family
- helping parents acquire job skills.

One of the most widely used models for helping parents use toys to teach their children was created by Nimnicht et al., at the Far West Parent/Child Toy Library Program. Parents are involved in eight two-hour sessions, usually meeting once a week. Child development topics are discussed and a new toy is introduced at each meeting. The toy as a means to boost children's problem-solving skills is demonstrated, discussed, and illustrated in films. Parents at the group meeting role-play with each other the many ways they could use a toy to promote thinking and problem solving. They use these ideas later at home with the toy to help the child make discoveries and increase his skills.

Stevens has reported that an eleven-week program of small group parent meetings which included toy/book demonstrations and lending produced significant IQ gains for children of project participants. He suggests that the parent consultants would have been even more effective had they provided feedback to a parent during his or her interaction with a child in the home. Programs that involve parents in their child's school learning may be particularly crucial for culturally different or non-English-speaking children. A variety of commercial programs exist to establish such linkages between home and school experiences. One such is Amanecer developed in San Antonio, Texas.

Based on the theories of Piaget, Montessori, and Maslow, the model was developed as part of the Head Start strategy for Spanish-speaking children. Teachers are helped to initiate parent contacts, plan parent learning activities, organize parent projects, and create a culturally sensitive learning environment. The goal is to increase the process by which parents become valuable resources in planning and implementing the curriculum for young children.

Parent workshops or group meetings are often inaugurated as supportive services to ensure at-home continuity of teaching with the learnings of the child in an educational setting. Karnes and colleagues provided a mothers' group meeting along with an enriched preschool for the children. However, no significant added effect of the parent group was found beyond score enhancement found for preschool alone.

In contrast, Gray has reported encouraging results for mother participation plus child preschool experience. IQs of children whose mothers were into the parent group remained relatively stable after two years: IQs of children with preschool only decreased further during that same time span. Boger and colleagues arranged for groups of mothers to meet in twelve weekly two-hour sessions with their children's teacher in a developmental or structured language workshop or in a placebo group workshop.

The mothers who participated in the specific language interaction groups increased their own language skills. Their children also increased in language skills and have a more positive perception of their mother's view of them compared to placebo treatment group children. This program has been replicated with rural as well as urban parents. "Education for Parenthood" recently has served as a parenting program curriculum for many Head Start project parenting groups. The program provides three learning modules: working with children; seeing development; and family and society. Parents gain insight not only into children's development but also into themselves as learners. Keeping a journal and learning to observe children are program techniques that help sensitize parents to their children. Lane the director of the NICE program in California, was an early believer in the importance of parent participation in the classroom. Lane further advanced the NICE program goal of helping parents to be more effective teachers of their own and others' children by creating training classes taught by the director and staff members of NICE. The classes met for two hours once a week for fifteen consecutive weeks. Each participant parent was required to spend one day per week at the nursery school trying out ideas discussed in the class. Each parent was required to learn to observe and record the behavior of a child and read the report in class.

In addition, parents shared their backgrounds, their dreams for their children, feelings about their own childhood, and problems they had with their children and with each other. The parents drew much closer together, although they came from quite different backgrounds. Mothers were judged by the staff to be competent enough to operate the school classes one day per week with the assistance of graduate students. Staff used this time for meetings. Several parents developed a degree of competency that qualified them as teacher aides. Parents became involved in assessing the program of the public schools to get to know the types of class programs their preschoolers would soon be entering. Parents developed considerable confidence in their own resources.

Public school systems, too, often use parents as supports for children's learning. The Benton Harbor Area schools in Michigan have formed a home-school-community partnership, in a Title I project called Project Help. This model provides for a group of teachers to design together with parents a series of activities that will work to support children's school learning in their community. Activities are written recipe-style on a single piece of paper. They are short, easy activities that use kitchen items or living room furniture, for example. These lessons build on school learnings. There are special advantages to the model when parents participate creatively in planning for experiences in the schools in which their children are already enrolled. As parents learn early education skills, they must examine their goals and values concerning children in order to develop curriculum, select facilities and equipment, and even hire teachers.

Parent education groups are often active in programs for handicapped children. Methods of encouraging parents to attend meetings include providing transportation, paying for baby-sitters, writing or calling parents in advance of meeting, and arranging small groups for those who seem uncomfortable at larger meetings. Other group techniques include showing parents videotapes of their interactions with their children and encouraging a parent-child album. The Portland Center for Hearing and Speech taught parents of language-delayed children in weekly sessions. Parents observed their children's language, enrichment program. The meetings had two purposes: (1) to discuss information about home management of communications problems; and (2) to provide emotional support for parents.

The children's progress during their eight-week summer session typically revealed an average of about six to nine months gain in general language functioning and in receptive vocabulary. What parts the parents' efforts played and what part the individualized curriculum played in such gains is not discernible, nor is it known how long these gains lasted. What is clear is that parents rated their own knowledge of factors affecting special problems higher after their group experience.

Some programs for handicapped children use a wide variety of parent involvement techniques. The Delayed Development Project in Stockton, California, for example, provides home visitation for children under eighteen months. From that age on, babies are induced into a program with individual therapy and small group activities. Parents spend one morning a week in school with their tots. "Dad's Day" classes are held on Saturdays. Evening group meetings with a psychologist allow parents to support each other as they discuss their fears, hopes, anxieties, and problems.

Bricker and Bricker, in their program for integration of Down's Syndrome and normal preschoolers have consistently involved parents in care-giving activities toward behavioral goals. Bassin & Drovetta report that parent-to-parent contact is particularly helpful when trained parents help those who are newly facing the problems that ensue with the birth of a handicapped child. Their St. Louis, Missouri, program trains parents to help each other with jargon-free explanations about disabilities, helpful hints on home training, and assistance in locating community resources. There are about 700 programs around the country that try to help pregnant teenagers and their babies.

"Education for Parenthood" was originally designed as a multimedia program to help teenagers learn about children and how to care for them. Badger brought groups of low-income teenage mothers into group meetings in a hospital setting during evenings when the teenagers were not at jobs or continuing their schooling. Her program offered a wide variety of information and skills at levels that these very young mothers can understand. Demonstrations of infant competencies, talks on good nutrition and infant care, encouragement of affectionate mother-infant contact were among the activities.

Young mothers were challenged when they exhibited attitudes of withdrawal and hopelessness. Honig noted that Badger's own enthusiasm for positive parenting practices was a major ingredient in encouraging some of these young mothers to become involved with their babies. Many programs for teen parents not only focus on parenting and child development skills, but they also encourage continuation toward a high school diploma by offering special educational programs housed in a building where infant care is also provided. Innovative and flexible programming is needed to deal with the national "epidemic" of teen parenting.

The Family Development Research Program and Children's Center in Syracuse, New York, has tried to actualize an "omnibus model". Paraprofessional home visitors, indigenous to the low-income community, brought nutritional, child development, and child care information to pregnant mothers.

After the infant's birth, the family was taught special games to encourage visual alerting, hand-eye coordinations, and vocalizations. Mothers were encouraged to improve their own and their babies' diets. At six months, infants entered the Children's Center, a developmental day-care program. Families continued to be visited by the Child Development Trainers (CDTs), and parents continued to receive child development information and skills until the child reached school age. Language, sensory-motor, and later proportional games and tasks as well as child-management ideas and techniques were presented. CDTs lent toys and books. They provided information and references to community resources to help with legal aid, health care, housing, food stamps, and other problems. They provided loyal friendships to mothers often beset with severe emotional, sexual, social, and financial crises. CDTs served as liaison persons between the parent and the center.

Complaint department, information clearing house about center activities, escort service for parents visiting the center, participant in parent group monthly discussion meetings, active worker at weekly parent workshops, bearer of special family news a teacher may need to know-all these roles filed by the CDT as her repertoire of family-facilitating skills expanded. CDTs held parent group meetings in homes for those parents who were interested in group discussion about special topics. Topics which parents requested included effective parent participation in the public school after the child entered the school, sexuality and early childhood, and working mothers and young children.

The FDRP gave particular attention to the importance of selection, preservice, and in-service training of the home visitors. The paraprofessionals initially underwent eight weeks of training in nutrition, health, interviewing techniques, and games and activities to facilitate early cognitive development.

At forty-eight months, FDRP children were significantly ahead of low-education matched control groups on all seven ITPA language subtests used. By seventy-two months, however, these differences were no longer found. Stanford-Binet mean scores for program children at forty-eight months and seventy-two months were 100 and 109 respectively, compared to 101 and 105 for low-education controls and 136 and 138 for high-education contrast group children. Thus, program children were functioning well in early elementary school grades but they lagged markedly in IQ scores compared to children from intact, college-educated families. One of the most comprehensive program efforts to involve families of preschoolers in enhancing living and learning conditions for their children is the Child and Family Resource Program (CFRP), a national Head Start demonstration program, which was initially funded in June 1973. CFRP uses Head Start as a base for developing a community-wide service delivery network.

A key feature of CFRP programs is flexibility and thoroughness in meeting family and child needs. This individualization and tailoring of programs to fit each family is a strength that augurs well for the success of CFRP programs. Another feature of CFRP programs is the attempt to involve resources in each community to serve the diagnostic and remediation needs of family members. A third is the provision of continuity of services from the prenatal period through early elementary school years. The fourth objective of CFRP is to enhance an build upon the strengths of the individual family as a child-rearing system with distinct values, culture, and aspirations. A variety of innovative programs for parents has arisen as parents needs are articulated ever more clearly.

Locales and program personnel may be non-traditional. Pediatricians' offices serve as a meeting place for parents as does the storefront "Parent Place" and outpatient waiting rooms of hospital pediatric services. Hot lines provide instant telephone information and comfort to parents who need help in coping with early child rearing and educating. Libraries institute toy and book lending programs. Grass-roots self-help parenting-education groups are being started in many communities by mothers who find they need to learn with each other and share their problems and adventures in child rearing. Programs that dovetail home visits and parenting activities with television programs for children have proved cost-effective and are widely accepted.

The Look-At-Me television series highlights discipline, family relationships, child emotions, and how parents can nurture child curiosity and learning. TV guides to stimulate family discussion are available from Prime Time School Television in Chicago. Many publications and audio-visual media are now available as self-help guides for parents. Some materials are designed primarily to help parents develop positive communication systems and loving relationships with children. Examples are books by Bessell and Kelly ad Ginott. Other packages can be used in parent groups with a leader. Gordon's "Parent Effectiveness Training" is the most famous of these programs. Parents are taught how to use "no lose" problem solving techniques, appropriate "I" and "You" messages, and "Active Listening" to help increase positive family communication. Interviews with parents who have undergone PET reveal ways in which the program helped families.

The Systematic Parent Effectiveness Training Program teaches parents how to analyze the goals of children's misbehaviors and positive behaviors and to respond in ways to increase the latter. Both these programs deal more with parents of school-age children. Some self-help materials are designed for specific parenting groups, such as Spanish-speaking parents or low-literacy parents. New Reader's Press in Syracuse, New York, has parenting materials and activities designed for readers with less than a fifth-grade education. Shure and Spivack have taken a problem-solving approach to training low-income parents and teachers of inner-city children to teach the children to generate solutions to interpersonal problems and to foresee consequences of their own behaviors in such a way that the children can make better adjustments: "To date, the most powerful ICPS mediator in young children appears to be the ability to conceptualize multiple solutions to interpersonal problems and, the ability to anticipate the consequences of acts". These findings continued to hold up in comparison to control children one year later.

Those mothers who consistently applied problem-solving techniques when real-life problems arose had children who improved most in ICPS thinking skills and subsequent behavioral adjustment. The kinds of dialogues and scripts that are taught, of course, require that parents acquire new thinking skills of their own. "Training parents to think through solutions to interpersonal problems and to anticipate the consequences of acts helps them appreciate the very thinking process they in turn learn to transmit to their children". Research findings from parent involvement programs lead to some considerations that should be weighed when launching, or evaluating parent programs.

1. Some parents in the program may do well with a one-year postnatal support service; others require long-term postnatal support services, even through the early grades of elementary school.

2. Some parents may feel uncomfortable about direct, immediate participation in certain models. After trust-building, a program can move into the second stage, such as parent participation in the classroom or parent group meetings.

3. Having parents present in classrooms without systematically helping them to notice how children learn and how to use positive reinforcing methods is "pseudo-parent involvement".

4. Parents may be an excellent source of help to other parents in a program. Parents with handicapped newborns may best accept help, advice, and information from other parents who have been through similar experiences.

5. Professionals may be best equipped to provide some parenting education services and interventions.

6. Trained paraprofessionals may be the most fitting choice for work with some groups of parents, whose children are at risk for cultural-educational retardation.

7. Flexibility is important if parent involvement efforts are to match the needs of families served.

8. A program may need to mix modalities of involvement. Home-based intervention, plus parent group meetings, plus parent participation in classroom, plus clinical therapy sessions, have been

used in intensive efforts to ameliorate and stabilize the family situation with abusive parents.

9. Parent involvement programs that focus only on cognitive development games, may not develop sufficient rapport with families so that home visits can be made regularly.

10. Fathers may need special parent involvement efforts. Tuck found that male workers with special training could best involve fathers living in a low-income urban housing project in learning and play interactions with their preschoolers.

11. Retraining or team-centered efforts may well be necessary or indispensable when a child-care program adds a parenting component.

12. Total reliance on volunteers to provide parenting training may jeopardize program goals.

13. New educational needs arise as children grow and a program continues. New developmental. Problems may become a concern to parents.

14. Strong support systems are imperative to prevent burn-out in parents and involves working with families with multiple problems.

15. Disturbances in the ecological system in which a family lives may vitiate parent involvement efforts focused exclusively on change in early education practices.

16. Charismatic leaders may be more responsible for significant program gains than a particular model, strategy, or theory that informs delivery services. Styles of communication, caring for families, and sharing developmental knowledge may be as

important as particular lesson plans, activities, or theories endorsed.

17. The focus of a parent involver's job may need to be widened if project successes are to accrue. Galvanizing parents to become their child's special early teacher and educational advocate for the future may also require offering help in some management skills, problem-solving strategies, job training, medical and other community service referrals, self-advocacy course for parents, and so on.
18. Assessment of parent involvement efforts requires the wisdom of Solomon. Program effects may be gained through vertical diffusion, with younger siblings.

Radin and collegues found that the effects of an intensive effort at parent involvement showed up one year later. Projects should measure target-child change and impact on the trained parent. Intangible changes in the child's surroundings may also positively affect the learning environment. Achievement scores may be significantly higher for experimental children even when IQ gains "wash out." Assessments that focus on psychometric measures only may overlook significant changes in unobtrusive measures or demographic variables. The number of repeat pregnancies which involved young parents may drop in comparison to untrained parents. Parents may take part more in neighhorhood and community groups.

Lazar and Darlington found two highly stable demographic differences for early education programs both with and without parent involvement components: (1) fewer children were retained in grade; and (2) fewer children were placed in special education classes.

Children of trained mothers may achieve a high school equivalency diploma more easily than controls. Assessments that lump all parents in the program together in contrast to untrained parents may underestimate program effects.

For the purpose of learning clinically more about the variables that might predict parent involvement success, it might be useful to break assessment findings into two kinds: (1) those that compare trained and untrained parents; and (2) those that compare trained parents who changed with those who did not and contrast both these groups with control parents.

8

Learning in Primary Classroom

The amount of time the pupil spends actively engaged on a particular topic is seen as the most important determinant of achievement on that topic. The measurement of this time is generally referred to as time on task, pupil involvement, or engagement. In this approach the pupil is the central focus, with the teacher seen as the manager of the attention and time of pupils in relation to the educational ends of the classroom. Research based on this approach has consistently linked pupil achievement to the quantity and pacing of instruction. Specifically the amount learned is related to opportunity to learn, measured, at its broadest, by the length of school day; by the time allowed for the study of different subjects in the curriculum; and by the amount of time pupils spend actively engaged on their tasks.

These findings have been developed into a prescriptive model of direct instruction from which teachers are urged to run structured, orderly, teacher-directed classrooms, with clear academic focus, frequent monitoring, and supervision, while maintaining a warm and encouraging climate. However, time, or involvement, while necessary conditions, are not sufficient for learning. Exhortations to increase curriculum time, or to improve level of pupils involvement, are of no avail if the quality of the curriculum tasks themselves is poor, not worthwhile, or not related to children's attainments.

Consequently, contemporary thinking about teaching and learning has shifted the focus from time to the nature and quality of classroom tasks as they are worked under normal classroom conditions and constraints, i.e. to the interaction of teachers, pupils, and tasks in complex social settings. This shift in focus is reflected in recent professional concerns about the appropriateness of tasks to children's attainments, which has centered on the concept of matching, i.e. the assignment to children of tasks which optimally sustain motivation, confidence, and progress in learning.

In a survey of over 500 primary schools in England, HMI concluded that teachers were underestimating the capabilities of their higher-attaining pupils, i.e., the top third of students in any class. In mathematics the provision of tasks that were too easy was evident in one half of the classrooms observed; and in geography, history, and science it was as high as two thirds. In later reports their concern has broadened to include low-attaining children.

In two recent surveys of schools catering for the ages ranging eight to thirteen years, they argued that neither the more able nor the less able were given enough suitable activities in the majority of schools, and concluded that overall, the content, level of demand and pace of work were most often directed towards children of average ability in the class. In many classes there was insufficient differentiation to cater for the full range of children's capabilities. However, the data on which these findings are based are, from a research perspective, unsatisfactory. HMI's observations of the match of tasks and children were unstructured, unstated, and undertaken without any clearly articulate view of learning or teaching.

Empirical research which has addressed this issue has been informed, at a theoretical level, by insights derived from cognitive psychology, and by theories of teaching which view classrooms as complex social settings. This theoretical background is considered briefly before the evidence available is summarised through the presentation of a model of classroom task processes. The adoption of cognitive psychological principles has moved the focus on learning from a behaviorist to a constructivist perspective.

The assumptions underpinning this perspective are that the task on which pupils work structure what information is selected from the environment and how it is processed, what information is selected from the environment and how it is processed. Learners, then, are not seen as passive recipients of sensory experience who can learn anything if provided with enough practice; rather they are seen as actively making use of cognitive strategies and previous knowledge to deal with cognitive limitations. In this conception, learners are active and interpretive, and learning is a covert, intellectual process providing the development and restructuring of existing conceptual schemes. As such, teaching effects learning through pupils' thought processes, i.e. teaching influences pupil thinking, pupil thinking mediates learning.

To monitor learning, an understanding of children's progressive performance on assigned tasks is required, and, to assess the impact of teaching on learning, it is necessary to ascertain the extent to which the intellectual demand in assigned work is matched to children's attainments. Further, since classrooms learning takes place within a complex social environment, it is necessary to understand the impact of social processes on children's task performances.

Doyle has produced the most elaborated model of classroom social processes. This views classroom as complex social settings within which teachers and students are in a continuous process of adaptation to each other and the classroom environment. Students must learn what the teacher will reward, and the teacher must learn what the students will deliver. Mutual accommodation leads to cooperation between teacher and taught, and co-operation, in this theory, is the keystone to a classroom life acceptable to the participants. This perspective emphasises the complex social interactions involved in classroom life, assigns a crucial role to the pupils in influencing the learning processes which teachers seek to manipulate, and places in central focus the role of assessment procedures.

In this perspective, studying matching as it actually occurs in classrooms entails observing which tasks teachers assign, how and why they assign them, how and why pupils interpret and work on them, and how and why teachers respond to pupils' work. Research undertaken from this perspective is still in its infancy. Nevertheless, the findings produced have been very fruitful in guiding attention to significant features of teacher and pupil behavior, and to aspects of classroom organisation, which have an impact on the quality of childrens learning experiences. Models are, by definition, simplified versions of reality, their role is to highlight the major influential factors in an area or process.

Teachers plan the tasks they will present to pupils, or will allow their pupils to choose, on the basis of clear and specific intentions, such as 'Angela needs work reinforcing symbol-sound relationship', or 'John is now sufficiently competent in the basic computation of Area and this should now be extended to applied or practical problems'. The tasks, once chosen, have to be presented to the child, group, or class in some way.

The presentation of tasks can take many forms, the major criterion being that children are clear what it is they are supposed to do. The pupils will then work on their tasks, demonstrating through their performances their conceptions and understandings of them. When the work is completed it might be expected that the teacher would assess or diagnose the work in some way, and that the knowledge of the child's understandings gained would thereby inform the teacher's next intention. This description is deceptively simple, however, since there is a possibility of a mismatch or an inappropriate link between every element of the model. These links are briefly considered below.

It has been argued that content, and the purposes for which it is taught, are at the very heart of teaching-learning processes. The focus of this model is in the purposes for which content is chosen, rather than on content *per se*. These purposes are defined in relation to the intellectual demand that content is designed to make on the learner, for example, to allow practice of previously encountered knowledge, to apply previously learned knowledge or skills in new contexts, and so on.

Despite the evident importance of content and purposes, their relationship, and their links with task selection and presentation, have rarely been studied although case studies have indicated that teachers often adhere to laudable aims while maintaining classroom processes that do relatively little to promote them. Recent studies have supported this by showing that the tasks teachers choose do not always match their intentions.

In one study 600 tasks in maths and language were observed in top infant and bottom junior classes, and for each task observed the teachers were interviewed prior to the school day regarding their purposes and intentions for target children, their rationale, and the actual tasks chosen. It was found that over 20 per cent of the tasks did not match the teachers' intentions. Some of these mismatches could be identified by comparison of the stated intention with the content of the task.

For example, one teacher gave a child an exercise designed to reinforce the relationship between the sound and the written symbol, whereas the task itself required the child to complete sentences containing missing words (i.e. there was no spoken component in the task). It was also fairly commonly found that teacher intentions to introduce new knowledge or skills to high attaining children in the class did not make the intended demand, since the pupils were already perfectly familiar with it. As such, a teacher intention for development actually turned out to be a task demanding consolidation through the practice of knowledge or skills already acquired.

A task may be inappropriately presented or specified by the teacher. Inappropriate specification can occur through lack of clarity, inadequate explanation, a lack of necessary resources materials, or a mismatch between what the teacher demands and what is assessed. With respect to this latter issue, it has been argued that teachers' evaluative comments need to be matched to the purposes of the task. Empirical studies of matching support the professional judgement of HMI. Among six-

and seven year olds, it has been found that only 40 per cent of tasks are matched to children's attainment, and there is a very clear trend for the under-estimation of high attainers in the class and the over-estimation of low attainers. This pattern was identical in maths and language work and has since been supported in a study of maths, language, topic works and art and craft in junior schools. When children have completed their work it would be expected that teachers would assess or diagnose it. Assessment is here defined in terms of judgements of right and wrong including ticking, crossing, and the provision of written comments.

Diagnosis, on the other hand, is defined as teacher attempts to acquire a clearer view of pupils understandings or misconceptions, by observation and careful questioning. The evidence is that teachers assess, but do not diagnose. Teachers appear to spend much time at their desks marking work while pupils queue for attention. Because of this pressure, the time spent with each child is short, interactions are not extensive, and they tend to be at a low level. Lack of diagnosis appears to be accompanied by teachers limiting their attention to the products of children's work, rather than focusing on the processes or strategies employed by children in arriving at that product. The quality of diagnosis is thereby diminished. Lack of diagnosis does, of course, mean that teachers have insufficient knowledge of the children's understandings to enable optimal decisions to be made concerning the next task intentions. It is clear from the evidence available so far that this, in part, explains the provision of inappropriate tasks to children.

In 1968 the publication of Rosenthal and Jacobson's American Study, *Pygmalion in the Classroom,* drew the attention of both educationalists and the popular press to the phenomenon that has come to be known as the teacher expectancy effect. Their study seemed to demonstrate that if teachers expected higher standards of work from some pupils than from others, then those former pupils would indeed do better over a school year. What made this study remarkable was that the results enabled the researchers to claim that, through their expectations, teachers had actually caused these differences, they had not merely predicted them. In this study, primary school teachers, at the start of a school year, were presented with information regarding their pupils. This information led the teachers to believe that some of their pupils were likely to be particularly prominent again during the school year ahead. In fact, the pupils thus identified as 'spurters' had been selected at random from each class. Any gains that were actually made, therefore, would be very unlikely to be the result of genuine extra potential, rather they would reflect the effects of a self-fulfilling prophecy. This experimental manipulation of the teachers' expectations by Rosenthal and Jacobson enabled them to rule out simple prediction as a possible explanation of any link established between what the teachers expected and what actually happened.

The results appeared to demonstrate that the expectations induced did indeed lead to higher levels of IQ in those children identified as spurters. In addition, at the end of the period of study, the teachers held generally more favourable attitudes towards the spurters than they did towards the other pupils. As the teachers could not remember by this stage which pupils had been identified as spurters and which had not, it seemed that they had genuinely developed a view of their class that had been determined by the bogus information that had been offered to them. In this study the information that had been provided by outsiders had been favourable towards the pupils that it concerned.

Under normal circumstances, Rosenthal and Jacobson assumed, teachers would form their own expectations concerning their pupils, and these could well be unfavourable. If the self fulfilling prophecy could operate to increase pupil performance with favourable expectations, as Rosenthal and Jacobson's study suggested, then it could also operate to depress performance if the expectations were unfavourable. If we also assume that teachers may not always form their own expectations on the basis of totally reliable and valid information, then we have to face the possibility that some pupils will be handicapped from the outset by the biasing effects of unfavourable teacher expectations.

A further study carried out by Rist at around the same time confirmed these fears. From an extended period of observation, Rist was able to investigate the ways in which a teacher's style of interaction with her pupils related to her early expectations for them. Rist's conclusion is a simple and in many respects a damning one. He took the view that children were effectively placed into different castes. These placements followed from early teacher judgements that seemed to have more to do with the clues available as to the children's socioeconomic status than their actual attainment or academic promise. Rist's data indicated that, having judged that a child had little potential, the teacher would then proceed to give him or her much less attention, and thereby make it very difficult for the child to prove the teacher wrong. Children placed in the lower groups on the basis of this apparently flimsy evidence generally stayed there.

The Pygmalion study has been subjected to close scrutiny and careful criticism over the years. These reviews indicate that different samples and context yield different results and that it is therefore important to exercise care in coming to any general conclusions. The teacher expectancy effect apparently does not operate in all classrooms, with all teachers, at all times. Nevertheless, there can now be little doubt that the effect can and does operate. Rosenthal himself has carried out a large-scale survey of research into the teacher expectancy effect, and has concluded that since his own Pygmalion Study more than four hundred further studies have demonstrated the existence of the effect. One individual study worthy of mention here was carried out by Crano and Mellon. By using data gathered over a number of years, they were able to test in a fairly direct manner the claim that expectations cause performance differences rather than simply predict them. The method they adopted enabled them to use the expectations that teachers had formed for themselves, rather than artificially inducing them as Rosenthal and Jacobson had done.

Crano and Mellon's results therefore have a greater likelihood of giving a valid picture of real classroom life. Their data show that expectations do have clear casual influence on pupil performance, particularly when the expectations are based on the teachers views of the social rather than the academic aspects of the pupil. That is, those pupils who are perceived as being well behaved, friendly, and pleasant to work with are the ones likely to benefit from positive expectations. Those perceived in the opposite way are those most likely to suffer.

Expectations relating to the actual academic ability of the pupil, while still important, were less likely to cause changes in pupil performance. In considering the processes likely to be involved in the teacher expectancy effect, this difference between the effects of social and academic expectations could well prove to be most important. What now remains to be done is the task of making clear just what is the nature of the process by which expectations are formed, transmitted and then acted upon. Several models of this exist. While these differ in detail they all share the same basic elements.

1. Expectations are formed from the information available to the teacher.
2. These expectations then lead to some systematic differences in teacher behaviour.
3. These differences are noted and responded to by the pupil, resulting in the pupil coming to match more closely to the original expectation.

One characteristic of the research available to date is that it has centered on the teacher. The data available are therefore more complete with respect to stages 1 and 2 than with respect to stage 3. It is clear however, that each stage needs to operate in order for the effect to take place. From an extensive review of studies Dusek and Joseph cautiously conclude that teachers' expectations do seem to be influenced by the attractiveness of the pupil, the pupil's classroom conduct, the school's cumulative records concerning the pupil, and the pupil's race and social class.

Perhaps surprisingly, given the current concern with gender differences in educational performance, the gender of the pupil did not influence expectations, but there was some evidence to suggest a possible link between teacher expectation and the sex role behavior of the pupil. Similarly, there was evidence suggestive of a possible effect of the teacher's experience with an older sibling, and the stereotyped views that a teacher may hold in respect to a particular name. It is immediately apparent that not all of these types of information will have a necessary connection with actual pupil ability. Their effect comes through the impact that they have upon the way in which the teacher responds to the pupil concerned.

Dusek and Joseph's reviews serve to remind us that we still know relatively little about the sources of information that teachers actually do use in building up their expectations for individual pupils. In particular, it is clear that we need to know more about the ways in which the nature of the classroom conditions that the teacher works under has an effect upon the kind of expectations that are formed, and the degree to which these might persist over time.

Rogers has suggested that the less advantageous a teacher's conditions of work may be, the more likely it is that relatively fixed expectations will be formed. The well-known work of Sharp and Green serves to illustrate these points. Under difficult working conditions teachers will have less time to reflect upon the developing abilities of each individual in their classes and will therefore be more likely to hold on to judgements arising from early impressions formed on the above types of clear, but not necessarily accurate, types of information.

Other reviewers, such as Blease have suggested that we also need to look at the extent to which expectations are shared by several teachers in the same school. Expectations that are shared by many teachers are more likely to influence a pupil than those that are unique to an individual member of staff. The consistent adoption of a development viewpoint is also necessary. The pieces of information that may play a critical role in determining early expectations may be less important later in the school year. Information critical in the formation of expectations for young primary school children may not be relevant in the formation of expectations for young adults towards the end of their secondary schooling.

A further review by Harris and Rosenthal has examined evidence relevant to the second and third stages listed above. Harris and Rosenthal draw together conscious observation relevant to the differences in teacher behavior that follow from differences in expectation, and the degree to which these differences in behavior in turn relate to pupil performance.

Teacher behavior was shown by the Harris and Rosenthal analysis to vary in a number of respects. Further, these variations were associated with the teachers' prior expectations, and equally important, with the pupils' later performance levels, in particular variations in expectation gave rise to differences in respect of: the amount of material that a teacher presented to a pupil; the degree of warmth and friendliness that is established in the relationship between the teacher and pupil; the degree to which the teacher will attempt to elicit responses from the pupil through questioning; and the degree to which the teacher would supply the pupil with positive feedback through praise, acceptance of pupil's ideas, and so on. In each case, the pupil for whom the higher expectations existed received the most favourable treatment.

Harris and Rosenthal have continued their analysis to demonstrate the degree to which each of these four areas of variation in teacher behaviour is associated with variations in levels of pupil performance. Such links are indeed found, particularly for those areas of teacher behaviour referred to as climate, input, and output. This review of research, then, establishes some important links. It shows that if a teacher has varying expectations for the performance of his or her pupils then there are likely to be predictable variations in that teacher's behavior towards those pupils.

The chain appears to be completed by the further demonstration that these differences in teacher behavior are also associated with levels of pupil performance. The final step in the chain, and the least adequately researched, concerns the nature of the pupil response. Whatever effects teacher expectancies might have upon pupils, they will not take place by directly influencing pupil ability. Rather the effects are likely to occur by promoting changes in pupil motivation and self-concept, which in turn enhance performance levels.

Both self-concept and motivation have been extensively researched in general terms, but are only recently being subjected to detailed and systematic study within the context of the classroom. A promising line of investigation relates concern with motivational processes to the work of social psychologists in the field of attribution theory.

The causes people believe to be responsible for their own successes and failures will determine the way in which they subsequently behave. Those who believe that their failures are caused by variable and, ideally, controllable causes are more likely to make a positive response to the failure, in attempting to overcome it, than are those who believe that the same degree of failure is caused by stable or uncontrollable factors.

For example, a failure attributed to lack of effort is more likely to be positively responded to than one attributed to lack of ability. Continued attributions for failure to lack of ability will progressively undermine the individual's confidence and feelings of self-worth until such time as they come to believe that success is unattainable. A school environment that encourages the pupils within it to have confidence in their abilities, to increase effort, and to search for successful solutions when confronted with initial failure, will increasingly improve the motivation of those individuals.

Recent research begins to show us how teacher behaviour can affect pupils' attributions. Two general points emerge from this literature. While the social aspects of the classroom are important, it is essential not to concentrate upon this at the expense of attention to the academic demands made on pupils.

Classroom Behaviour

Direct observational procedures may be concerned with behaviours as they occur either under naturalistic or controlled situations. Naturalistic observations are concerned mainly with viewing the child in his every day environment, where behaviour can unfold naturally and is not influenced or cased by the observer or his cohorts. Two naturalistic observational techniques are observations in unstructured environments and observations in selected situations. The technique known as 'observations in contrived situations' is a controlled observation technique. In controlled observations the environment is subtly modified by the observer in such a way that behaviour of interest to the observer may be elected from according to S Welck' "tempered naturalness."

Observations in unstructured environments are concerned with situations in which the subject moves freely about in his everyday environment (e.g. his neighbourhood), unrestricted by the observer. Such behaviour is usually assessed by any number of different types of 'trailing' techniques, unusually referred to as specimen description techniques.

These techniques involve following the subject and recording, usually in a detailed sequential narration, his predominant modes of response to various situations he encounters. The specimen description technique can also be used in the classroom situation.

Welck indicated that there are several reasons why an investigator might decide to modify a natural setting, but basically it is because he cannot afford to just wait for something relevant to happen. Techniques used for observations in contrived situations also provide more control, and the results may be generalizable to other conditions which are similar. An example of an observation in contrived situations technique is the instrument Reaction to Entry of Teachers, developed by the staff of the National Institute of Mental Health (undated). In general, the true purpose of the modified situation is hidden from the subject, and he is not (or should not be) aware that he is being observed.

Observations in selected situations refer to a class of techniques that are designed to assess behaviour in given situations (e.g. in the classroom, on the playground, at home, etc.). These procedures are employed because many interesting behaviours occur more frequently under certain conditions than under others. Also, researchers and educators are vitally concerned with classroom behaviour. Almost every type of device and technique available has been used to gather observational data in the classroom. Welck considers two processes basic to the observational process; recording and encoding. Recording means that a considerable portion of observational research consists of making extensive records of events which at some later time are subject to analysis. Encoding is "the simplification of records through ratings, categories, or frequency counts."

Welck's distinction, however, does not do justice to the observational processes which use encoding techniques as relational processes which use encoding techniques as recording procedures. Another way of looking at these processes is possible.

Webb et al., for example, speak of 'accretion,' a process whereby materials are "deposited" and later examined by behavioural trace measures. This is an arresting distinction, and is one of which we should be more aware. We may note in this respect that the initial collection or accretion of observational data employs direct observational procedures; the analysis of the already-collected data employs behavioural trace procedures. In any invent, we shall use the term "accretion" to refer to any process whereby behavioural data are gathered for future analysis. Classroom behaviours can be witnessed live by an observer, or recorded mechanically by a technician, using a videotape recorder, for example.

Behaviours observed "live" may be encoded on the scene or otherwise described to be processed later. Regardless of approach, the end result is the accretion of data that are to be analyzed statistically at some future time. There are ten basic accretion devices by which observational data may be "deposited" physically: cinematic, audience, photographic, typographic, miscellaneous mechanical devices, self—as instrument, diagrammatic, notational, marking, and written. These accretion devices can be combined to form a more extensive set of devices.

Cinematic procedures, in the form of motion picture films, have gained in popularity as an accretion device. The cinematic/audient combination, which may be in the form of a film with sound or video tape with sound, is even more popularly employed.

Loomis and Meyer had two observers watch subjects and describe on tape everything that occurred. The observer's voice was analyzed as well as content. Sher and Horner used two tracks—one to record what the subject said and the other to keep a record of what the subject was doing. These data were later transcribed for analysis (audient-typographic). Caldwell (undated) uses the audient-marking procedure, whereby narrative description behaviours is tape-recorded and then coded. The audient written approach was used by Schoggen. He used a "Stenomask" into which he narratively described what was going on in the classroom. He obtained a degree of freedom in that he could move about and talk without disturbing anyone. He later wrote down his impressions. Withal used time-lapse photography, a photographic data accretion device. Gump obtained a specimen description of a classroom, but supplemented his data by use of photographs (photographic/written). Chapple invented the "interaction chronograph," which was similar in many respects to a typewriter, the keys differed, and were in fact, codes for behaviour. The typographic device is used often to transcribe audiently obtained observational data. There are a number of different miscellaneous type data accretion devices. Hargreaves and Starkweather used a voice spectrometer to examine emotive quality. Crawford and Nicora used an ultrasonic device to examine classroom movement.

Self-as-instrument devices refer to any procedure in which the observer himself is behaving as if he were the recording device. The observer becomes both a cinematic and audient device, and tends to rely upon memory for recording visual and auditory events. Later the observer attempts to recall what it was that transcribed.

Lofland and Schwartz and Schwartz discuss the participant observer approach, which involves the observer living with the type of persons he is concerned, self-as-instrument device, and have developed scales after he has gathered his inferences about S (Self -as-instrument marking).

Coller used the diagrammatic device (which, by definition, also employs notations) to display pictorially a day in the life of a classroom. Coller also used the diagrammatic/Written device to describe more fully what the diagrams and the notations on it represented. Wrightstone used a notational system to describe how students at their seats in a classroom were reacting in respect to the lesson.

Marking, of course, is an obvious encoding procedure (a diagrammatic and/or national system may also be an encoding procedure), and may be employed as a supplementary process for many of the devices mentioned.

The observational instruments developed by Medley and Smith and Wilensky are typical marking procedures. The Educational instrument, which employed both marking and narrative description (Marking/written). The written devices are well known (e.g., specimen description, diary description, anecdotal records, etc.) The work of Kounin and of Barker and Wright are good examples of this method. How to implement a chosen accretion device in the classroom is a problem for the developer of an observational instrument. Wright and Gordon and Jester (in press) have considered this issue.

For example, Wright attempted to schematize six basic methods used in observational child study. Diary description, specimen description, time sampling, even sampling, trait ratings, and field unit analysis. These methods may be distinguished from one another on the basis of "Continuum averages," "material coverages," "recording technique," and "analysis procedure." Gordon and Jester added to the number of basic methods by dividing the time sampling category into "time/signs" and "time/categories," and by adding "level of cognitive interaction."

There are three fundamental data systems; field, sign, and category. Field data system refers to that situation in which the observer is not pre-set by instruction to look for and assess specific behaviours.

Instead, the observer is to respond to filed forces and describe, within predetermined limits, all that occurs. Sign data system refers to that situation in which the observer is not pre-set by instruction to look for an assess specific behaviours. Instead, the observer is to respond to field forces and describe, within predetermined limits, all that occurs. Sign data system refers to the approach during which O lists "beforehand a number of specific acts or incidents of behaviour which may or may not occur during a period of observation." O, however, is present by the sign system to look only for certain behaviours.

We distinguish between two types of sign systems: the discrete and the hierarchical. Sign/discrete systems refer to those observation schedules whose categorical boundaries do not approach the equal appearing interval type of scale.

The categories in the sign/discrete system often are orthogonal to one another and cannot be construed as belonging to the same continuum.

The sign/hierarchical systems also tend to have discrete categories, but a clear representation of a hierarchy or taxonomy is present in the items. (note that a debate still exists as to whether or not the evaluative dimension of the cognitive taxonomy is actually the highest level of cognition).

Category data system refers to the attempt to limit the observation to one general aspect of classroom behaviour. The procedure, as described by Medley and Mitzel, is to "construct a definite set of categories into one, and only one, of which every unit observed can be classified."

There are three types of category systems: discrete, hierarchical, and interval rating. As in the case of sign systems, discrete category systems refer to those observational schedules whose categorical boundaries do not approach the equal-appearing interval type of scale. Likewise, the categorical boundaries of the hierarchical type of category system tend to be discrete, but a clear representation of a hierarchy or taxonomy is present. The interval rating type of category system provides the observer with scales that tend to approach the equal-appearing interval type; there is a distinct continuum.

In general, a category system differs from a sign system in that the category system is supposed to be exhaustive of behaviours of the type to be observed. Both the category and sign systems differ from field systems, primarily because the O is pre-set by the sign and category systems to look at very specific behaviours.

The sampling unit dimension is divided into three factors: time/events, events, and situational/events. The use of events in all three factors is to acknowledge that, regardless of what sampling plan is employed by O, the basic unit of analysis is a behavioural action-an event. When O samples behaviour using the time/event factor, he typically employs a fixed time for obtaining an observation; only those behaviours occurring during a fixed time unit are treated as data.

If the sampling unit is the events factor, O will describe, check, code, and /or rate only when a critical, topical or specified event occurs. Observations terminate for the target person or class when the event occurs.

The situational/events factor refers to a sampling plan during which time the variable, and the observation terminates only after some specified situation ends—the class, or snack period, for example. We may disregard here the fact that the time/events sampling units may be repeated during a defined situation.

Event sampling, a procedure described by Wright as one which "singles out naturally segregated behavioural events of one or another class and records these events as they arise and unfold, " is typically employed as a situational/events measure. Wright defined trait ratings as a process that "selects dimensions of behaviour and bases judgments about them on observations during extended sequences of behaviour".

Possession ratings would approach this definition. Other rating schemes, termed intercession ratings, are used during a session, sometimes in a time sampling format. Intersession ratings are used from one session to another until all items are observed and rated. Goodlad, Klein and associates developed an anecdotal record type of procedure in which they supplied O with a list of topics they were to observe intentionally. Such a procedure tends to create a closed system and provides different types of data. The anecdotal record/critical incidents and formatted anecdotal record tend to point up these differences. One final significant additional is the point-time sampling procedure. In this procedure the O examines the behaviour of the target person only long enough to be sure what the behaviour is, and then checks off the behaviour in the appropriate category.

The behavioural technologist entering the typical classroom can be at once both overwhelmed by the range and variety of potential reinforces available to teachers and dismayed by the infrequency with which potential reinforcers are used. In the author's experience with all kinds of classroom behaviour problems, it seems that 80 to 90 per cent of such problems can be handled by little more than a change in the teacher's verbal behaviour, e.g., when she says what to whom.

Continuing our discussions in chapter 4 regarding modeling, research conducted within this framework has shown that modeling influences can produce three separable types of effects depending on the different processes involved.

First, observers can acquire new patterns of behaviour by watching the performances of others. This observational learning effect is demonstrated most clearly when models exhibit novel response which observers have not yet learned to make and which they later reproduce in substantially identical form.

A second major function of modeling influences is to strengthen or to weaken inhibition of previously learned responses. The effects that modeled activities have on behavioural restraints are largely determined by observation of rewarding and punishing consequences accompanying the actions.

Inhibitory effects are indicated when observers show either decrements in the modeled class of behaviour or a general reduction of responsiveness as a result of seeing the model's behaviour produce punishing consequences. Studies of effectiveness in classroom management have under-scored the importance of an efficient activity system in establishing and maintaining order in classrooms.

This chapter contains a report of research conducted to define more fully the procedural knowledge and the interpretive processes teachers use to manage classrooms successfully. The findings of this research as well as the concepts used to guide the inquiry have considerable practical significance for beginning and experienced teachers.

The first study focused on how teachers achieved and sustained order in their classes throughout the year. For this study, narrative descriptions of class sessions conducted by seven junior high school English teachers were analyzed in an effort to specify more fully what a teacher needs to know in order to manage classrooms.

For the second study narrative descriptions of class sessions were used to construct models of how four junior high school English teachers understood the problem of order and its solution in their classrooms. These models of teacher comprehension provide insight into the knowledge structures and cognitive processes that teachers use to interpret classroom scenes and decide how to act to achieve order. In discussing the findings of these studies, particular attention is given to implications for classroom practice.

The concept of a classroom activity can be defined as a bonded segment of classroom time characterized by an identifiable arrangement of people and space; a focal content or concern; and a pattern or programme of action for participants. Classroom activities are commonly labeled by seating arrangements or by content. Other key dimensions of an activity are duration, the physical space in which work occurs, the type and number of students, the props and resources used, and the expected behaviour of students and the teacher.

Activities, in other words, represent the various ways in which groups are structured, information is communicated, and resources are used in classrooms. Successful teaching is grounded in the management of these units of classroom organization. At the same time, classroom management is fundamentally a cognitive enterprise. Managerial skill, in other words, rests on how a teacher interprets classroom events and thinks about the problem of order in classroom situations.

Cultivation of Thinking

Methods of instruction developed over centuries for selected populations of students left too much implicit and relied too heavily on the ingenuity and application of gifted teachers and students to be adequate for a mass educational system.

The current educational challenge requires more explicit theories of thinking processes and attempt to meet goals formulated in an elite educational system within a system intended for everyone. Current cognitive research offers promise in providing such theories, for it is showing that some of the features of thinking traditionally associated with the high literacy tradition are in fact characteristic even of the most basic skills in the school curriculum when they are learned successfully. While it is difficult to define higher-order thinking exactly, it is not very difficult to recognize it when it occurs.

The process of reading which emerges in current psychological and artificial intelligence accounts, is one in which a reader uses a combination of what is written, what he or she already knows, and various general processes to construct a plausible representation of what the author presumably had in mind. The mental representation constructed by the reader does not exactly match what the texts says—not even try to, except under social circumstances. Instead it attempts to represent the situation the author had in mind or the argument the author hoped to build. The reader's representation omits details that do not seem central to the message. It also adds information that is needed to make the message coherent and sensible.

Usually, these processes go on so automatically that skilled readers are quite unaware of them. Only when the flow of comprehension breaks down do competent readers become aware of their inferential and interpretive processes. Yet our models of skilled reading suggest that inferences are being drawn and interpretations being made patterns as texts are aloud. The disruptions in comprehension that can be caused by minor modifications at key points in the text, provide convincing evidence of inferential work in the reader's efforts to make sense of even quite simple texts.

This broad analysis of comprehension as a meaning imposing process that depends on the reader's knowledge of text structure as well as linguistic, topical, and inferential knowledge, is common to all current cognitive theories of reading. There are important differences among theories with respect to specific aspects of these processes—their timing, the kinds of cues that set them in motion, the ways in which knowledge is organized—but there are no disagreements regarding the general characterization of comprehension.

A point on which research still does not provide a clear answer is the extent to which meaning imposition proceeds strategically—that is, in deliberate, self-conscious fashion—as opposed to automatically and unconsciously. Much evidence suggests that, for an individual who is skilled as a reader and not totally new to the topic of the text, most of the work of building a text representation goes on quite unconsciously, through processes of automatic activation. The process slows down, requires deliberate attention, and becomes accessible to conscious awareness under special conditions: when there is an anomaly in the text or some unusual linguistic construction; when the topical domain is so unfamiliar that the reader lacks necessary prior knowledge for interpretation; when a particularly complicated chain of reasoning is presented; or when the reader wants to study and remember the text rather than just read and understand it.

There is considerably more research needed to establish the kinds of teaching that are likely to produce general improvements in students' abilities to comprehend and interpret texts. It is striking, however, that the kinds of proposals emerging from cognitive research on reading comprehension are highly convergent with processes of textual exegesis and analysis, techniques that are common in high-level courses in literature, philosophy, and other disciplines in which multiple interpretations of texts are discussed as part of instruction.

Cognitive theory is suggesting that processes traditionally reserved for advanced students-that is, for a minority who had developed skill and taste for interpretive mental work might be taught to all readers, including young children and, perhaps especially, those who learn with difficulty. These processes, cognitive researchers are saying, are what we mean by reading skill. Not to teach them is to ignore the most important aspects of reading. This convergence of cognitive research on reading with traditional high literacy competencies offers some promise that the goal of extending high literacy standards to the mass educational system can actually be achieved.

9
Language in Primary Children

Language is what people say, not what some people think they ought to say. Speech acts are in turn located in larger units of discourse, such as conversation, arguments, interviews, and narrations. For the analysis of the actual linguistic forms that individuals use in speaking to one another cannot be separated from such social processes as showing respect and deference, taking turns at talk, and correctly beginning and ending interactions. Analysts of verbal interaction have focused on such issues as the determination of units of talk, the development of systems of transcription, and the discovery of general principles of language use. Researches in the area of reading have investigated the effects of various instructional methods used in beginning reading: the language experience approach versus phonics, linguistic readers versus basals, the initial teaching alphabet versus the standard alphabet, and so on. These investigations, however, have yielded little information about the best way to teach children to read:

It should be acknowledged, however, that several large studies, in which many individual studies of instructional methods have been surveyed or in which their results have been analyzed as a group, have found small but significant differences in favour of methods emphasizing some kind of systematic phonies instruction. The significant effect found for sound-symbol methods could have been "due to chance in the testing of many effects".

Others have pointed out that competing explanations were not adequately discounted and that the results could have been due to higher learning time for students in some programs, unusual teacher characteristics, a better match between teaching and testing in experimental programs, and differences in pace and task selection. It appears, then, that this line of inquiry is beset with problems and yields conflicting results. Because the question of which method is best has generally proved to be an unproductive one, this review will not provide any discussion of research specifically aimed at comparing instructional methods used in beginning reading. It has often been assumed that children know little or nothing about written language before they receive formal instruction in school. Evidence indicates, however, that children do have extensive knowledge of some aspects of written language.

Many preschoolers have knowledge about the graphic features of print. They know that the features of lines used in print are different from lines used to make pictures or other nonprint configurations. The features contrasted in one study of three-to six-and-one-half-year-olds were pictures versus writing, linear versus nonlinear arrangement of units, internally varied versus repetitive sequences of units, and multiple units versus single units. Still other displays contained Roman or cursive letters and words, artificial letters, Hebrew letters, a Mayan design, and Chinese characters. Even the youngest children distinguished between pictures and writing, though they often labeled as writing nonpictorial displays that were not writing, basing judgments on gross features of the displays, such as linearity, variety of units, and multiplicity of units. The older children tended to base judgments on actual features of individual units within a display rather than on features of the total display.

Thus, the more that units in the display resembled actual letters occurring in the child's environment the greater the tendency for the display to be labeled as writing, regardless of the display's general characteristics. A similar developmental trend has been found in studies of preschool children's productions of writing.

In a recent study, four-year-olds were instructed to "write everything you can write." Each child's scribble resembled the writing system to which the child had been exposed most frequently, even though no child's sample contained real units of print. Nejeeba, the child attempting to write Arabic, told the researcher that Arabic uses "a lot more dots than English". This research indicates that before children receive formal instruction in reading and writing, and often before they accurately name letters or recognize words, they abstract features of writing from the print they encounter from exposure to print provided in their everyday environments.

Young children may, of course, differentiate among graphic displays, that is, determine visually some of its properties, but not understand how to use it or what purposes it serves. For example, children who can detect differences in pictorial and print displays and label one writing and not the other may point to pictures rather than print in a storybook when indicating what the reader looks at.

In short, children may recognize print versus nonprint but know nothing of the reading process. Some research has indicated that young children know little about what a reader does or what the reading process entails. Two studies of five-year-olds, for example, demonstrated that many children did not know what adults do when they read or that words rather than pictures in books are what one reads.

Research by Hiebert, however, suggests that many preschoolers may know more than earlier research has revealed. Early studies posed questions in abstract situations rather than in more concrete contextualized situations where children could show rather than tell what they know. In addition, the children studied previously may not have been provided opportunities to interact with print in their daily lives. In Hiebert's study, understanding of the reading process was measured by three tasks.

In one, the researcher read silently and orally from a book and also stared silently at an object. Children were asked to name each activity performed by the researcher.

The second task asked children to read a "secret message". This stimulus was used to ask children about their reading ability and to infer their understanding of the reading process if they attempted to "read" the page.

The third task used several books: (1) one with pictures and text; (2) one with pictures only; (3) one with text only; and (4) one with blank pages.

Children were asked if each book could be read by someone who could read and if yes, what such a reader would look at. These tasks were designed to reveal children's basic ideas about reading, such as whether reading requires speaking while looking at a book or can be done silently and whether print versus pictures are what one looks at to read. Hiebert also investigated preschoolers' understanding of the functions of writing. Story situations were used. For example, children were shown Christmas packages and asked how one would know to which family member each package was to be given. Each package was tagged with a news label. If the child did not refer to this label, he or she was asked who it was for. Three stories used a model town complete with buildings, street signs, road signs, and toy cars. One of these presented two cars approaching an intersection. Children were asked how the drivers would know what to do to avoid a crash. A fifth story used materials and directions for a children's game. The experimenter explained that children wanted to play this new game but did not know how. Additional evidence that preschool children develop knowledge about reading processes or about what one does while reading comes from studies of children's story-reading behaviour. Doake and Rossman, for example, found that the preschool children they studied increased their awareness over time, that readers look at the text when they read, and that reading involves looking at print in a book, not just saying words of a story that you know while looking at the pictures.

Young children may know that one looks at words to read and that reading serves a variety of purposes, but not what characteristics distinguish a word from other segments of print, or how to determine if a print display shown to them is a word or something that does not qualify as a word. In a study by Pick et al., children were presented print displays on white cards. Word displays included single-letter words, long letter strings, short letter strings likely to be unfamiliar to the children, and fifteen five-letter words. Nonword displays included single letters; two long letter strings; ten four-letter consonant clusters; ten strings of misoriented letters, of which five could be words and five that could not; four groups of meaningful initials sounded like real words. Variables contrasted were length of a letter string, whether a string was an actual word, vowel and consonant strings only versus strings with both consonant and vowels, letter orientation, and meaning. The subjects were twenty-three-four-year-old nursery school children, older by one-half year than the oldest nursery school children, seventeen kindergarten children, older by one-half year than the oldest nursery school children; sixteen first-grade children, and thirteen second and third grade children. Children were asked to sort the cards into those that had words and those that did not.

Younger nursery school children were significantly more likely than older nursery school children to accept single letters as words, whether they were words or not. The preschool children also accepted a higher percentage of the very long letter strings as words. This tendency decreased with age, with the oldest children accepting very long strings only when these were real words. The percentage of vowel-only and consonant-only clusters accepted as words decreases with age, with significant differences occurring both between nursery school and kindergarten and kindergarten and first grade.

Acceptance of strings containing declined significantly between the nursery and kindergarten groups and again between kindergarten and first grade groups. Acceptance of pronounceable non-kindergarten and between the nursery and kindergarten groups and again between kindergarten and first grade groups. Acceptance of pronounceable non-words that sounded like meaningful words decreased between nursery school ad kindergarten and between first and second grade but even the oldest children still accepted a large percentage of them as words.

Acceptance of pronounceable clusters that were not meaningful declined with age, with sharp declines between kindergarten and first grade and between first grade and second grade. These results indicate that before the beginning of formal instruction in reading, children begin to understand something about word structure. Between kindergarten and first grade when formal instruction has still been somewhat minimal, substantial gains are made. The youngest children were more likely to classify both single letters and letter strings as words. But by five, children knew that words generally are composed of several letters and that letters and words are different entities. Older children also rejected very long strings, unless they were real words, indicating that they knew a word is not defined simply by a string of letters, but by internal characteristics of the string as well, such as the arrangement of the letters and whether when sounded out they result in a meaningful word.

Similarly, by kindergarten age, children more and more rejected strings that were all vowels or all consonants, indicating again that they knew that wordness is determined by characteristics within the letter strings-that there are permissible strings and nonpermissible strings. A letter string by itself does not constitute wordness. As children got older, particularly between kindergarten and first grade, they rejected letter strings that were pronounceable but meaningless, as well as pronounceable nonwords that were meaningful, with the former showing the stronger decline. Apparently, as children get older they use their ability to sound out strings, as well as their knowledge of how words look, to judge wordness. If sounding out results in a meaningful word, they are likely to judge that the letter string is a word. Other studies and clinical observations have yielded similar results. When matching speech to print in storybooks, for example, the youngest and/or least experienced preschoolers often point to individual letters as if each were a word or syllable.

Additional evidence comes from a second study by Hiebert in which children between three and four-and-one-half were shown cards in context and out of context, and were asked 'What might this say?' Confusion between letters and words should have caused children to respond to single word displays with multiword responses. Yet, a high percentage of the responses for both in-context and out-of-context displays consisted of single words.

Most children knew how to make correct printed word to spoken word correspondences, indicating that they knew, at minimum, that words consist of letter clusters and single letters are not words. Even kindergarten and first grade children, however, cannot accurately determine what a printed word is when asked to respond to various print displays.

Meltzer and Herse asked kindergarten and first grade children to use scissors to cut off words from printed sentences. Children sometimes cut off one word, sometimes two, and sometimes only part of a word, indicating that they did not judge words in a line of print as clusters of letters set off from other clusters by space. The difference between the performance of these children and younger children who accurately point to individual printed words when reading storybooks could be due to their inability to monitor the print by using knowledge of what it said.

In short, being able to detect individual words in print or in speech may be facilitated when the child knows what the print presented says. Getting the match between speech and print to come out right can serve as a monitor to judge what constitutes a word in both speech and print. Support for this hypothesis comes from a study of children just finishing the first month of school. Children were first taught a short poem orally. Then the researcher read the first line aloud and pointed along each word. Then the child was asked to finger-point and read the second, third, and fourth lines, which were framed with index cards. After each line was read, the examiner pronounced two target words within the line and asked the child to locate these. Next, the examiner and the child read the entire poem together twice as the examiner pointed to each word. The examiner then pointed to individual words within the poem and asked the child to pronounce them. Finally, the printed poem was taken away, and the child was asked to pronounce six words isolated from the text, one at a time. The four measures of word concepts were ability to: (1) point to words as one reads aloud; (2) recognise specific words within one line; (3) recognise specific words any where in the poem; and (4) recognize sight words.

Although there was a wide range of success on this count, many children performed well, indicating that they could isolate words in both speech and print. Still other evidence of young children's understanding of word structure comes from their attempts to create words with manipulative alphabet materials or by writing rather than from their judgments about wordness in terms of displays of print presented to them.

Research and clinical observations reveal that preschool children may at first string letters together at random to make words. Such behaviour often occurs spontaneously as children play with alphabet materials. The child tells the adult that the creation is a "word" and even labels it, or the child may ask the adult." What does this word say?" At this stage, the child seems to know that words are composed of more than one unit, but not that such strings are organized in specific ways internally. Absent are visual criteria for permissible letter combinations, as well as any notion that the sequence of letters in a printed word must be related to the sequence of sounds in the spoken word. When the letter realizations dawns on children, they may give up visual criteria of wordness used earlier and rely on phonetic relationships when creating words even if knowledge of letter-sound relationships is limited to only one element of the word. Henderson has designated a preliterate phonetic stage of spelling in which dog is spelled D or DJ, and candy, K or KDE, by different children. What is common to all spellings for a given word at this stage is that letters selected to spell it must bear some phonetic relationship to the spoken word. What is different about various spellings is that at times children have used just one letter to spell the word, while at other times they have used more than one letter. It is impossible to know from Henderson's data if different children consistently used one strategy and not the other and if the same children used both strategies on different occasions.

If they did not know how to represent more than one sound, they may have used only one letter rather than violate their knowledge that when making words, letters must be selected with this criterion in mind. Instead, they may have violated their knowledge that words consist of more than one letter.

Children lacking knowledge of phonetic relationships may use longer letter strings to make words because they judge wordness on the basis of characteristics they have obtained merely from seeing words; words are letter strings. Without phonetic constraints as a guide, stringing may get out of hand. In addition, if the child does not know that words in a line are surrounded by space, then exposure to printed text, as opposed to single words such as names or traffic signs, may lead them to believe that words can be very long.

The number of letters used to make a particular word may be influenced by knowledge of the object whose name is spelled. Papandropoulou and Sinelair and Berthoud Papandropoulou, for example, found that preschool children often justified a word's length in terms of characteristics of its referent, not in terms of the necessity to mach print to length of utterance. Crocodile is longer than cat because crocodiles are longer than cats. Typewriter is long because typewriters have lots of letters. Children who make judgments based on these criteria must know a little about the actual determinants of word structure, particularly that a printed word is related to its spoken counterpart.

Apparently, knowing that a printed word is related to the spoken word in a specific way—that letters used to make a word must represent sounds in the spoken word—is a late development for many children. Henderson has suggested that the preliterate phonetic stage emerges by late kindergarten or beginning first grade. The second stage, called letter name strategy stage, emerges by mid-first grade. More complicated and sophisticated phonetic strategies appear by grade two and beyond. However, Read has reported preschool children as young as three-and one-half using phonetic strategies. Bissex, in a case study of her son, reports such behaviour beginning at five. The early emergence of phonetic strategies to create words in some preschool children seems to be related to the print-rich environments these children were reared in.

The ingredients for precocious development seem clear: printed materials of various kinds; materials for creating print of one's own; adult mediation of print in the environment such as naming letters, writing the child's name, and modeling reading and writing; reading to children; answering the child's questions; and allowing the child wide latitude in exploring how words are created. Variations in documentation of children's knowledge of wordness appear to have two major sources: (1) variations in the populations studied; and (2) differences in definitions or aspects of wordness and methodologies used to study these.

In summary, we can say only that some older preschool and kindergarten children seem to know something about what distinguishes words from nonwords, using both visual and meaning criteria, and that some older preschool and kindergarten children have general notions about criteria one must use to create words. But many children do not have such knowledge even upon entry into or completion of, first grade. They do not know a letter from a word or how words are constructed either by visual criteria or in relation to the spoken words they represent. Without it, they are likely to be confused by reading instruction. Speech may be represented in writing in a number of ways for example, at the word or syllable level. English orthography is based on representation of smaller segments; it is alphabetic.

The linguistic unit represented by letters is the individual phoneme or sound. To use such a system, a reader must be able to segment and analyze oral language at the phonemic level. Researchers have tried to determine if young children can do this. The research indicates that analysis at the phonemic level is extremely difficult for the preschool and kindergarten age child. Liberman et al., asked nursery, kindergarten, and first grade children to repeat a word or sound spoken by the researcher and to tap on the table with a dowel the number of segments contained in the stimulus item.

Nursery school children could not segment stimuli into phonemes, although about half could segment words into syllables. About one fifth of the kindergarten children could segment by phonemes, while about half could segment by syllables. About 70 per cent of the first graders could segment by phonemes, and 90 per cent could segment by syllables. Other researchers have also indicated that young children cannot analyze speech at the phonemic level and that this inability is related to difficulty in learning to read. Without the ability to segment at the phonemic level, that is, to hear three segments in bat, it would be difficult to know how speech is mapped on to an alphabetic orthography that provides one letter for each sound.

The major difficulty in segmenting speech into phonemes seems to arise because there is no distinct acoustic segment which marks phonemes. In bat, for example, the initial and final consonants are, in the conversion to sound, folded into the medial vowel, with the result that information about successive segments is transmitted more or less simultaneously on the same parts of the sound. Syllables, in contrast, are marked by a "peak of acoustic energy".

Our perception that words consist of distinct sounds is not as much a matter of perceptual reality as it is of conceptual development. We come to think of words in terms of individual sound segments, though they do not exist in "physical" reality. Although some children arrive at this basic insight before they receive formal reading instruction, most children develop it only before they receive formal reading instruction, most children develop it only after exposure to formal reading instruction. The insight escapes a few children even after considerable instruction, and many of these children have great difficulty in learning to read. The absence of this insight is not due to faulty auditory or speech perception. A child who detects that the words bad and bat sound different, may not be able to segment each into three parts and say in which segment the difference occurs. The problem is centered more on becoming aware of analysis in speech at a level that is tied to printed letters; it involves knowing how to map speech to print. Conscious analysis at this level would not be necessary or useful if our orthography were not alphabetic. Experience with speech alone, even speech organized to highlight differences at the phoneme level, may not be enough. The idea of phonemes may not emerge in any concrete way unless the child is confronted with print and must find a use for all of the letters that make up the child's name or the words in a line of text in a favourite storybook.

Print freezes the continuous stream of speech into perceptually manipulable blocks and begins to pull a child's tacit knowledge about words to the surface where an explicit understanding can begin to develop. Print appears to play a crucial but paradoxical role in turning the transparency of spoken language into the opaqueness of an object that can be studied—paradoxical because print is supposed to be a second order abstraction from reality, with spoken language being a first order abstraction. Logically, it would appear that print would be more difficult to grasp conceptually than spoken language. If we assume that to understand print entails a fairly elaborate explanation of its characteristics and function, then print may indeed be more difficult. If on the other hand we admit the virtues of tacit knowledge, then we see where print, by being a common and fairly stable symbolic system in the environment, draws the young child's attention to ward the abstract symbolic structure of language.

The same monitoring of speech used to find word segments corresponding to each letter cluster marked by space when following along a known story, poem or text could lead ultimately to monitoring of speech to find segments that correspond to each letter within the cluster making a word. Solving this puzzle, or realising that it is a puzzle needing a solution, would seem to lead a child to the needed discovery.

In Morris' study, there was a significant correlation between locating individual words in a poem known orally and performing successfully on a phoneme segmentation test. Knowing what words in print are and locating them were related to the ability to segment speech into phonemes. We can only speculate that being able to match words in speech to words in prints is a necessary step in the development of the ability to segment speech into phonemes and match these to letters within a word.

Oral knowledge of the text may be able to force changes in our understandings about print, and understandings of print may be able to force changes in understandings about language. This review would be incomplete without a brief discussion of children who learn to read before they begin formal instruction. Reports of these children have been provided by Durkin, Plessas and Oakes, Sutton, Krippner, Torrey, Forester, Doake, and Witty and Coomer. For the most part, parents of such children did not set out to teach their children to read. In virtually all cases, however, children have come from print-rich environments. Being read to frequently was an experience common to almost all of these children. In addition, environmental print was interpreted by parents and read to the children. These children were also given materials such as paper and pencils or crayons, chalkboards, and manipulative alphabet materials. Finally, their parents responded to questions and requests. Parents also read the same stories over and over, pointed out words when the child asked "Where does it say?", provided appropriated demonstrations when children asked, for example, "How does an 'e' go?", and provided the letter when asked "How do you spell?" While not setting out to teach children to read and not doing so in a formal way, the parents, nevertheless, provided essential experiences. It is difficult to translate research findings into suggestions for practice.

Most of the research tells us what children can and cannot do, but little about what determines these abilities. In addition, we know little about how some of these concepts and abilities are related to each other or what other concepts and abilities, as yet unknown, are also critical.

Despite these limitations, some tentative decisions can be made about practices that may be promising, and related issues can be considered. Because some preschool and kindergarten children have considerable knowledge about written language before receiving formal instruction, some researchers have claimed that learning to read is "natural," as natural as learning to speak.

Other claim that learning to read is not "natural" because most children become readers only after specific tutoring. Learning to speak is natural, but learning to read is different, they claim. Perhaps both views are incorrect; perhaps learning to read is not different from learning to speak, and perhaps neither occurs "naturally".

The frequency with which a behaviour occurs does not necessarily indicate anything about the basis for its development. We cannot assume, simply because oral language acquisition is almost universal, that it is innate or "natural," developing without environmental supports, or even instruction of a sort. Assuming that environmental supports for languages are virtually universal-robust and redundant-the universality of languages acquisition may depend not only on characteristics of the child but also on the environment.

Because these characteristics have become commonplace, we fail to recognize their contribution and believe that language acquisition is "natural." In formal development when control of the trunk is achieved in stable sitting posture, there is a smooth transition to bridging and creeping. In our sample, most of our babies achieved stability in sitting well within the range of sighted babies. Most of our babies demonstrated the ability to support themselves on hands and knees within the range for sighted babies. Then, something that should appear on the developmental timetable did not appear. The baby did not creep. Since locating and reaching a toy on sound cues are the only ways in which the blind child can find equivalence for reaching and attaining an object on sight, there was no motive for reach. The sighted child, in the same posture, will reach for the out-of-reach toy which propels him forward. It is the visual incentive that initiates the creeping pattern. At every point where vision would normally intervene to promote a new phase in locomotor development we had to help the baby find an adaptive solution. The prone position, for example, is not an "interesting" position for the blind baby. The sighted baby spends long in prone, with head elevated, "just looking around." The blind baby, without such incentives, may resist the prone position. We build in "interest" in prone through speaking to the baby, through dangle toys or other devices..... Practicing pulling to stand and cruising will be "more interesting" in the familiar space of a playpen with favourite toys offering sound-touch incentives. Even motor development, typically thought to be controlled by genetic or maturational factors, is dependent on objects and people that are approached with the guidance of vision in sighted children. These supports are so abundant in most children's environments that it takes a study of visually impaired children to make us aware of their role.

Extensive research has recently been conducted on the effects of adult language on infant language development. Adult linguistic input is often extensive, and the quality of the adult language influences the infant's language development. Evidence that written language acquisition occurs without formal instruction only when appropriate social and physical environments are provided comes from almost every study of children who have learned read before they received formal instruction in school. Most of these children had extensive experience with print and tools for creating it, as well as interactions with parents who answered their children's questions, modeled reading, and read to them frequently. The fact that parents did not set out to teach their children to read and to write, and were often not aware that they were doing so, does not mean that they did not provide crucial experiences and supports. The evidence suggests that they did. The term "natural" is not very useful. We might be wiser to think of the "given" characteristics of children as "invariant functions," to borrow an idea and terminology from Piaget. What is "given" are modes of adaptation or particular orientations to circumstances. The structure of intelligence, or what we come to know, is created or constructed through interactions between the child and the environment.

Knowledge construction in a particular domain depends on access to experiences out of which that kind of knowledge can be created. Without such access, a "natural" learner cannot come to know. All environments, no matter how commonplace, are contrived—they could be different. Experiences relating to some kinds of knowledge such as number, space, and classification are so redundant, however, that universal acquisition of concepts could occur without adults being aware that they and the physical environment have made a contribution. The same may be said for oral language, but with a difference: a strong social environment would also be required. We need to read to them or respond positively to their questions, and no pencils or crayons and paper on which to attempt to write. The current disparities in the occurrence of oral and written language in the population may be due to disparities in the universal availability of environments that support each.

If written language acquisition is in the way suggested, then we must do more than wait for it to emerge "naturally." We probably need not employ the "formal" instructional programs currently used in many primary grade classrooms. But "informal approaches" to reading instruction cannot be devoid of contact with print in context. Exposure to print experiences—actually, involvement in print experiences—can be incidental, but not accidental. Environments that are robust and redundant with print experiences must be deliberately contrived. We must adopt the processes as well as the content of effective parental practices.

The practice of reading stories to young children, for example, often distorts and makes ineffective the parental reading situation. Parents read to individual children or to two or three who are in their lap or sitting close. Teachers read to groups of children sitting at a distance. Parents allow children to select the book to be read and reread the same book over and over again, both at the same sitting and over a period of weeks or months; teachers often select the book that is to be read and read it once at each sitting and infrequently in the course of a week or month. Parents allow children to turn the pages, pause to look at pictures or to ask questions, and read along if they wish. Teachers, on the other hand, are more likely to set the pace, turn the pages, and discourage reading along during the story episode. Parents keep their children's books accessible over a number of years: teachers often keep books out of children's reach, particularly if the books have been obtained from a library, and they return borrowed books promptly, allowing children little long-term access. It is not easy to employ the informal methods used by effective parents, and it may be unrealistic to think that they can be adopted completely.

We need to study exactly what effective parents do and then think carefully about how essential features of these practices can be adapted to classrooms. In the meantime, we fact do not. The evidence denies this, although the methods they use differ significantly from those typically used in schools. Formal reading instruction typically involves the teaching of isolated skills in a predetermined sequence. These procedures are based on the nations that reading must be simplified if children are to understand it and that learning is primarily linear, a matter of gradually building up associations until everything comes together. Arguments against using reductionist simplification strategies are often based on evidence that some children learn to read before receiving such instruction and that these instances demonstrate that no simplification is necessary and may even be a hindrance. At issue here are basic assumptions about knowledge.

The direct teaching of subskills assumes that knowledge exists in external reality and that learning is a matter of getting what is "out there" into children's heads. However, a different assumption about knowledge is that it exists neither in external reality nor within the learner, but rather is constructed through interactions between the two. If knowledge is derived from actions on objects or experiences, then a learner must be placed in a situation where such acting can occur. Phonemes do not exist as perceptible units of separate sounds. They "cannot be segmented physically because the acoustic properties of formants of any letter in a syllable are spread across the entire syllable",

Our knowledge of distinct sounds does not exist as such in objective reality but is constructed somehow from interactions with speech and print. The problem with much subskill instruction as practiced is that it makes an erroneous assumption about the nature of this knowledge. Sounds are regarded as out there and objective, something children can hear. When teachers talk about the sounds that certain letters make, they may know what they mean, but many children don't.

One reason why children who learn to read with holistic methods before they enter school usually become such good readers may be because they have access to experiences that are complex enough that essential knowledge about the reading process can be derived. But we should not jump too quickly to the assumption that no simplification of the reading situation has been provided. The simplification, however, is not reductionist. A discussion of learning in other areas will serve as an introduction to a discussion of the kind of simplification that may occur. A complicated 'form box' frustrates children one or one-and-one-half years old. We provide simple form boxes at first. We give children one-piece puzzles at first, too, not ten-piece puzzles. If we misjudge a young child's ability to interact with such materials, however, or if for some reason the child selects a toy too complex, we usually comment on the baby's behaviour in sentences such as "He likes to open the lid and put all of the shapes in and then dump them out again," or "Wooden objects are great for teething", or "Look, he likes to put his fingers through the holes in the lid and then pull it up to see them sticking through the other side."

In short, we change our expectations and behaviour in relation to the baby and the objects, and the baby copes with the physical objects by doing much more with them than was intended by their designers. The baby, or even an older child in a similar situation, does not become frustrated with being unable to perform the intended task "correctly' because no one demands that it be performed in a certain "fluent" way.

We commonly accommodate or "simplify" situations for children by allowing them to add behaviours that are not an essential part of the task for those more experienced. In addition, parents often add something to the situation to keep it within the child's realm of experience and ability. We add training wheels to bicycles and thickness to the diameters of pencils and the pages of infant picture books. Perhaps most important, we add social interaction that provides redundancy. This may be especially true of the language we use with very young children: "Moerk, What's this? Yes, that's your nose. What's this? Yes, that's your mouth. What are these? Uh-huh, those are your eyes. Where are my eyes? Yes, those are my eyes. Where's my nose?" These additions simplify situations, but they do not destroy the essential nature of language, puzzles, bicycles, form boxes, or whatever. They allow children to construct essential knowledge-knowledge perhaps unattainable unless children can act on the "whole ball of wax."

These informal observations and speculations suggest that we might start children on the course of understanding written language by providing "real" reading experiences, but with supports not needed by the mature reader. If we consider storybooks, for example, redundancy is added in a number of ways: rhyme and repetition of phrases make learning the story line easy, pictures support the text and serve as clues to what a page says, and the adult's social behaviour of reading the story again and again gives the child a way of knowing what the print says without having had to decipher it.

Storybooks seem to fit perfectly the little text, few pages, and uncomplicated plots, do not result in distortion of the essential characteristics of written language: and other simplifications are additions or redundancies, both physical and social. In addition, the situation can be simplified by other additions that consist of information provided by interactions with the adult: "We must start at the front, not the back, of the books"; "Move your finger, you're covering the words and I can't see to read them"; "Wait a minute: I haven't finished reading that page yet"; "Yes, Max does have a wolf suit on just like it says right here"; "You have to point to each word as you say a word, not to each letter, like this.

"Finally, the child's knowledge of the story, obtained from having heard it read, provides an important means for discovering mysteries of print—it becomes a monitoring device as was discussed earlier.

Many aspects of reading may be understood only when approached in this manner, for they are complicated rules, to surface structure information. But we will probably not be served well by thinking in dichotomies that suggest that we must simplify situations by cutting them apart or that we must keep them totally complex.

Experiences of the sort described above might be called simplified complexities. We need to create and use these in beginning reading instructions. The roots of literacy are growing strongly long before schools begin instruction. Children learn that print represents meaning. They learn general and specific meanings of specific print sequences in situational contexts: stop signs, cereal boxes, toothpaste cartons. At the same time, children develop some awareness of the form of spring: directionality, letter names, key features. They distinguish print from pictures. They can handle books and know the basic function of books, letters, newspapers.

Literacy development in school needs to be built on this base. It must be seen as an extension of natural development. Literacy development in schools is often not based on natural development because the reading behaviours children present upon entrance are not recognized as the precursors of skilled performance in reading and writing. Traditional diagnostic tools often require all-or-none responses: accurate naming of letters, and so on. Most standardized tests are based on reductionist principles that assume precursors of final knowledge to be recognizable, perfect pieces of final knowledge. Errors indicate deficiencies—the absence of specific pieces of knowledge.

The qualitative differences are due to the use of different generalizations or rules to organize and manipulate the surface structures of various aspects of language. Errors in this view do not indicate the absence of knowledge but rather the presence of different knowledge. With respect to letter orientation, for example, we can assume that in the beginning many reversals are due to application of a generalization children bring with them from experience with the three-dimensional word: orientation is irrelevant to naming objects: therefore, letters may face any direction, and indeed they do in children's early writing.

Somewhat later, children realise that orientation of two-dimensional symbols is meaningful. They then seek rules for orientation by observing letters themselves. If almost all of the left-right asymmetrical letters face right, then all left-right asymmetrical letters must face right, even the J which, of course is an exception. This behaviour is similar to a child's assumptions about inflections in oral language: if the past tense of most verbs is formed by adding 'ed' then the past tense of all verbs must be formed in this way, the child reasons. The result is the creation of words such as teached, runned, swinged, and so on.

When such errors are assumed to be failures to make discriminations rather than to be applications of different rules, teachers assume children cannot see orientation, that they are unable to perceive it. Training in seeing is often provided, and children are told to look carefully at their writing. But when teachers assume instead that children can see orientation, but have not mastered general rules and their exceptions—that the problem is one of knowing, not perceiving—training in visual discrimination is not provided. Indeed, the problem isn't seen as a problem in need of training at all. It is assumed that these errors will be corrected as children use print more and more just as errors in oral language are corrected.

Instructional activities provided are thus less specific and trivial, and more meaningful and comprehensive. Errors due to application of different underlying rules by children can also be seen in their early spellings. Children's early categories of sounds are not identical to the categories used by adults. For example, they typically spell words containing 'tr' with the letters 'ch' because the 't' preceeding an 'r' is affricated just as 'ch' is. If this phonetic feature, rather than place of articulation, is used as the basis for categorizing sounds, then 'tr' will be considered more closely related to 'ch' than to 't' as in toy or top. In other words, our categories of phonemes—the distinct sounds we recognize in standard spelling—are not the same as the young child's.

Specific developmental stages have been documented for phonological development and its impact on how children spell words which they do not know by sight. In addition, young children generally assume that spelling is phonetic. They have yet to understand that phonetic relations are often violated in standard spelling in order to preserve lexical relationships or similar meanings in words as in 'nation and nationally', 'medicine and medical', 'muscle and muscular'. English orthography is based on phonetic and lexical considerations. Young children, however, are "super-phoneticians." What they discern in the phonetic sequence of spoken words is quite free of higher level orthographic overlay, and so they proceed to construct each word by setting out each named letter to its sound.

It is probably a mistake to view children's early spelling as evidence that they know nothing about spelling and to seek to remedy this perceived problem by presenting word lists whose spellings are to be learned one-by one. The problem is of a different order, one of underlying rules and generalizations, one most easily corrected by continued exposure to written words and the need to create them.

It seems inefficient to provide instruction focusing on learning to spell single words when rules relating to many words can be abstracted from broader experiences which would contribute as well to many other literacy skills and keep children meaningfully engaged in, rather than bored with or afraid of, literacy development. The research reviewed here holds much promise for informing us about what is involved in learning to read.

Of particular interest are the studies indicating the development of preschool children who grow up in socially mediated literate environments we need also to know more about exactly what these children know and how they develop such knowledge if we are to develop early childhood programs that lead to the same results. In the meantime, we can attempt to approximate in classrooms both the social and physical environments that appear to foster literacy development in young children.

We need to abandon ideas and practices that assume early literacy development to be simply a matter of teaching children a few basic sk.ils such as alphabet recognition or litter-sound associations. Limiting children's reading experiences to contacts with bits and pieces of print isolated from meaningful contexts may actually prevent them from developing broader and more complex insights that are the key to understanding what writ-classrooms; we need to learn to make it easier. This will require that we provide experiences with real, whole print that we have often assumed in the past to be too complex for young children to understand.

Inculcation of Discussion Techniques

The inculcation of discussion techniques, and development of respect for views of average minds, will reduce his being disliked by average minds. Such techniques will also equip the child for better team work. Discussion as a process makes a group think together, in a constructive style, for learning, for problem-solving and for decision-making on plans of action. The child has to be educated on the following:

(i) A participant in discussion is a learner, not a teacher.

(ii) Discussion is a process of reflective thinking, and not for selling of predetermined ideas.

(iii) It is an approach of a critic rather than that of a propagandist.

(iv) Through discussion, consent and consensus are achieved and conflict is eliminated.

The process of discussion demands faith in truth and faith in human nature. Parents should educate their children in senior classes that the process of discussion covers the following:

(a) Purpose

(b) Objectives

(c) Agenda

(d) Participants

(e) Time and Place

(f) Chairman or moderator

(g) Scope and limits

(h) Evaluation of discussion

(i) Means of following up

Training of an able child could be done by making him think imaginatively, e.g.:

(i) to offer suggestions without defenses;

(ii) to add to given set of ideas;

(iii) to defer solutions until all ideas have been enumerated.

Discussion is a method for developing creative approaches to knowledge, An able child as a participant should also be taught to:

(a) listen to others for their positive contributions;

(b) speak to others with vigour and clarify one's own points, well synthesized, before concluding the views.

Language experience also demands two more skills to be achieved. They are: talking and listening. These skills are developed through the following ways of oral communication;

(i) conversation and discussion;

(ii) telling experiences;

(iii) narrating stories;

(iv) use of common courtesies;

(v) using telephones;

(vi) giving direction and explanation.

Parents should emphasise;

(a) pleasing voice quality, distinct enunciation and correct pronunciation;

(b) poise and self-assurance in different situations;

(c) standardised variety common over language style other than dialect.;

(d) to agree and disagree courteously;

(e) habit of correct speech.

Oral expression provides an important avenue of cultural interpretation. In many countries there is always a sharp difference between the home-language and the school language. This gap has to be filled by the help of parents. The capacity of sound listening includes ability to synthesise the component parts of a speech in order to find out central ideas; ability to distinguish between relevant and irrelevant parts of what one listens; ability to make logical inferences of what one listens to; and ability to make full use of contextual skills. Parents need to develop these characteristics in the child.

The parents need to see that the child is trained in the following aspects of good listening:

(i) adoption of positive approach to what has been heard, for finding the meaning;

ii) analysing the speaker's meaning;

(iii) accurate perception and orientation; and

(iv) integration of meaning into objective concepts.

Some training on coordinate process of discussion, like—reception of ideas, digestion of new points and transmission of one's views, will equip an able child for positive roles in life.

For conveying one's views and feeling in a discussion, the child should be given demonstration of the following in a rehearsal type of guidance by parents:

(a) Effective poise-concerning preparedness, calmness, courteous attitude and confidence;

(b) Meeting of questions objectively and rationally. One should neither personalise nor assign motives to objections raised;

(c) Avoid too many gestures and movements while speaking;

(d) The voice should be easily heard, be pleasant in quality, well-modulated to portray mood and meaning. In fact, the voice should reveal the speaker's personality;

(e) Effective articulation combines techniques of subordination and stress;

(f) Regulating the words spoken per unit of time, rhythm and pause.

The best way of developing good speaking ability is to make a child deliver speeches from time to time under parental guidance, keeping in view the points stated above. It has often been assumed that children know little or nothing about written language before they receive formal instruction in school. Evidence indicates, however, that children do have extensive knowledge of some aspects of written language.

10

Visual Arts in Primary Education

In the recent past, working with art materials has been thought therapeutic to the emotional health of young children. It has been valued as a release from anxiety and inhibition and as an appropriate outlet for aggressions and fantasies. Similarly, it is understood to supply adults with insight into the emotions of children and it is thought conducive to the development of creative capacities. Interwoven with these goals has been the belief that both the therapeutic and the creative functions of art will occur best without direction from the teacher. Schaffer-Simmern joins the teacher not to interfere with the natural unfolding of artistic activity. Serious attention to children's art began at the end of the nineteenth century.

Numerous descriptive accounts of the developmental changes in drawings were written in biographies of infants by parent-psychologists. These studies established a serious attitude toward children's art work and also set forth a sequence of natural development in drawing that began with scribbles, passed through a phase of schematic work, and achieved more adultlike representations in later childhood. At the same time that these studies wee taking place, there was a shift in education toward a more child-centered pedagogy. Another important factor contributing to an emphasis on freer forms of artistic activity was the emergence of the Modern movement in art. Expressionism, Surrealism, and Cubism came into being and were recognized as style during this period. Indeed, in 1913 the famous Armory Show held in New York, Chicago and Boston heralded to the Americans art as expression, experiment, and individual innovation.

These historical trends in the study of child development; the liberalization of educational practice through the work of Froebel, Cizek, Dewey, and others; the relating of art of unconscious needs by Freud; and the emergence of innovation and expression as explicit values in art—came together in the work of Victor Lowenfeld, an Austrian art educator who came to the United States at the time of Hitler's rise to power in Germany. Lowenfeld was personally affected by the inflexible dogmatism and disregard for individual differences in German educational practices at the time. He believed that such training had made the eventual acceptance of Nazi totalitarianism possible. His book, *Creative and Mental Growth,* first published in 1947 proposed freedom for the child, nonintervention by the teacher, respect for the sequence of developmental stages, and mental health-cum-creativity as the ultimate goals of art in the schools. Creativity was associated with innovation and was held to be innate, emerging organically with development.

The role of the teacher was to keep damaging influences out so that the natural unfolding of creativity would not be stunted or impaired. This book was the single most influential factor in American art education in twenty years following its publication. Viewed in historical context, it is possible to understand how this point of view came to permeate American educational thought and practice. It is interesting to note that despite widespread interest there has been comparatively little empirical research on creativity in early childhood art. In the visual arts most studies have been efforts to determine or describe attributes of creativity. The drawbacks of Lowenfeld's program are evident in the light of contemporary developmental psychology.

Current theory holds that development is the result of interactions between genetically prompted structures in the child and stimulation from the environment; consequently, children are believed to need stimulation to progress normally. Lowenfeld acknowledged the need for outside stimulation when he advised teachers to evoke children's memories of real-life experiences as sources of content. At the same time, he called for isolation from drawing from his program for young children. In so doing he eliminated important experiences and rich sources of artistic stimulation. It seems only reasonable to suppose that children deprived of these sources would lack knowledge and skill and it is probably not extreme to attribute some portion of the ineptitude felt by many adolescent children to these omissions. It may be that Lowenfeld believed outside influences would stifle children because he equated children's creative processes with those of adults.

However, children's artistic activities differ significantly form those of adults. For children, making art is the creation of order in a relatively limited and disorganized state of knowledge. With few rules and minimal information children strive to organize and image their thoughts and feelings about the world of experience. Adult artists, working with much more information and many more rules strive to move beyond conventional rules and constraints to imagine new visions or reality. The children's goal is order; the freshness of their work is a sign of their lack of rules as well as their nascent ingenuity in the creation of meaning. Conversely, for artists the goal achieve and the struggle is to achieve subservience of order to freshness of vision.

Lowenfeld seems not to have recognized this crucial difference and to have transposed the adult need for freedom form cultural constraints to freedom from culture for children. Apparently, he was unable to imagine how adult artistic influences might beneficially be provided for children. This may be because he had no general theory of cognitive-affective development in art and could not select content from artistic sources in accordance with an organized view of children's developmental needs and abilities. His own discussion of developmental stages in art is limited to a descriptive account of imagery and reference to emotional needs and benefits. There is little mention of cognitive processes or theory. Since he had omitted drawing from observation from his program for young children, the stages he described were based on memory work and offer a restricted picture of children's abilities. His caution is understandable; and, indeed, without a deep understanding of children's artistic processes, teachers may impose on them as she feared. But with the awareness of this problem and more insight into child development, no such negative outcome need occur.

This discussion has called into question some current educational beliefs and practices. Among them are that: (1) the role of teachers is to help children make images of the sort described by Lowenfeld but otherwise to refrain from intervention; (2) a major purpose of art in the schools is to provide opportunities for uninhibited expression; and (3) children should not be exposed to adult art forms or work from observation. These beliefs and practices are contrary to the dynamics of child development, and their revision through study of cognitive-affective processes in art is necessary to foster the creation of meaning in art education.

The study of meaning creation may fruitfully be approached through the analysis of the processes of symbolization as discussed in developmental psychology. In order to avoid confusion with more current uses of the words symbolization and representation, it will be helpful to clarify the meanings as used here.

Symbolization is the more general of the two referring to any and all events in which people use some means to call to mind nonpresent persons, objects, or events. Gestures, words, graphic images, play, and dreams are all vehicles of symbolization. A symbol is more usually thought of as an image that refers to another entity metaphorically—for example, when a lion is used to denote strength. This form is subsumed, together with all other forms of reference, in the term symbolization as it will be used here. Representation refers to a limited subsets of visual symbolization as discussed in developmental psychology. In order to avoid confusion with more current uses of the words symbolization and representation, it will be helpful to clarify the meanings as used here.

Symbolization is the more general of the two referring to any and all events in which people use some means to call to mind nonpresent persons, objects, or events. Gestures, words, graphic images, play and dreams are all vehicles of symbolization. A symbol is more usually thought of as an image that refers to another entity metaphorically, for example, when a lion is used to denote strength. This form is subsumed, together with all other forms of reference, in the term symbolization as it will be used here.

Representation refers to a limited subset of visual symbolizations in which some physical quality of a symbolizing medium is in an isomorphic correspondence with some physical quality of a referent. Thus, in a painting of a tree there is physical correspondence of shapes and colours between tree and painted lines. There are nonobjective as well as objective forms of symbolic reference. In nonobjective symbols, expressive properties of symbols are understood to convey meaning without referring to concrete objects. For example, lines can convey qualities such as speed or uprising movement and emotions such as excitement or depression without depicting objects.

The dynamic nature of the process of symbolization is most powerfully etched in the theory of Western and Kaplan. Their theory proposes that a symbol and the concept of the object to which it refers are created in relation to each other by"form-building processes." It is the activity of these form-building processes that brings experience into realization for children as well as for adults. Symbolization takes place in several modes; gesture, language, play, and the arts.

However, the arts are distinguished from other modes of symbolization by three significant characteristics. First, in art, deliberate consideration is given to aesthetic and formal qualities. The way in which a symbol is designed is as important as the object or event to which it refers. Second, in a work of art, conscious attention is given to emotional content both by the artist and by the audience. This is not true in more objective modes of communication. Third, these two attributes are united in a work of art because emotional content is embodied in the formal qualities as well as represented in the imagery.

Because of the interplay between thought and feeling in form and content, it is possible in the arts to symbolize the complex blend of objective and expressive qualities in the experience of real life. Through art the inner and outer worlds of experience may be brought into relation. Thus, the arts serve a particular psychological function: to capture and embody meanings that bridge thought and feeling. The artist, in fact, every thinker needs such a medium, a vehicle for organizing and thinking about experience. And although some psychologists associate thought with logical operations and abstract verbal generalization, the artist, thinking in a medium, thinks differently. He thinks forms, and people talking, and images, and rhythms.

When the artist thinks in this way certain so-called logical distinctions disappear, for example, the distinction between intellect and emotion. In life we simultaneously grasp and experience and feel it emotionally; we understand that someone is helping us with no apparent benefit to himself and we feel gratitude. We feel the grayness of the day as rain approaches and feel the melancholy. In a medium, an artist can simultaneously communicate event and feeling.

Doyle also refers to the medium as "a kind of reality principle" because its characteristic make specific demands on artists and set up limits against which they must test their dawning conceptualizations. In this respect, materials serve a function similar to that proposed by Erikson for the rules or limits in play. These, he says, provide the structure for "leeway" in play so that the "free" experimentation that develops mastery can take place.

In the visual arts, the physical and visual properties of materials provide structure and anchor the form-building process in the concrete. Three different components of knowledge are used in forming a symbol: the symbolizer's knowledge of the material, of the referent, and of the possible modes of correspondence between them. What finally appears in the symbol is a selection from the sum total of information the symbol maker has about the referent and about the material. This selection is based on the symbol maker's understanding of how the two may be related as well as factors relating to the symbol maker's personal and immediate intention. In order to understand any given symbol one must consider all three components of the process; and to understand children's symbolization, it is necessary to study the development of all three components.

Better understanding of the development of the three components of symbolization would enable teachers to design appropriate curricula using a full range of resources. It would also enable them to plan lessons and curricula that engage in the creation of the most substantive sorts of meaning from the point of view of the child. Several comprehensive studies cover the first years of artistic activity during which children come to understand the nature of materials. Those of Biber Kellogg and Smith are based on collections of spontaneous drawings and paintings. Biber offers careful analysis of the characteristic of children's drawings in relation to cognitive and affective development; Kellogg provides a classification system of typical configurations; and Smith traces the evolution of visual concepts and includes step-by-step process records of paintings and drawings. There is one full-length case study on an individual child; Arnheim discusses the period theoretically. The account that follows draws on all these sources generally but relies most specifically on Smith.

The influence of a material of the form of the symbol has been a major point for a number of authors. These investigators have emphasized the fact that a given material elicits and also limits the content of a symbol; some have discussed the child's gradual acquisition of information about materials, but there has been relatively little recognition that it is necessary for children to learn the nature of material before they can use them in symbols.

Works of art are made of substances manipulated into patterns of lines, colours, and shapes. In order to arrange a material into such patterns, it is necessary to understand its physical properties, its visual properties, and the performatory actions of hand and eye that produce such patterns. Perceptual response to visual properties such as shape and colour is present very early. By the end of the first year of life, sensory response is much like that of children's understandings of such stimuli.

However, the ability to respond to visual configurations, as for example a straight line, does not make it possible to produce controlled versions of them, as childrens scribbles and copying problems make clear. Nor can we attribute the disorderly appearance of these early efforts to the child's limited motor skills; the drawings would be more random if they were the product of poor control. It seems more likely that in the beginning, children lack the necessary concepts of physical and visual properties to give direction to their hands. This interpretation is suggested by the logic of the sequence in which their abilities emerge. As children grow their work demonstrates an orderly progression of visual properties from simple to ever more complex. In the beginning, with no concepts of the possible visible consequences, children move arm and hand in reflex-like motoric rhythms. These movements produce characteristic forms in the material which over time, the child begins to recognize and diffrentiate.

Piaget and Inhelder suggest that the origin of drawing is the rhythmic pattern of the child's undifferentiated state, the fundamental elements of drawing from which more complex concepts will be developed. Smith traces the evolution of the concepts of line, shape, and picture space in three to five-year-olds. Lines begin as traces of rhythmic zigzag movements, as noted by Piaget and Inhelder; thereafter, children master, in order, discontinuity versus continuity, straightness versus curvedness, changes in direction, orientation, and intersection, thus becoming able to control line on paper. In the course of this evolution, and early capacity to produce vertical lines was noted. Construction of the concept of graphic verticals may depend on body factors and also on the coordination of the orientation of line within the axes-frame of the paper space. A further extension of these vertical and horizontal coordinations may be the child's preference for perpendicular angles. The capacity to produce controlled shapes emerges from the capacity to produce controlled lines. Children of three and four first create rectangular shapes by drawing a set of parallel verticals and then adding a set of parallel horizontals to them. Only later do they draw a continuous pathway around the perimeter of the shape.

Spielman reasons that children's first lines are understood by them as autonomous entities and that when used to form a shape, they lose their autonomy. Thus, the child requires more time to develop the capacity to draw controlled shapes with a continuous line. Eventually, children construct a complement of visual concepts of line, space, shape, and colour that make it possible for them to create organized designs of considerable complexity. It is assumed that the necessary physical concepts of materials are constructed at the same time.

The role of motor activity in the construction of both these sets of concepts would be central in the theory of Piaget. Whatever role it does in fact play, it is clear that children teach themselves the performance skills and motor sequences required to create controlled forms of visual graphic elements through manipulative experimentation with materials. Children come to know the different capacities of materials but they also come to generalize properties of materials that are not medium-specific. They are more likely to discover these similarities and differences because their initial movements with each material are very similar. However, because of the different physical and visual properties of each material, similar movements produce different results. Repeated back and forth motions produce patches of colour in paint, tangled lines in crayon, and coils or balls in clay. Nevertheless, some similarities emerge; and in time, it is possible for children to produce similar shapes in different media. Thus, manipulation leads to both differentiation and generalization of properties may be seen in other media.

Golomb writes of development in the use of play-dough as well as drawing. Hirsch traces development of concepts in block-building. It is essential to the creation of meaning with materials for the child to develop a deep and rich understanding of the physical and visual properties of materials. In order for this to take place, opportunities for experimentation with appropriate materials over sufficient time are necessary. More empirical research is needed to determine clearly the evolution of the capacity to produce basic visual elements and also to combine them in designs.

The development of an understanding of the physical and visual properties of materials occupies the child's first several years of working with materials. Sometime during the third or fourth year after the child is knowledgeable about materials, the innate capacity for symbolization begins to emerge in the use of materials, and another dimension of expression is added to children's work. Although the capacity for symbolization is first evident during the second year beginning with gestured imitations, it evolves rapidly to include other forms including language and play. Nevertheless, the representational shaping of art materials begins considerably later, during the third and fourth years following the development of basic understanding of materials.

Werner and Kaplan hold that the form a symbol takes is the consequence of the maker's conception of the material, the referent, and of the possible correspondence derived from objective similarities familiar to adults but also from another less familiar mode of correspondence based on physiognomic perception. Werner proposed that we have a set of perceptions that respond to expressive characteristics in phenomena. He called this mode of perception physiognomic and described it as more dependent on physical sensation and emotion than on logic. It is natural to young children, available to adults, and much used by artists.

Through it, nonobjective imagery is perceived as expressing emotions and concepts, objective imagery is given emotional force, and composition is used to convey meaning. Through it, we may perceive lines as sad, trees as suffering, and compositions as turbulent. Some characteristics of children's drawings based on physiognomic perception make them difficult for adults to understand; the objective contours of shapes may be ignored and objects may be rendered in simple circles or lines; spatial relationships are simplified and based on typological concepts; movement is often used as feature of correspondence.

In addition, the images of children offer grew correspondences while those of adults are redundant, offering multiple cues from lines, spaces, colour, and spatial arrangements. For example, a child may call a vertical line "a tall building". In this example, verticality and relative length are the only correspondences the child feels are necessary. Thus, children create sparse images using expressive features, such as movement in line for correspondence, and omitting more objective geometric properties of shape and spatial arrangement. However, difficult it may be to decode individual configurations, these images in particular deserve serious study, for they embody the foundation of expression in art. In their fusion of form and content, of expressive and objective correspondences, resides the germ of all later creations of meaning and the bridging of thought and feeling through visual means. Children often begin symbolizing by naming configurations they have already made. In this proto-symbolic activity, the child's choice of referent is prompted by the configuration of the finished drawing. As a consequence, the choice of referents reflects children's interpretations of properties in the material more than it does their need to present a particular theme. There is an interesting consequence of the influence of materials on the choice of referents at this time.

Since different materials have different properties, typical referents identified by young children differ from material to material. In paint, frequently named referents are smoke, rain, and fire; those in clay are food in various forms; and those in blocks are buildings and portable objects. Names are often prompted by favourite design configurations. For example, a circle with radiating lines is a common design. It combines a number of visual concepts the child has recently learned, including straight and curved lines, enclosure, spacing at regular intervals along a line, orientation of lines, joining of lines at perpendicular angles, and so forth.

When beginning to symbolize,the child often calls this configuration "a spider". Physiognomic perception is involved in this creation of a relationship between the lines and the child's conception of a spider. It involves affect in that spiders are frightening and lines that poke or just spider is perceived with global simplicity as a mass in the middle of the many radiating lines. A common early planned symbol is that of "a man" or "a person," and a common form of it is the so-called tadpole man, that is, a configuration composed simply of a circle with two descending lines. Inside the circle there are usually other circles or lines standing for eyes, nose, and mouth. There is no trunk depicted in the drawing and a number of explanations have been offered for this omission.

Arnheim and Golomb consider that the circle represents head and body in one shape, standing syncretically for the total figure. Piaget and Inhelder, citing Luquet, hold that the trunk is omitted because of the child's inability to synthesize. Freeman suggests that the head-legs configuration may be the result of an end-anchoring memory effect. Kellogg and Smith refer to the influence of the child's prior knowledge of circular designs on the configuration.

Goodnow studies the influence of the children's rules of sequencing and layout. Werner attributes the large size of faces in general to emotional perspective, that is, emphasis on features with emotional salience. The pattern of this group of interpretations in suggestive. One group of observers focuses on the child's conception of the referent; another, on the child's conception of the material, and another, on the mode of correspondence between material and referent. The most penetrating explanation will probably be found in an interpretation that takes each of the three components of symbol formation into account.

In general, the rules of relationship between materials and referent shift with development from expressive and simplified relationships to ever more differentiated objective and conceptual relationships. The shift to more conceptual relationships is particularly evident in the representation of the three-dimensional world on the two-dimensional surface. Studies record the gradual introduction of occlusion, vertical positioning, and obliques to indicate recession into space in drawing; but specific rules of correspondence are still to be identified. The shift from simple to more complex rules of representations is paralleled by the child's growing awareness of modes of correspondences. Korzenik studied the child's gradual recognition of the necessity for communicative imagery.

Children of five blame any lack of understanding on the viewer, while older children recognize themselves as responsible for making the image comprehensible. Elkind also reports on the development of metasymbolic awareness. Research is needed to clarify these aspects of correspondence and to examine other areas of correspondence as well. Among these is correspondence in three dimensional media and how expressive correspondences continue to be used and elaborated in older children.It is important to attend to the child's gradually evolving understanding of experiences of objects and events. This constitutes the reservoir of information about referents upon which the child draws in forming a symbol. Here particularly, it is important to attend to the child's evolving understanding of what constitutes an appropriate referent for an image. For example, the child of five to seven may understand the act of representation as the depiction of a generic form rather than of an individual object, and thus choose salient parts for their ability to offer categorical definition.

Children's use of simple categorical thought during this age span has been observed in a variety of symbolic modes. If in their early planned representations, children have in mind an illustration of a generic car, house, or tree, that might account in part for some of the simplicity of these configurations. Certainly, it is true that there is a developmental shift from representation of basic types such as a person to representation of more differentiated types such as a little girl. Later, children come to add individual objects to their array of possible referents for images. If this progression is the result of changing definitions of an acceptable referent, then the attitude educators have had toward early so-called stereotypes needs to be revised.

Rand and Wagner, tracking developmental change in children's representations of a motivated act, observe a similar sequence and note that it is the adult finally who sees the general in the specific. A charming example of changes is the definition of the referents offered by S. Fein. Here, a pictorial record of one child's horse drawing from earliest representations of essential horseness to adolescent consideration of the social context is offered. Children's development of the concept of space has received a great deal of attention, and the theme of perspective taking in particular has been much studied. This topic is of interest in relation to children's ability to use the convention of perspective.

The research derives from a particular study carried out by Piaget and Inhelder in which children, looking at a model of three mountains, were asked to identify viewpoints other than their own. The Piagetian study found that children of six to eight choose their own for all viewpoints, while children of nine to ten distinguish those of others.

Piaget and Inhelder suggest that egocentrism declines as the result of internal coordination of all possible viewpoints and that one consequence of this coordination is older children's ability to use the rules of perspective. However, subsequent studies have challenged the Piagetian account. Some have considered social influences and some, the rotation of the display rather than the subject. Many of these report fewer egocentric errors from younger children than did the Piagetian study. The question of children's perspective-talking ability and its relation to drawing is unresolved and needs further study.

Conscientious assessment of art forms must take into account the child's changing conceptualization of each of the three components of symbolization. This is true for researchers as it is for teachers. Recognition that a number of factors impinge on the representational process is growing, and many observers are questioning the practice of interpreting art products as indicators of any one factor but the three components of symbolization deserve much more recognition. Several other factors may need attention as well. These are central processes, emotional status, performatory processes, and the development of the child's capacity to respond to works of art.

While the presence and nature of such a central symbolizing function is yet to be determined, the importance of considering such a possibility is underscored by observations of the unlikely ability of the blind to make simple drawings. If those who have no visual experience of objects or images can make rudimentary drawings, it may be that there are general capacities for making symbolic correspondences buried deep in the human mind. The role of memory has been largely disregarded in the children's art literature.

It has been assumed that there is no significant difference in young children's work made from memory or from observation, because children at five, six, and seven seem to ignore the scene in front of them. Goodenough and Eng express this conviction and cite a study by Kershensteiner in which young children, when asked to draw a schoolmate, drew other poses in addition to the one before them. However, several recent studies put this assumption to question. Children drawing from observation have been found to produce more articulate contours, to include more details, and to use occlusion at a younger age. Furthermore, when assisted in the recall of details by dictation, children's representations are more detailed and well integrated. Thus, some simplifications in children's art may reflect difficulties in accessing from memory. The effects of drawing from observation and the role of memory in young children's art require further study. The processes lived in producing appropriate hand movements also deserve more attention.

Olson has given particular attention to the problem of performance and Rand has examined task analysis, motor skills, and motor training in drawing. Studies in which figures are assembled from provided parts indicate greater ability to include parts and to relate parts to the whole. Goodnow has carried out a particularly fruitful series of studies on children's sequencing, economy of means, and rules of layout. Others who have looked at sequencing in drawing are Ames, Freeman, and Smith. Children's art is often used as means of personality assessment and diagnosis. However, more research on the role of needs and emotions in the formation of symbols by normal children is needed.

A better understanding of the interplay of cognitive and affective factors in the forming of children's imagery would offer a more well- balanced, thorough, and comprehensive view of what constitutes normal expression of emotions in art. This review of factors influencing graphic symbolization has included a wide range of issues including central processing, performatory processing, emotional status, and the three components of symbol formation.

As research continues, one can only hope that more precise means of studying relevant influences and their interactions will be found. Interest in children's responses to works of art has been growing for some time. Much of it reports children's art preferences based on criteria such as colour and subject matter. Children's increasing preference for realism is another frequent observation.

Developmental stages of aesthetic experience based on experimental data have also been formulated. In yet other studies it is reported that preference for complexity increases with age and so do comprehension of style and aesthetic principles. Gardner, Winner, and Kircher asked children questions relating to artistic training, media, display, formal properties, and the sources of works of art. They report the relative inaccuracy of younger children's replies. A related area of investigation is of picture perception. Factors involved in the recognition of images have been studied by a number of investigators. Perception of depth cues in flat images has received particular attention.

Research on children's responses to art has much helpful information to offer teachers. It is essential in educating children to understand artistic meaning to provide which lessons and curricula must be designed. Teachers need to know much more about the aesthetic understandings and interests of children and to present much more of the world of fine arts to them.Current research has begun to identify cognitive benefits to children resulting from participation in the arts. Ives and Pond, in reviewing this material cite studies of improvements in cognitive abilities after children engage in activities including fantasy and dramatic play. They also discuss a renewed interest in mental imagery and its functional effect in problem solving. In addition, Greenfield and others have found parallels between some children's manipulative activities and other cognitive task.

These studies point to the intellectual as well as the affective significance of art activities and underscore the need for art in education.There is a glaring and puzzling lack of research in the areas of special needs and disadvantaged children. Among the few studies on special needs children are reports on learning disabled children by Walker and development of representation in retardates by Golomb and Barr-Grossman; a case study of a very atypical autistic girl by Selfe; and a diagnosis and remediation program proposed by Gair.

In the area of the disadvantaged, Eisner reports on drawing abilities; Castrup, Ain, and Scott offer an art skills instrument for inner city and suburban preschoolers; Renick reports on an assessment of reasoning and perception in black and white children and Mills offers a study of the effect of an art program on the reading scores of rural children. There is a pressing need for more extensive study of the art of special needs and disadvantaged children.

A number of consequences for education form this view of art. Among them is the belief that children will gain the most benefit from art programs designed to enhance their capacity to create meaning with visual materials and that this may best be approached by structuring curricula around the three components of symbol formation; concepts of the material, of the referent, and of the modes of correspondence between them.

The visual arts are a particularly appropriate means of expression for young children because art materials are concrete, allowing for direct manipulation and immediate feedback. However, to achieve the most from working with them, it is important for children to conceptualize as fully as possible their physical, visual, and expressive properties. To plan for this, teachers need to understand the development of these concepts from their origin in motoric activities, to their use in objective and nonobjective forms of symbolization. Attention to conceptualization of referents is also required. Teachers need to help children select developmentally appropriate objects and events as subjects and to help them expand their range of responses to these experiences.

Direct as well as indirect experiences of objects, events, and works of art are needed in the classroom.

The parallel development of children's objective and expressive modes of correspondence requires particular emphasis. These two modes of symbolization emerge in a fused state, and they become differentiated, they interact in changing patterns. This interaction is central to the creation of meaning in art and deserves much more attention from researcher and teacher alike. Children's changing concepts of what constitutes an appropriate referent for an image is another important consideration. More accurate knowledge about this, together with more accurate knowledge of how children believe it possible to relate lines, shapes, and colours to such a referent will make it possible for teachers to offer developmentally relevant assistance in the process of forming symbols rather than to avoid this for fear imposing adult modes of correspondence on children.

More research is needed that is sensitive to the complex interplay of forces influencing the forms of imagery. Information from research will make it possible for teachers to be more active in helping children in work with materials and, in addition, it will help them offer adult works of art to children with more assurance and success. With the creation of meaning as a goal and attention to children's cognitive-affective development as safeguard, far more comprehensive and substantive art programs are possible. Children can be offered information and experience of the everyday world and of art without harm if these are selected and presented with respect for the children's growing capacities and individual differences. The media are usually designed to entertain and to induce the desire to buy, not to teach young children.

Television is a potential source of general information and laguage training as well as of social knowledge. Studies indicate, first grades in a town receiving television broadcasts had more advanced vocabularies than those in a town without television. The vast amount of time that young children devote to mass media affects their aggressiveness, morality, anxiety, social knowledge, cognitive functioning, and positive interpersonal behaviour.

Enhancing cognitive development is an essential and worthy goal, yet it threatens to overshadow social and economical development, especially in educational programs for the disadvantaged. Current educational thinking gives relatively little attention to teaching cooperation, consideration for others, non-violent ways of copying with frustration, and mature modes of moral judgment, to mention only a few specifics. Thus, most children can profit from education in these areas, and disadvantaged children probably have as much need for opportunities to learn interpersonal skills as they do for education in abstract concepts and Standard English.

11
Child-Centered Basic Education

The child has got its own unique individuality. One child differs from another. He is not a mere passive being to be easily moulded at a will. He rather is an active being engaged in some sort of activity to satisfy some need. That is why he can not be confined within the four walls of a school, nor can his education be confined to books alone. He loves freedom; he is ceaselessly active; he is self-guided and self-dependent by disposition. Therefore such a social atmosphere should be created in school as can enable the child to acquire social fitness while developing his individual qualities. This aim can be achieved by introducing crafts into the curriculum. For an all-round development of the child it is necessary that an intimate contact be established between school, home and community.

In this triangle of development child, parents and teacher-all the three are correlated. John Dewey, a great American educationist, defines education as the reconstruction of one's experiences while participating in social activities. From this very point of view, school is called not a mere miniature of society, but the society itself. School life should be the mirror of all the home and social activities. Vinoba has expressed the same idea when he says that sociology should aim at the creation of a school home and that education should aim at the establishment of a home school. What he means to say is that school should be turned into home and home into school.

In other words, school should not remain confined within its four walls, but extend to home and the community. This scheme will not only educate children, but also provide them social training.The scheme recommends compulsory basic national education for children between six and fourteen. In a democratic country compulsory education up to a definite stage is absolutely indispensable.

One of the fundamental concepts of the scheme is that education should begin not only from birth, but from conception to death. Western educationists express the same ideas when they say that education should extend from 'cradle to grave'.

Education should cover the whole period from infancy to maturity. Then will it be a truly public education. In order to systematise the scheme from this point of view experiments are being made with the compulsory education of children as also with pre-basic, post basic and adult education. It is to be noted that in some parts basic education has been confined to the primary education of the fifth standard only. But in the original scheme eight years' systematic education has been recommended.

In the fundamental concept of this scheme self-sufficiency has been given an important place. Under this scheme the salary of the teacher will be covered by the earnings from craft-work, though the point has been quite controversial. However, it may safely be accepted that the productive aspect of education is not less important than its creative aspect and hence it cannot be ignored. In fact, production is the measure with which the worth of work done methodically can be judged.

Work done with scientific knowledge becomes the medium of education. Skill comes as a result of work done with intelligence. With skill in work, understanding becomes sharp. Therefore, production can not be ignored. From the stand-point of education as well as economics proper attention should be paid to production. This does not at all imply that basic education teaches the processes of productive crafts for the sake of production alone. The sponsors of this scheme have unequivocally said that crafts are taught only as the medium of education, so that the physical, mental and moral capacities of the child could be developed properly.

Craft possesses the invisible magnetic power of correlating various branches of knowledge. The fruitful processes involved in craft work illuminate various subjects of study. Craft work is introduced in the scheme of education with this aim in view. If it is ignored, the educational importance of crafts work is lost. Basic education having been accepted as the national pattern of education at the elementary level, both the Central and the State Government are committed to transform all the elementary schools into Basic schools in due course of time. This process has already begun. But there are certain difficulties which stand in the way of speedy progress of Basic education in the country.

The transformation of the present system of elementary education into the Basic system is a huge problem. In the face of the prevailing condition in our country and the human and material resources at our disposal this transformation cannot take place all at once.

The problem of opening new Basic schools is in itself bristled with various difficulties. But the conversion of the existing non-Basic schools is a still more baffling and more stupendous problem. One can realize the immensity of the problem in quantitatives terms by looking at the figures given in the "Review of Education in India, 1947-61." Considering that the whole of elementary education has to be reorientated on Basic lines, the process has not advanced very far yet. In 1950-51 the number of children going to Basic schools accounted for 13.1 per cent of the total number of children enrolled in the elementary school; the proportion increased to nearly 17.2 per cent by the end of the First Plan and is estimated to have risen to 23.3 per cent by March, 1961.

This shows clearly that it would take a long time to establish the Basic system of education as the only pattern at the elementary stage. It is, therefore, essential to devise ways and means to bring about such changes in the existing elementary schools, as could pave the way for their complete change over to the Basic pattern at a later date when necessary resources would have been secured for this purpose.

The changes to be introduced immediately must, in the nature of things, be such as would not entail expenditure beyond the present allocations made for education. It means that only those activities of Basic education which are inexpensive should be initiated in the ordinary elementary schools at once. But this is not to say that no additional amount would be needed at all to run the new programme. This would certainly require some financial resources, but these would be of a magnitude that could easily be met by making necessary adjustments in the normal budget for education. If these activities are to help in orienting elementary schools towards the basic pattern, certain conditions must be fulfilled. First, these activities have to be integrated in the curriculum of the schools, so that they may contribute to the aims of Basic education. They should not be treated as mere extra-curricular activities unrelated to the main work of the school. These activities would lose much of their value and significance as media of education, if they were conducted in a mechanical way devoid of the real spirit. Secondly, there must be a proper evaluation of the outcome of these activities. It must be assessed as to what impact they have made on the learner, how he has become a better person both as an individual and as a member of his community as a result of this programme. These requirements can be met only when teaching and administrative personnel are so prepared professionally as to enable them to shoulder the specific responsibilities of the orientation programme.

The teacher and administrators of elementary schools should not only have the skill to organize the activities, but they must have an insight into the objective which these activities are intended to serve. As to the activities to be introduced in the elementary school, these may be of various kinds. There are certain activities which are suitable for all schools, as for example, health activities, social service, cultural activities, etc, while there are others which may suit only certain schools, for instance, a school having a sizeable piece of land with irrigation facilities may practice flower and vegetable gardening. What particular activities a given school should start would obviously depend on the availability of the material resources needed and the nature and strength of the school staff. Whatever activities a school selects for itself, must be properly planned, executed and evaluated; and what is even more important, they must be fully utilized as media of education.

For instance, an activity like the bringing out of a children's wall-magazine on the occasion of our Independence Day would require well thought-out planning as to its content, time, cost, contributors, editors, supervisor, etc. In order to make this activity educationally more meaningful, it would be necessary to organize individual study collective teaching, workshop, seminar, etc, on various topics relating to the Indian freedom movement. This would not only enrich the knowledge of the children involved in this activity, but inculcate in them certain virtues like initiative, resourcefulness, cooperativeness, sense of responsibility, etc. After an activity is carried out in this manner, evaluation of its process as well as of its end-result becomes a useful exercise in learning from one's own achievement and shortcomings, success and failure.

When all these conditions are fulfilled, the activity concerned no longer remains an isolated routine unconnected with the main educational programme of the school or a mere pastime. It then gets integrated into the total curriculum, becomes a veritable source of effective learning experiences; and as such it contributes to the achievement of educational objectives. So far as the syllabus of various academic subjects is concerned, the same prescribed for Basic schools should be introduced forthwith in all elementary schools.

The diversity existing in this matter has already proved detrimental to the best interests of Basic education. Interested parties in certain places have begun voicing the demand to do away with Basic education in the name of academic standards; and there seems to be a tendency towards making the subject matter of the Basic syllabus heavier in response to the subject-centred curriculum of the high school. Thus, the emphasis laid on the life-centred curriculum in Basic education is virtually shifted to the subject-matter. This shift is fraught with dangerous consequences, inasmuch as it would eliminate the progressive element of Basic education.

It is, therefore, essential that while devising the same subject-matter, both for Basic and non-Basic schools, the guiding principle must be its relevance to the life of the community and experiences of the child rather than its usefulness for higher education. The orientation programme indicated above can, however, be implemented only by such teachers and educational administrators who understand its implications thoroughly. This would necessitate organizing short courses or seminars for them.

Some suitable system has to be evolved for this. It is suggested that a mobile training squad be set up to give short orientation courses at places convenient for teachers of a particular area. The district supervisory staff should preferably undergo an intensive orientation course in Basic education for two to four weeks.

Such courses may be organized by Postgraduate Basic Training Colleges during the long vocations at the instance of the Department of Education in the State concerned. In order to facilitate and expedite the orientation programme, certain changes in the administrative set-up of education are deemed necessary. The officer who is in charge of elementary education of the State at the Headquarters of the Director of Education should also be made responsible for Basic education and the orientation programme.

This officer should have a sufficiently high status to get the orientation programme executed without unnecessary delay caused by the usual official routine. He should indeed be assisted by an Officer-on-Special-Duty who must be a specialist in Basic education. Some of the important problems concerning the orientation of elementary schools towards the Basic pattern have been briefly discussed above. Their solution needs a nation-wide effort at all levels—government, community and the school.

"What shape will education take after the Basic stage?" has been one of the complicated issues connected with Basic education from its inception. This question has been posed not only by the conservative section of our educators, who always find difficulties-real or imaginary-in accepting a new idea, but even by those who have enthusiastically supported the scheme of Basic education and worked for it. In the beginning, however, this might have been brushed aside as a theoretical question, but now when in certain areas this scheme has been in operation for a number of years and full-fledged Basic schools have come into existence, the question of post-Basic education has assumed a practical importance.

The number of Basic schools in most of the States in India is very small and the number of non-Basic schools, therefore, very large. We have thus the picture of Education Departments running a few Basic schools here and there with ordinary Elementary schools almost everywhere. This state of affairs has now continued for some years.

It is clear that the methods followed till now of developing Basic education, i.e., by creating small compact areas of Basic schools in selected places, will no longer suffice. Creation of compact areas might have been a good procedure before, but now the process will be very different. Compact areas have continued in various States without spreading or multiplying. The gulf between the small compact areas of Basic schools and the remaining vast non-Basic areas has come to be accepted as a matter of course by the Education Departments concerned.

Instead of compact areas affecting and vitalising the remaining areas, what has happened in practice is that the larger areas of non-Basic schools have adversely affected and weakened the morale of the Basic patches. This has unfortunately resulted in more than one State, in regarding Basic schools and Basic training schools as schools kept in quarantine! If this position is allowed to continue, it will retard the spread of Basic education in the country. But the conversion of all elementary schools into full-fledged Basic schools will take time and much effort.

An ordinary school will become a full Basic school only when a number of things are done including, chiefly the introduction of systematic craft and other productive work and the technique of correlated teaching. These two important items cannot be introduced without Basic-trained teachers and adequate equipment and supply of raw materials. Efficient craft and other productive work and the correlated technique of teaching will, therefore, have to wait till a sufficient number of Basic-trained teachers becomes available. There is thus bound to be an interim period of waiting. It is of great importance that this period of waiting should be used to turn all Elementary schools in the direction of Basic education. It is at this point that we must remember that there are some important aspects of Basic education which can be introductedd into all Elementary schools without delay. It is for us to pick out these features and introduce them *en mass* into all Elementary schools thus bringing them much closer to Basic education. This is not difficult and is well worth doing.

Features of Basic Education

Let us therefore be clear in our minds that if all Elementary schools become Basic schools and if a period of waiting is unavoidable, then it certainly stands to reason that we should introduce into all Elementary schools the features of Basic education during the interim period. We should also understands why these features are good in themselves and can at the same time being Basic education nearer to the children. What these feature of Basic education are and how they may be introduced into all Elementary schools is the subject matter.

Whether all Elementary schools are converted into full-fledged Basic schools in course of time or only brought closer to Basic education without delay will depend on how the teachers concerned respond to the wither programme. The essential preliminary step, therefore, is to secure the cooperation of teachers through understanding and reasoning. We will have to deal with a vast number of teachers with no Basic-training and probably without any training at all. How shall we enlighten and enthuse the teachers, who have all along worked in ordinary schools in the old way? When we attempt to do this, we shall find at once that the majority of teachers have certain misconceptions about Basic education which strongly persist in their minds and which will make them hesitate. We must, therefore, clear these misconceptions.

The first misconception is that Basic education is something very difficult to understand and practise. Let us make it clear beyond doubt that there is nothing mystic or hidden about Basic education. Let us present Basic education as improved elementary education and frighten nobody by saying that Basic education is meant to uproot or throw away what is going on in Elementary education. Let us explain that Basic education is meant to fulfil the best intentions with which elementary education must be concerned. Let no one create the impression that Basic education must grow in total hostility to Elementary education as it has developed. We certainly want radical changes, but these changes will not destroy, but only fulfil. We must admit that it is a long time since everybody agreed that Elementary education should not be only book-centred, though unfortunately it has in practice, largely continued to be so. Is it not also true that for a long time subjects like Nature Study, Chemistry, Physics, General Science, etc., have not been taught exclusively from and through books and that increasing efforts have been made to teach them in and through work in the garden, laboratory and workshop? Has not some kind of manual or craft work come to be considered already as essential for the all-round education of children?

Elementary education has thus tended to improve, become more real and to come closer to Basic education without many of us knowing about it. Several of the good trends which have remained as an undercurrent in Elementary education are now sought to be brought up and made systematic, precise and added to in Basic education. If all those concerned, and especially the teachers, will approach Basic education from this angle, the whole question of changing over from the present elementary education into the Basic pattern will become easier and more fruitful.

Another misconception is that any productive work in Elementary schools will become the sweated labour of children. This is a very wrong idea and must be fully exposed. Productive work is not something that is unrelated to the capacity of children at different age levels in Basic education. It is not an end in itself in Basic education. It is only means to learning. When productive work becomes the medium of learning and is carefully regulated to suit different age levels of children, the whole idea of sweated labour is liquidated. It is the essence of basic education that whatever productive work is given to children should be such that the children can do it without any undue physical strain. That is why the younger children have only the *taklis* to work with. Even the small *charkha* comes only later. When programmes of learning are drawn out of work with the *takli* or the *charkha* or in the garden, then work becomes interesting and joyful. Work, as a vehicle of learning, is far removed from drudgery. Sweated child labour is the very negation of Basic education and will defeat it completely. Teachers should know that they can add to the happiness of children at work by encouraging children to organise and do their work on their own and with only unobtrusive guidance from without.

A third misconception relates to self-sufficiency in Basic schools. Many teachers are frightened and worried at the thought that their salaries will be paid only when what is produced by children is sold profitably. What an absurd idea! Nobody at any time suggested anything so stupid. Teachers must and will be paid as usual by the management or local bodies or government. What has been suggested is merely that there will be an income side to school budget and not merely an expenditure side. If several lakhs of children in thousands of Basic schools do, some productive work or other and do it well, then surely what is produced must fetch an income which will not be inconsiderable. Those who pay for education will find that such income might well lighten their burden. The more efficient Basic schools are, the better and more systematic will be their productive work fetching relatively better incomes. Why should this be considered an unreasonable idea? If money is spent in raw materials, equipment and productive work, there must be an income from production. But, the main object of productive work is education through such work and income is only a corollary.

A fourth misconception is that because time is given to craft or productive work, much time is taken away from learning and, therefore, learning in Basic school will necessarily be less than in a non-Basic school. When we had education through books alone, it was thought that the more boys and girls studied books, the more educated they became. We have now begun to realise that a great deal of education takes place through activities and that, therefore, the more activities we provide the more learning there will be. Activities and productive work thus are replacing books more and more and the old importance of books must shift to activities. There can, therefore, be no question that learning becomes less, because children give time to activities and organized productive work.

Many teachers think that education in Basic schools can only be through craft or other productive work. This is an erroneous idea. Basic education clearly lays down that learning various subjects takes place not only through activities and productive work, but equally through the close study of an association with the natural and social environment of the growing child. Take your lesson from the natural environment, from productive work and from the social environment, is the challenge of Basic education. Productive work, therefore, covers only one third of the catchment area of learning in Basic education. Any intelligent teacher can bring the mind of the child into increasing touch with innumerable matters of interest in the natural and social environments and thus give the child much necessary knowledge. There will hardly be any child who will not find spontaneous delight in its natural and social environment. But the misconception to be cleared is that Basic education does not lay down that every subject must be taught only in correlation with productive work. Besides a number of important activities that distinguish Basic education from the older system are the technique of correlated teaching and such productive work as becomes the medium for learning. We have agreed that both these features will have to wait for the trained Basic teacher and the supply of craft equipment, etc.

But if these two features are kept apart, there will still remain a number of activities and studies which even ordinary teachers should be able to manage with benefit to the children in their educational process and will, at the same time, pull all Elementary schools very much closer to Basic education. Such activities do not involve any considerable expenditure and when carried out carefully and systematically can lead to excellent results in terms of Basic education. Teachers with average intelligence and capacity can help boys and girls to organise such activities and, at the same time, explain the 'why' and the 'how' of all the processes involved. When this is done, we shall turn all Elementary schools successfully in the direction of Basic education and prepare the way for it to come in fully.

Organization of Activities

In this programme, activities will certainly be important, but of equal importance will be all the necessary answers to every question the child-mind will raise concerning them. The activities may be grouped under the following heads:

Increasing the Sense of Self-reliance and Responsibility

Let the children understand that the school belongs to them and that each one of them, as a member of the school community, must maintain certain standards of conduct, work and learning.

The cleanliness of the school and the premises, the care of the school property, keeping time and ringing the bell, maintaining daily records of work and studies, writing reports, editing a school bulletin, individual and collective disciplines inside the community, etc., should be progressively and increasingly left in the hands of the children themselves. For this, the children should be encouraged to set up their own General Assembly which will elect from month to month or for shorter periods their own Cabinet of children, the members of which will undertake one or the other of the several duties in the school community. There will be a student Chief Minister and other Ministers associated with him or her. There will be student Ministers for sanitation, gardening, entertainment, class arrangements, supply of drinking water, excursions, etc. The General Assembly may meet from time to time to consider the report of the Chief Minister of the work done during the tenure of his Cabinet and all such reports should be open to comments and criticisms by the members of the Assembly.

Misconduct and irregularities on the part of children will also come before the Assembly and will be dealt with by it. Innumerable projects which will develop responsibility and self-reliance in the children can be woven round this type of student self-government. This is a common feature already in most Basic schools and is one of the bright features of the present situation in Basic education. Teachers should help in this process without obtruding too much into the picture and by giving friendly guidance from behind. But the teachers should be vigilant and keep watch over the whole situation so that the freedom given to children does not degenerate into endless little squabbles and general confusion.

Increasing Purposeful Activities

Increased activities in various directions will come forth form the above programme of Student self-Government. Activities will commence as soon as the children arrive in the school.

The following is an illustrative list of the activities which will have for their object, formation and stabilising of good habits, accruing knowledge about many matters important in daily life, developing a broad and healthy outlook and cultivating a keen awareness and alertness of mind.

1. Attending to and checking up personal cleanliness, then the cleanliness of the school and the premises. This will mean washing, cleaning, sweeping, dusting, etc.
2. Providing clean drinking water and storing it in different classrooms.
3. Gathering together in a morning assembly for non-sectarian community prayers or flag salutation, etc.
4. Arranging class furniture like black boards, desks, benches, etc., and decorating classrooms in various artistic ways. One good idea would be to keep small painted mud pots with green leaves and flowers inside as in a flower vase.
5. Maintaining a board to give important news and announcements.

6. Preparation of a school album.
7. Organising a small museum in any one of the classrooms with materials collected from nature and the community, demonstrating the flora and fauna of the locality as also simple products of local handicrafts; even a collection of stones of different shapes and quality-can be attractive.
8. Organising midday meals whenever and wherever possible, picnics and excursions and occasional experiments in community cooling.
9. Training in group-singing.
10. Growing vegetables and simple agricultural.
11. Clay modelling, coloured paper work, simple cardboard work, spinning or any other craft which will be inexpensive in the locality.
12. Celebration of local festivals and important national days with the school and the community joining together.
13. Organising games, simple dramas, plays festivals, etc.
14. Organising small projects like a Post Office, Railway Station, Dispensary, etc., to give children knowledge of such institutions.
15. For older children in upper classes, participation in sowing, transplanting, reaping, fencing, drawing water from wells and tanks, disinfecting drinking water and dirty places, etc.
16. Apart from school sanitation,village sanitation, at least once a month.

17. Growing flowers in the schools and in the homes and making small children's parks, etc.

18. Preparation of easy charts, manuscripts and simple learning aids with the help of teachers.

19. Tree planting and taking care of trees in and near schools and in the home and village or street.

20. Making soak-pits to canalise drainage.

21. Making simple trench urinals and latrines and how to maintain them clean.

22. Composting manure by collecting refuse material from the village and making use of green leaves and grass.

23. Running a manuscript magazine and collecting local information and data for publication in it.

24. Regular and organised visits to study existing workshops in villages, towns or streets, like carpentry, blacksmithy, pottery, handloom, printing press, tailory and institutions like the Post Office, the Panchayat, the hospital, the bank, the market and the temple, church or mosque, etc., boys and girls being encouraged to observe and understand what is going on in such places and then to produce little manuscript pamphlets on them; also children may get some initial training in one or the other of the workshops.

25. Collecting local proverbs, anecdotes, folk songs and folk tales, etc., and recording them.

26. Easy study in common aliments and disease current in the locality and how to help such cases. Elementary knowledge of First-aid and preventive work in the case of epidemics for the elder children.

27. Making shadow-poles to study the movement of the sun, rain gauge and the weather cook.

28. Elementary knowledge of surveying, sketching and mapping.

29. Elementary study of the stars.

30. Familiarity with the handling of such instruments as the thermometer, barometer, balances, clock, etc.

31. Learning cycling and swimming by the elder children.

32. Learning to understand, appreciate ad practise the Cooperative Method of Organisation and Work for Social and Economic Development. Small suitable projects like a Cooperative Store for Stationery, etc., and for the higher classes of the Senior Basic, a small Students' Bank may well be organised. It is of the utmost importance that boys and girls should grow up with a grasp of the principles of cooperation.

33. The Basic education syllabus may be adopted in all elementary schools so that teachers and children may get used to its contents and its special trends. There should be no difficulty about this and the adoption of the basic syllabus can helpfully precede the coming in later of the technique of correlated teaching.

Let no teacher be frightened by this list. It is for him to pick and choose. There may be many other suitable activities not included in the list. The teacher would be free, therefore, to choose an activity other than what is mentioned and is encouraged to take up a variety of useful activities which will give them the joy of discovery and the joy of learning. Wherever a teacher has taught a boy or a girl to love work, there Basic education has already started. Ordinary in present day schools, children learn to dislike work.

Increasing Freedom for Self-Development

Where self-reliance and responsibility are sought to be cultivated and where children are taught increasingly to take part in purposeful activities, it is very necessary to cultivate a growing sense of freedom from fear and coercion. Let there be no cane in a school and let no teacher frighten or threaten a child into doing or learning anything. Nothing is learnt or done effectively except in freedom and in joy anything. This does not at all mean that discipline, orderliness and good conduct are not necessary. It only means that these should come more from within than imposed from without. There is no doubt that student self-government and increased activities will bring more initiative and freedom and joy to children, but they have to be carefully nurtured and sustained. Teachers would encourage children to make their own rules and regulations and maintain these through their General Assembly and elected Cabinet. Freedom in doing and learning will certainly mean freedom for children for self-expression without fear and inhibition. Group discussions should increase and take the place of teaching and learning. Teachers should not only permit, but deliberately encourage children to ask questions and express doubts.

Children should be free to ask questions and seek information not only from teachers, but from elders in the family and the community and from visitors and guests. Dictation of notes and asking children to learn lessons by heart should be more and more given up in favour of free discussion and clear understanding. The importance of textbooks must progressively shift to learning from and through activities and throughlife situations. At every possible point, children should be encouraged to come out with their own suggestions, proposals and plans for various activities and studies. Freedom and initiative depend on each; neither can be produced to order. Both will accrue from very many factors and teachers must take care of such factors. Timid and nervous children will not blossom out into freedom and initiative by being ordered to do so. Conditions will have to be created in which such a change can occur. Every teacher must think out this problem of freedom for children with real understanding of the needs of the child-mind.

It is by no means a new idea that the school and the community should remain as close to each other as possible. But this has not happened in our country and the school has very often remained as some kind of an office and apart from the community. In the rural areas, nature and the community are much mixed together. Teachers should bring children out to look at and take a keen interest in the natural and social life around the school.

The school children should be able to recognise flowers, plants, trees, birds, insects, animals, etc., and to know something positive about all of them. Linking Nature with the community will be such things as irrigation and drinking water wells, tanks, canals, rivers, dams; foot paths, roads, telegraphic wires; and cultivated fields and gardens, etc. These should also be observed and studied. Innumerable factors in the life of the community around, if pointed out and explained to children will fascinate them.

The way people work to earn their living, what they eat, how they dress, their festivals, amusements, etc., will all be relevant. It is not enough that children should come across all these in a causal way and then absorb wrong impressions. Details of the life and nature around the school and in the surrounding community can become very entertaining and enlightening points for easy interrelated studies concerning the natural, economic and social problems in the midst of which children have to live and grow.

Children should be taken out to watch farmers, carpenters, black-smiths, potters, etc., at work and encouraged to ask all the questions they wish to and answers should be given carefully and fully. Let farmers, village craftsmen and fathers, mothers, relations and friends come into the school to help children whenever they can to develop their kitchen garden or try their hand at some simple craft or other. Whenever there is a local festival or a national day let school children organise them or participate in them inside and outside the school. Elder children may help in sanitation, in setting up exhibitions and making other arrangement during local festivals including the supply of clean drinking water. Simple conversational study circles may be organised in which the children and the elders will sit together to discuss topical questions and other matters of interest. Active participation in some of the activities going on in the National Extension Blocks will help students to understand at first hand issues connected with community development. In this connection, teachers should encourage boys and girls to keep brief, simple but systematic records of all work done. Such reports should be read, discussed and evaluated.

For the senior children in the upper grades, it would be a good idea that two log books are maintained in every school. One log book would be to record from day to day information and data collected about things and happenings in the natural environment. A drought or a flood will have many consequences and these may be observed and recorded. The second log book should contain a record of things and happenings in the social environment, as for instance, a festival, an epidemic, a visit by some well-known person, a village quarrel etc.

Teachers should encourage children in every school to organise their own games and play-time without obtruding into the programme. Play festivals should be arranged periodically. Singing, recitations, simple dramas and other entertainments should be organised through the children and by the children. Such entertainments can also furnish much worthwhile knowledge. For instance, the tragedies that come into the life of the community through insanitaiton may be dramatised and this can carry more conviction to children than many classroom lessons. Group singing and dancing should be encouraged as items of pure happiness and relaxation. Easy *asanas* should be taught in every school to improve bodily and mental health. Let teachers take all the care necessary to see that children bubble with happiness inside schools instead of feeling frightened and suppressed. Even if this much is achieved and nothing else, it will be a great gain. The sorrows and fears of our children who are very often ill-nourished, ill-clothed and frightened and suppressed are among the major evils of our national life.

Index